GEOGRAPHY
Through Enquiry

*Approaches to teaching and
learning in th...   ...ol*

D0488612

Author: Margaret Roberts taught in comprehensive schools in London, Leicestershire and Sheffield before moving to Sheffield University's Division of Education where she was responsible for the geography PGCE course for over 20 years. During this time she carried out extensive research into the national curriculum and enquiry learning. Since her retirement in 2006 Margaret has been President of the Geographical Association (2008–09), edited the journal *Teaching Geography* and in 2011 ran ten workshops on 'Geographical Inquiry' for geography teachers in Singapore. Her book, *Learning Through Enquiry*, was published by the Geographical Association in 2003.

ISBN 978-1-84377-337-5

First published 2013

Impression number 10 9 8 7 6 5 4 3 2 1

Year 2015 2014 2013

Published by the Geographical Association, 160 Solly Street, Sheffield S1 4BF

Company number 07139068

Website: www.geography.org.uk

E-mail: info@geography.org.uk

The Geographical Association is a registered charity: no. 1135148

The GA would be happy to hear from other potential authors who have ideas for geography books. You may contact the Publications Manager via the GA at the address above.

Copy edited by Fran Royle

Index compiled by Liz Cook

Designed and typeset by Ledgard Jepson Ltd

Printed and bound in Northern Ireland by W&G Baird

Disclaimer: Every effort has been made to identify and contact the original sources of copyright material. If there have been any inadvertent breaches of copyright we apologise.

CONTENTS

Contents

Preface

This book is written for people interested in the geographical education of students aged 11–18. It is primarily intended for geography teachers and for those preparing to become teachers but I hope it will also be of interest to policy makers and people carrying out research into geographical education. I draw mainly on my experience and knowledge of geographical education in secondary schools in England, but the ideas and examples presented in the book are also applicable to geographical education in other countries and to those teaching geography in upper primary schools. Although an enquiry approach is highly relevant to fieldwork investigations I have chosen to focus on classroom practice as less has been written about the meaning of enquiry in the classroom than enquiry in the field.

Since the publication of *Learning Through Enquiry* in 2003, there has been increasing advocacy of enquiry-based learning by universities, examination syllabuses and national curriculum documents across the world. The term 'enquiry-based learning' is generally used as an umbrella term to cover a range of approaches in which students are actively engaged in investigating questions, problems and issues. These approaches can vary from investigations that are guided by teachers and tutors to those in which there is more student self-direction. This book recognises that sometimes in secondary schools, because of the constraints of a national curriculum or an examination syllabus, enquiry has to be strongly guided. The book also recognises that there are advantages in students having opportunities to take more control over their own learning by being involved in choosing what to investigate and how to do so.

There is nothing specifically geographical about 'enquiry' and most of the skills developed through an enquiry approach are relevant to other subjects. I think, however, that it is a mistake to think of enquiry mainly in terms of students learning valuable generic skills. If these skills are to be worth learning, then students need to apply them to something worth knowing about and worth understanding. When universities use enquiry-based learning modules, the aim is for students to increase their understanding of their subject disciplines. The title of this book emphasises this approach; I am interested in how students can learn geography through enquiry and not simply on how they can learn generic skills through geography.

This book grew out of work I did in 2011 in Singapore. The Singapore government was revising the O-level geography syllabus and had chosen to endorse an enquiry-based approach to the learning of geography. I was invited to run courses for teachers on 'inquiry' prior to the introduction of the new syllabus. I had to consider what an enquiry approach might mean in relation to a prescribed examination syllabus and, together with Singaporean colleagues, how the needs of the teachers could be met through the course. After piloting the course and revising it, we ran it ten times. Each course was evaluated and we modified and developed some of the activities in light of our discussions.

In addition to my work in Singapore, my thinking about enquiry has been informed by my work as a PGCE tutor at the University of Sheffield, through my research and through discussions with those in the geographical education research community. My thinking has been extended by my experiences as External Examiner for two PGCE courses and by extensive reading. Although this book developed from *Learning Through Enquiry*, it is not simply an update. It differs in significant ways:

▲ I have written *Geography Through Enquiry* with the whole secondary school age range in mind, including the years in which students are studying for external examinations. The previous book was focused on key stage 3.

▲ When I wrote *Learning Through Enquiry* in 2003, it was in the context of geographical education in England at the time; it took account of the demands of the national curriculum and of the generic national strategies. This book has been written with a wider audience in mind. It has been informed not only by developments in the

UK but also by my work in Singapore and my study of national curriculum documents of other countries.

▲ Where there is an overlap between this book and the previous one, e.g. on essential characteristics of enquiry, on the role of the teacher, on constructivism and on using questionnaires, I have re-written these sections and added further thoughts based on additional experience and reading.

▲ The chapters on representation, controversial issues, reasoning and argumentation, developing conceptual understanding and dialogic teaching are new and develop ideas which I think are important to consider when adopting an enquiry approach.

▲ This book, like the previous one, refers to a large number of classroom activities, most of which are new. Those that appeared in *Learning Through Enquiry* have been updated or applied to different examples.

This book is in two parts. Chapters 1–12 might be considered more theoretical and Chapters 13–21 more practical. The distinction between theory and practice, however, seems artificial to me. All classroom practice is necessarily underpinned by assumptions or implicit theories about how students learn, how they are motivated, the role of the teacher etc. It seemed important to me, therefore, to set out in the first part of this book the assumptions that underpin my ideas about geography, teaching and learning and enquiry. I also wanted to focus on aspects of learning geography through enquiry that are not usually listed in sequences of the enquiry process. If students are to develop conceptual understanding and to learn to think and argue geographically, then ways of incorporating these aspects of learning into an enquiry approach need to be considered. I wanted to emphasise the importance of discussion in learning geography so have incorporated recent research into dialogic teaching. Also, as most of what is studied in geography is inherently value-laden, I wanted to explore some aspects of teaching controversial issues. I hope that geography departments will use some of these chapters as a focus for departmental discussion.

Each of Chapters 13–21 focuses on a particular classroom activity that can be used to contribute to an enquiry approach. I have reflected and commented on their use and identified some of the issues that have arisen when using them. I hope that those who use the book will adapt and develop these activities so that they meet the needs of their own students. I would emphasise, however, that enquiry means much more than selecting one or more of these activities and slotting them into a unit of work. Adopting an enquiry approach requires the establishment of a classroom culture in which constant questioning is valued and in which units of work are focused on investigating interesting and challenging geographical questions through the study of geographical source materials.

For those looking for ideas for research, I have included a few suggestions at the end of each chapter together with references specific to that chapter. There is also a short bibliography of books that have been influential on my thinking, including some that I have not referred to specifically in the chapters.

Acknowledgements

I have developed my ideas related to enquiry throughout my career as a classroom teacher in London and Leicestershire, as a lecturer and geography PGCE tutor at the University of Sheffield, as External Examiner and through my research and reading.

In my early career I was fortunate enough to work alongside three inspirational teachers of English: Douglas Barnes in London, Michael Armstrong and the late Pat D'Arcy in Leicestershire. By involving me in the Language across the Curriculum movement and by introducing me to the ideas of Vygotsky and Bruner, they transformed my views of teaching and learning. I appreciate the support and encouragement they have given me throughout my career.

My thinking owes a lot to the research of others, within the field of geographical education and also to research related to classroom talk, science education and history education. As a university lecturer I had opportunities to carry out research into the national curriculum, classroom practice and to liaise with a wider research community through the International Geographic Union and Geography Tutors' Conferences. I am very grateful for what I have learnt through the educational research community. I would like to give particular thanks to Eleanor Rawling and David Lambert for encouraging me to continue thinking and writing about enquiry.

I have had the privilege of observing many geography lessons, both as PGCE tutor at the University of Sheffield and as an External Examiner for PGCE courses. These lessons gave me the opportunity to reflect on the possibilities for implementing enquiry approaches in widely different contexts. I would like to thank the geography departments I visited, the student teachers I observed and the colleagues with whom I was able to discuss these lessons. I also learnt from the many University of Sheffield PGCE students I worked with and would like to thank two of them, Rachel Atherton and Emma Rawlings Smith, for providing examples for me to use in this book.

I learned a lot from working alongside my colleagues Chris Winter and Jane Ferretti at the University of Sheffield and appreciated being able to discuss my ideas on enquiry, curriculum and pedagogy with them. I would also like to thank Jane for providing me with an example of how she used the layers of inference framework with teachers and PGCE students, together with comments on its use.

I would like to thank the colleagues I worked with in Singapore in 2011 for encouraging me to write this book. I found it extremely stimulating to develop my ideas in a different cultural context for a different secondary school curriculum. I would like to thank Elaine Lim Pik Ying and Siew Hong Ang for inviting me to run courses for teachers in Singapore and to thank them and the team of geography teachers seconded to the Singapore Government for their support in helping me develop the course to meet their needs. During each of the ten courses on which I worked, I was supported by a team of teachers and seconded teachers and would like to thank all of them. I owe particular thanks to Kai Ling Leong, Wendy Li-Jin Tan and Josef Tan who were involved in most of the courses and in the post-course reflections, evaluations and discussions.

Lastly, I would like to thank all those at the Geographical Association who have been involved in this publication, with special thanks to Dorcas Brown who had responsibility for transforming the many files I sent her into this book.

Margaret Roberts
April 2013

CHAPTER 01

Learning through enquiry: some frequently asked questions

"When I use a word" said Humpty Dumpty, "it means just what I choose it to mean – neither more nor less" (Lewis Carroll, *Alice Through the Looking Glass*, 1871)

Introduction

The concept of an enquiry approach to teaching and learning has attracted a lot of attention in the last few decades, but its origins date back to the work of Dewey and Vygotsky in the first half of the 20th century. In the UK various aspects of enquiry have their advocates in all phases of education from primary to postgraduate and in a wide range of disciplines. Other countries, such as Singapore, Australia, the Netherlands, Germany and the USA, have also developed initiatives which encourage an enquiry approach in both schools and higher education. So, although this book focuses on secondary school geography, 'enquiry' is not specifically geographical, nor is it limited to secondary schools. It is not possible to give one definition of 'enquiry' which would apply in all contexts, as what an enquiry approach means in practice is related to the specific contexts in which it is developed. For secondary school geography teachers the context includes the country, the school and locality in which they teach and the opportunities provided within requirements set by a national curriculum or external examinations.

Regardless of its context, some big questions need to be asked about geographical enquiry. How does enquiry relate to the nature of geography as a discipline and to its key concepts? What are the purposes of geographical education and how might enquiry contribute to achieving them? How does adopting an enquiry approach impact on curriculum planning and classroom practice? These big questions are considered throughout the book; in this introductory chapter, however, I want to address a few questions which I have encountered frequently and which might be in readers' minds at the outset. 'Why adopt an enquiry approach?' and 'What is the role of the geography teacher in an enquiry approach?' are addressed in Chapters 2 and 3.

What exactly is geographical enquiry?

In 1996 I carried out some research into how geography departments in England were incorporating enquiry into their plans for the 1995 geography national curriculum. In spite of using the same national curriculum document, teachers' interpretations of what they needed to do in relation to enquiry varied considerably according to what they understood by 'enquiry' (Figure 1.1). Although geographical enquiry was commonly associated with fieldwork, independent learning and a sequence of investigation, teachers attached different degrees of importance to these aspects and this had an impact on classroom practice. Where enquiry was associated strongly with fieldwork there was little enquiry work in the classroom. These differences in understanding had their origins in when and how teachers had studied geography at university and to the public examination syllabuses they had used.

What is the difference between 'enquiry' and 'inquiry'?

Should it be 'enquiry' with an 'e' or 'inquiry' with an 'i'? Is there a difference and does it matter? In the UK, in educational contexts, the words are used interchangeably, with 'enquiry' being by far the most common spelling. In general usage, however, there are some differences in meaning between 'enquiry' and 'inquiry' in British English. The verb 'to enquire' is used in relation to asking questions about something and the noun with an 'e' is used, for example, in telephone 'directory enquiries'. The verb 'to inquire' is used in relation to investigating something and the noun with an 'i' is used, for example, in judicial or public inquiries. In American English, both in educational and general usage, inquiry with an 'i' is the most common usage. From my reading of the literature there seems to be no significant difference between the meaning of British English 'enquiry' and American English 'inquiry' when used in educational contexts.

Figure 1.1: Different understandings of 'enquiry'. Source: Roberts, 1998.

Extracts from transcripts of interviews carried out in 1996 with geography teachers in five different geography departments.

A *'We look upon enquiry as being a situation where students, preferably outside school, have an opportunity for independent learning based on a set of problems or hypotheses, for which they can find the information and formulate answers. They have to set a hypothesis, because otherwise I don't see how they can go through the whole enquiry process.'*

B *'Instead of somebody standing at the front telling you the information you try and find out yourself through other means.'*

C *'Enquiry is when you formulate what you are going to look at and you find your own evidence. It is where people decide their own learning pathways, basically, and the nearer you get to handing the whole learning process over to the kids, the nearer you are to true enquiry-based learning.'*

D *'It is enquiry-based when they go out and they are doing a bit on their own. Then they go home and do some follow-up work.'*

E *'I see enquiry as a form of problem solving where they have to go through a route of asking questions: How are they going to find it out? What is their response to it? I see it as a wide process but using a variety of evidence. They have to search out what is relevant, make connections. We don't do much number crunching. For most of the enquiry, values and attitudes come into it.'*

F *'Supported self study, where you have got a job, you have the resources and the students make their way through to a particular finished product. It is basically the route followed through in the MEG syllabus B: identify the problem, identify the method, identify resources, do something, appraise it and re-plan.'*

What do I understand by geographical enquiry?

It seems important, at this point, to outline what I mean by enquiry. My thinking about enquiry has developed throughout my career as a teacher and teacher educator, influenced by my experience as a practitioner, by the people I have worked with and by what I have read. There are three important aspects of my thinking.

First, I think of enquiry not simply as a set of skills but as an approach to teaching and learning geography. I think it is important that, when students are learning geography through enquiry,

they extend their geographical knowledge and understanding at the same time as they learn skills, both skills specific to geography and generic skills used in other subjects and contexts.

Second, I think that what students learn and how they learn are inextricably related; I do not think that curriculum can be separated from pedagogy. How students learn influences what they learn. When we plan an enquiry-based unit of work, we have to focus on both what is being investigated and how it is to be investigated.

Third, I think that what students learn is influenced by the knowledge they bring to the classroom and the extent to which we enable them to make use of this. All students have their own varied personal geographies, developed through their everyday direct experiences of the world and their indirect experiences, via the media and other people. Their personal geographies include knowledge of places and environments, ways of thinking about the world and explaining it to themselves, even if these are false or naïve. Their prior knowledge also includes the geography they have already learned in school, some of which might be through other subjects in the curriculum. I think that in an enquiry approach to learning it is essential that students are enabled to connect their prior knowledge and experience with what they are investigating.

Is geographical enquiry best suited to fieldwork?

Clearly, there are many advantages to investigating geography in the field: students can relate more easily to what they are studying because they can experience it directly with their senses; they can collect their own first-hand data; they can develop a deeper understanding of data they are using because they know how they were collected, the categories used, etc.; and they can become aware of the subjectivities involved in the way that data are represented. However, I think that the key elements of an enquiry approach, identified in the next section, are as applicable in the classroom as in the field.

What are the key elements of enquiry?

I think that there are four characteristics, or elements, of an enquiry approach to learning geography through enquiry (Figure 1.2). I will explain my rationale for choosing these elements more fully in Chapter 2. Figure 1.2 is an adaptation of the framework for geographical enquiry that I produced for *Learning Through Enquiry* (Roberts,

2003). The original framework had arrows linking the boxes, suggesting that the elements occurred in a sequence. Omitting the arrows emphasises that each element could occur at any stage of the enquiry process.

First, I think that enquiry should be question-driven. An enquiry approach is an investigative approach to knowledge and knowledge construction. Geographical knowledge has been constructed by geographers in response to questions that have made them curious, have made them want to know something. I think that students need to become aware of the key questions that frame units of work and that these questions become their own. We need to create a 'need to know', to create question 'hooks' in students' minds. The importance of this can be illustrated by something one of my daughters said when she was ten. She came home from school one day declaring that she hated school. When I asked her why, she replied, 'I can't stand teachers standing there all day telling me things I don't want to know'. I found this remark provocative and significant. Of my three children, Elizabeth had always been the most curious, constantly asking questions from an early age. She had a great need to know about everything she encountered. Yet in spite of a carefully planned curriculum at her school, teachers were not giving her the opportunity to find out things she wanted to know. Many students experience being told things they don't want to know. I am not arguing for a curriculum determined entirely by what students want to study, but for the need to spark students' curiosity in what they are investigating. This is crucial at the start of a new unit of work, but it is also important to maintain curiosity and encourage a questioning attitude throughout it.

Figure 1.2: Essential elements of learning geography through enquiry.

Enquiry is question-driven
The teacher sparks curiosity, creating a need to know. Students:

▲ are curious

▲ speculate

▲ hypothesise

▲ use imagination

▲ generate ideas

▲ identify issues

▲ ask questions

▲ plan how to research

Enquiry is supported by evidence
The teacher enables students to use sources of geographical information as evidence. Students:

▲ search for information

▲ collect evidence

▲ select evidence

▲ sort information

▲ classify information

Enquiry requires thinking geographically
The teacher provides opportunities for students to make sense and exercise reasoning. Students:

▲ relate existing knowledge to new knowledge

▲ describe

▲ explain

▲ compare

▲ contrast

▲ analyse

▲ interpret

▲ recognise relationships

▲ analyse values

▲ clarify values

▲ reach conclusions

Enquiry is reflective
The teacher provides opportunities for both students and teacher to reflect on learning. Students are critical in relation to:

▲ sources of information

▲ skills and techniques used

▲ criteria for making judgements

▲ opinions

▲ what has been learnt

▲ how it has been learnt

▲ how the enquiry could be improved

▲ how the enquiry could be further developed

▲ the value of what has been learnt

Second, I think that enquiry should be supported by evidence. In investigating the key question of an enquiry, students need to study sources of geographical information. In the classroom, most sources are based on secondary data, but these might be supplemented occasionally with first-hand data collected in the field, or from a questionnaire survey, or based on students' own first-hand experiences. Using geographical evidence is not just one stage of the enquiry process. Sources can be used to provoke curiosity. Students use them to make sense of what they are studying, support their arguments and justify their conclusions.

Third, I think that enquiry should provide opportunities for students to make sense of geographical information for themselves, to make connections of all kinds. They need make connections between what they already know and new information. They need to make connections between different pieces of new information. Learning through enquiry means much more than finding answers to questions. It requires students to reason and to think critically. It means having the opportunity to reach conclusions and make judgements based on evidence. Making sense is not a discrete stage in the enquiry process: reasoned thinking is required at all stages.

Fourth, if students are to make sense not only of the evidence provided but of a unit of work as a whole, then they need to reflect on what they have learnt. They need to reflect on the extent to which they have answered or explored the questions posed at the outset, the extent to which evidence was sufficient, on whether the techniques they have used to analyse or interpret source materials were appropriate and whether the conclusions and judgements they reached were sufficiently supported by the evidence. They might reflect on what further questions could be investigated. In addition to reflecting on what they have learnt in terms of content they could also reflect on how they have learnt and how they might apply this method to future investigations. Although I have referred to reflection taking place at the end of an investigation, an enquiry approach could encourage a constantly reflective attitude towards knowledge and learning.

How does geographical enquiry relate to other educational initiatives?

Over the last 15 years there have been many initiatives advocating new ways of teaching and learning and new ways of developing the curriculum. I have often been asked how learning through enquiry relates to these.

Many of these initiatives refer to 'competence' which has been defined as:

'A competence is more than just knowledge or skills. It involves the ability to meet complex demands, by drawing on and mobilising psychosocial resources (including skills and attitudes) in a particular context. For example, the ability to communicate effectively is a competence that may draw on an individual's knowledge of language, practical IT skills and attitudes towards those with whom he or she is communicating' (Ananiadou and Claro, 2009, p. 8).

The documents I refer to use the terms 'competency' and 'competence' in the singular and 'competences' and 'competencies' in the plural and refer to 'competency-based approaches'. In what follows I have used the terminology found in the original documents, even when different plurals are used in the same document.

EBL, IBL and PBL in higher education

During the last 15 years many universities in the UK and worldwide have introduced enquiry-based learning in undergraduate courses across a range of disciplines. Some universities, e.g. Manchester, Birmingham and Reading, refer to it as EBL, while others, e.g. Sheffield, refer to it as IBL (inquiry-based learning), the term used in the USA. There is no significant difference in meaning between EBL and IBL. They are both similar to my understanding of enquiry; they:

▲ emphasise engagement with, and acquisition of, subject knowledge

▲ recognise that it can develop a broad range of skills

▲ include a range of practices ('a cluster of approaches', 'a broad umbrella term') to suit different disciplines and different time scales

▲ include less structured approaches than where the tutor determines the question or provides resources

▲ recognise that the tutor has an important supportive role.

Problem-based learning (PBL) is a particular type of EBL in which a problem is presented to students who work in small groups to make the decisions about issues to investigate and how to investigate them. The terms EBL and IBL are used more flexibly than PBL to include a range of approaches (Figure 1.3).

OBE, SBE and UbD

Outcomes-based education (OBE), standards-based education (SBE) (Figure 1.4) and understanding by design (UbD) (Figure 1.5) are approaches to curriculum planning rather than approaches to teaching and learning in the classroom. Instead of starting curriculum planning by thinking about what should go into the curriculum, these approaches start by considering what students should have learnt by the end of a programme of study. This is not an entirely new approach to curriculum planning as teachers have always considered aims, goals and purposes, though not always related to very specific outcomes.

Outcomes-based education (OBE) is an approach to education in which all decisions about the curriculum, including classroom activities and types of assessment, are driven by the outcomes students should achieve by the end of the course. OBE was developed mostly with generic outcomes, e.g. problem-solving skills. Standards-based education (SBE) evolved from OBE, with subject-specific standards being defined as the start of curriculum planning.

OBE and SBE have their roots in Tyler's objectives model of curriculum planning (Tyler, 1949). OBE was developed in the USA in the 1980s by William Spady. Its approach was adopted for statutory curriculum documents in the USA, Australia, South Africa and Hong Kong but has been abandoned in Australia (Donnelly, 2007) and South Africa. In the USA it has developed into SBE.

Extracts from *The Sheffield Companion to Inquiry Based Learning*

'*IBL describes a cluster of strongly student-centred learning and teaching approaches in which students' inquiry or research drives the learning experience*' (p. 8).

'*IBL is an empowering, engaging approach with benefits for subject learning as well as for the development of a wide range of attributes and skills in areas including initiative, critical judgment, openness, creativity and independence of mind*' (p. 8).

'*We take it to include approaches in which academic staff set the questions and offer a great deal of guidance on the inquiry process as well as those in which students have a larger degree of freedom and control in relation to both inquiry questions and inquiry processes and procedures*' (p. 8).

'*IBL is a flexible approach that can take a variety of forms. It can be used to foster acquisition of clearly-defined, "certain" knowledge such as the conceptual foundations of a scientific discipline. Alternatively it can be used to engage students with uncertainty, multiple perspectives and contestation through exploration of open-ended questions and problems to which single right answers do not exist*' (p. 8).

'*As well as developing students' subject knowledge and "transferable" skills, IBL can in a positive way challenge limiting beliefs and expectations that they may have about their role in learning and knowledge building*' (p. 40).

Characteristics of IBL

In IBL, students:

▲ learn through a process of inquiry, often co-operatively with peers and using digital information and technologies

▲ apply principles and practices of academic or professional inquiry, scholarship or research

▲ engage with questions and problems that often are open-ended

▲ explore a knowledge-base actively, critically and creatively

▲ participate in building new meaning and knowledge

▲ develop process knowledge and skills in inquiry methods and in other areas including information literacy, reflection and group-work

▲ gain opportunities to share their results of their inquiries with each other and with wider audiences.

Extracts from *Guide to Curriculum Design: Enquiry-based learning, University of Manchester*

Enquiry-based learning (EBL) is used here as a broad umbrella term to describe approaches to learning that are driven by a process of enquiry. We can outline some of the characteristics of EBL as follows:

▲ engagement – with a complex problem or scenario – that is sufficiently open-ended to allow a variety of responses or solutions

▲ students direct the lines of enquiry and the methods employed

▲ the enquiry requires students to draw on existing knowledge and to identify their required learning needs

▲ tasks stimulate curiosity in the students, encouraging them to actively explore and seek out new evidence.

Responsibility falls to the student for analysing and presenting that evidence in appropriate ways and in support of their own response to the problem.

'*Enquiries may be framed so that students engage with a specific set of resources*' (p. 3).

'*EBL thus represents a shift away from more passive methods, which involve the transmission of knowledge to students, to more facilitative teaching methods through which students are expected to construct their own knowledge and understandings by engaging in supported processes of enquiry, often carried out in small groups*' (pp. 4–5).

Figure 1.3: IBL and EBL in higher education. Sources: Levy *et al.*, 2012; Kahn and O'Rourke, 2004.

Aims	To clarify the outcomes of an educational programme before determining teaching and learning activities.
	To expect all students to be able to achieve.
	To recognise what each student has achieved.
Key characteristics	Emphasis in planning is on outputs rather than inputs, with 'performance outcomes' being identified at different levels.
	Emphasis on criteria-based, formative assessment based on levels of performance outcomes, rather than summative assessment.
	All instructional resources, teaching and learning activities and assessments are designed to support the intended outcome.
	Intended for all learners: all students are expected to achieve outcomes or standards.
Differences	OBE is generally associated with more generic outcomes focusing on attitudes, dispositions and competencies, whereas SBE is based on subject knowledge, understanding and skills.
	OBE is generally associated with more student-centred approaches to teaching whereas SBE tends to include more formal instructional activities.

Figure 1.4: Outcomes-based education (OBE) and standards-based education (SBE): aims, key characteristics and differences. Sources: Tyler, 1949; Donnelly, 2007.

Aims	To clarify educational goals.
	To provide a framework to support teachers' planning.
	To enable students to develop understanding.
	To produce a curriculum that focuses on essential questions.
Key characteristics	UbD is a tool for planning curriculum units, not individual lessons.
	Planning starts with identifying learning outcomes, referred to as 'backward design' and then devising activities to achieve them.
	The emphasis is on developing six 'facets' of understanding: explain, interpret, apply, have perspective, empathise, have self-knowledge.
	There is an emphasis on transferable skills and what students can do with knowledge.
	It challenges the idea of teaching knowledge and skills first and then teaching for meaning later. Teaching for meaning is important from the outset.
	UbD includes assessment of understanding in performance tasks.
	UbD proposes an instructional sequence:
	▲ begin with problem
	▲ introduce essential questions
	▲ preview performance task
	▲ provide direct instruction, practice and opportunities for discussion
	▲ provide an application task
	▲ lead a whole-class discussion
	▲ provide applications for small groups
	▲ revisit the original question
	▲ give performance task
	▲ give students opportunities to reflect.
	The key concepts, essential questions and evaluative criteria are made explicit to students.

Figure 1.5: Understanding by design (UbD): aims and key characteristics. Sources: Wiggins and McTighe, 2008, 2011.

OBE, SBE and UbD are based on a technical, managerial view of curriculum planning, rooted in Tyler's objectives model (Tyler, 1949) and are driven by a desire for measurable outcomes and accountability. They all differ from the enquiry approach suggested in this book in that they are based on predetermined measurable outcomes of learning. This book emphasises learning as a developmental process and values unanticipated outcomes and outcomes that are not easily measured as well as expected, more measurable outcomes.

Each approach relates in some ways to the ideas presented in this book, but there are significant differences.

▲ OBE often claims to be enquiry-based and based on constructivist ideas but it emphasises generic skills rather than the development of knowledge and understanding. Unlike enquiry-based learning, which is becoming more widely advocated, OBE has been much criticised and has been abandoned as an approach or modified as SBE.

▲ SBE values the development of subject knowledge, but its emphasis on predetermined measurable outcomes limits the scope of learning through enquiry.

▲ UbD values the development of understanding and attention to key questions, but is less concerned with the acquisition of subject knowledge.

UbD is a framework for designing curriculum units, performance assessments and instruction. UbD was developed in the USA by Grant Wiggins and Jay McTighe. Their first publication, *Understanding by Design Book*, was published in 1998.

Opening Minds

Opening Minds (OM) (Figure 1.6), a competency-based approach to the curriculum, has been adopted by over 200 schools in England. It is advocated as a whole-school approach and has encouraged the development of integrated courses. Geography usually ceases to be taught as a separate subject in secondary school year groups in which the OM approach has been adopted. Geographical subject knowledge tends to be included because it relates to one of the integrated themes and can be used to achieve particular competencies.

Like the enquiry approach to learning, OM encourages students to be more actively engaged in their learning, but its purposes are different. By focusing on competencies, it underemphasises the educational value of acquiring knowledge and developing understanding. It gives more emphasis to developing the competencies needed by employers and the global economy than to goals related to students' intellectual or personal development. The competencies emphasise managing information rather than investigating issues and challenging viewpoints. As Winter (2011) points out, 'The OM competency curriculum pays scant attention to developing students' critical capacities and the word "political" is absent' (p. 353). The enquiry approach suggested in this book advocates a more critical engagement with knowledge than can be achieved through focusing on competencies.

Aims	To better equip young people to meet the challenges of the 21st century.
	To prepare students so they can be successful in the modern-day world and workplace.
	To develop the skills valued by employers (CBI/NUS, 2011).
Key characteristics	Emphasis on development of competences.
	Seen as an alternative way of teaching subject knowledge, but the content is seen as 'the means to the end rather than the end itself'.
	Schools are encouraged to adopt Opening Minds as a framework for the whole-school curriculum, but schools develop their own ways of incorporating its approach in to the curriculum.
	Students are taught by one teacher for the majority of their curriculum.
	Competences are developed through the study of common themes, such as Smart Brain, Breaking News, Global Affairs, Time and Fair Trade. Subject boundaries are blurred. The subjects most commonly combined include geography, history and RE.
	A mixture of teaching and learning activities are used, with the emphasis on students taking responsibility for managing and measuring their own competence development.

Figure 1.6: Opening Minds: aims and key characteristics. Source: Opening Minds website.

The Royal Society of Arts piloted OM during 2004–06. In 2011 it was being implemented in over 200 secondary schools. OM is a competence-based curriculum, focusing on five key competencies (sometimes abbreviated to CLIPS):

1. Citizenship
2. Learning
3. Managing information
4. Relating to people
5. Managing situations.

Building Learning Power

Schools in the UK and internationally have adopted Building Learning Power (BLP) principles. Like the Opening Minds initiative, BLP encourages a whole-school approach so that all parts of the curriculum are developed according to its ideas (Figure 1.7). Although it encourages teachers to have a dual focus on the content as well as the development of students' capacity to learn, there is more emphasis on the 'how' than the 'what' of learning. Its first framework, which relates to students' minds, encourages many 'dispositions' that are desirable for learning through enquiry, e.g. inquisitiveness, but there seems to be more emphasis on developing students' dispositions than on getting students to extend their knowledge and understanding within subject areas.

In its second framework, 'the teacher's palette', BLP identifies many ways in which teachers can support learners in the classroom. This framework could well be used by geography teachers planning an enquiry approach in the classroom.

BLP is about creating a whole-school culture that focuses on developing students' capacity to learn.

There are two BLP frameworks:

▲ The 'Learning Powered Mind' diagram illustrates aspects of learning power (resilience, resourcefulness, reflectiveness and reciprocity) and is designed to help teachers plan effective activities for students.

▲ The Teacher's Palette sets out the teacher's role under four headings – explaining, commentating, orchestrating and modelling – and is designed to help schools change the school culture.

Building Learning Power was developed in the UK by Professor Guy Claxton. His first book on BLP, *Building Learning Power: Helping young people become better learners*, was published in 2002. Since then he has written five further books on BLP.

Enquiring Minds

Enquiring Minds was a research and development project, developed by Futurelab, and launched in Bristol in 2005 (Figure 1.8). It promotes a student-centred enquiry approach, with an emphasis on students taking responsibility for the content and direction of their own learning. One student said, 'It is about doing what you're interested in, researching what you want about what you like' (Morgan *et al.*, 2007, p. 5). It shares some of the characteristics of the understanding of enquiry presented in this book in its emphasis on constructivism, the importance of interaction between teacher and student and in being concerned with the construction of knowledge as well as the development of skills. However, it is difficult to give students the freedom it advocates within the constraints of national curricula and examination syllabuses.

Aims	To prepare young people for life in a 21st-century world which is full of 'change, complexity, risk and individual opportunity'.
	To develop students' emotional, social resources so that they enjoy challenge and cope well with uncertainty and complexity.
	To develop students' confidence and real-world intelligence.
Key characteristics	Emphasis on 'building learning power' and on 'expanding students' generic capacity' to learn.
	Focus more on the 'how' of learning than on what is learnt.
	Identifies 17 learning capacities grouped into four clusters: resilience, resourcefulness, reciprocity and reflection (the four Rs).
	Refers to 'dispositions' rather than skills.
	Aims to change of the learning culture of the whole school, with all teachers involved.
	Encourages 'split screen thinking' in planning and in the classroom. The teacher always has a dual focus: the content of the lesson and the development of students' learning capacity.
	Rooted in research into the nature of learning and practitioner research.

Figure 1.7: Building Learning Power: aims and key characteristics. Source: Building Learning Power website.

Aims	Enquiring Minds aims to support students to be:
	▲ inquisitive and curious about things that they experience in their everyday lives
	▲ able to pose problems, ask questions, and recognise issues that they would like to explore
	▲ able to develop an understanding that all knowledge changes over time as people challenge, shape and contribute to it
	▲ confident that they too can challenge, shape and contribute to knowledge
	▲ aware that there are always multiple perspectives for looking at, analysing and understanding things
	▲ able to propose solutions to problems and questions, and to know how to pursue these solutions.
Key characteristics	'An approach to teaching and learning that takes seriously the ideas, interests, concerns and ways of thinking that students bring to school'
	Students take increasing responsibility for the content and purpose of their learning.
	Emphasises the construction of knowledge in the classroom and the role of both teachers and students in its co-construction, using both students' knowledge and disciplined subject knowledge.
	Recognises that educational innovation needs to be context driven and shaped by teachers in schools.
	Recognises that outcomes of learning might be unanticipated.
	Promotes an enquiry-based, problem-solving approach to teaching and learning which enables students to engage with 'useful knowledge'.
	Based on a social constructivist view of knowledge and learning.

Figure 1.8: Enquiring Minds: aims and key characteristics. Source: Morgan *et al.*, 2007.

Other frequently asked questions

This section includes some additional questions asked by teachers I worked with in Singapore and how I responded to them (Roberts, 2012).

Is it true that geographical enquiry requires more classroom time?

In some ways this is true because in enquiry-based geography there needs to be time for students to make sense for themselves through studying data, through discussion, writing and representing their ideas graphically. In addition to learning the content of the lesson, they are learning much more; they are learning skills of analysis and interpretation, of debate, of reaching their own conclusions. If an enquiry approach is to be adopted, syllabuses should have fewer topics so that there is time in the classroom for students both to develop geographical knowledge and understanding and also to develop the wide range of skills needed for enquiry and relevant to life in the 21st century.

Could geographical enquiry help to improve test scores?

This depends on what is tested. If the test assesses students' ability to remember and reproduce geographical information, then it might not, although some students might recall more because they have been more actively engaged. However, if the test assesses students' ability to analyse given data or to discuss a geographical issue, then geographical enquiry is likely to improve test scores as students would have had more classroom experience of analysing data, discussing issues and thinking for themselves.

How is enquiry-based learning different from problem-based learning?

Problem-based learning is a form of enquiry, but is student-led and open-ended. My own understanding of enquiry makes it more flexible for adaptation for examination classes studying courses that have predetermined outcomes in terms of knowledge, understanding and skills. In these classes most enquiry work would be strongly teacher guided.

Singaporean teachers were also concerned about the additional time needed to prepare resources and units of work. The Singapore government has provided support, through the team of seconded geography teachers who work for the government, to enable teachers to work collaboratively to prepare resources and ideas and to share these online.

Summary

What enquiry means cannot be defined precisely because it has developed different meanings in different contexts to meet different needs. Some key characteristics of learning geography through enquiry can be identified. The emphasis in this book is on enquiry as an approach to developing students' knowledge and understanding of the discipline of geography, not simply on acquiring a range of skills. Various national and international initiatives have given more emphasis to skills and cross-curricular approaches. Where schools have adopted these, enabling students to learn geography through enquiry is a challenge.

Suggestions for research

1. Investigate the extent to which 'enquiry' is included in geography and other subjects in one school's curriculum. Identify similarities and differences in understanding and practice within and between departments. Data could be collected through questionnaires, through semi-structured interviews and from curriculum documents, e.g. schemes of work, and through lesson observation.

2. What relationships are there between the prescribed curriculum (by national curriculum or examination boards), the described curriculum (by schemes of work and units of work) and the enacted curriculum (what actually happens in the classroom) in relation to an enquiry approach?

3. Explore the meaning of enquiry as set out in curriculum documents of other countries, in documents related to higher education and in documents related to 21st-century initiatives.

References

Ananiadou, K. and Claro, M. (2009) '21st Century skills and Competences for New Millennium Learners in OECD countries', *OECD Education Working Papers*, No. 41, OECD Publishing. Available online at *http://dx.doi.org/10.1787/218525261154* (last accessed 11 January 2013).

Building Learning Power website: *www.buildinglearningpower.co.uk* (last accessed 11 January 2013).

Carroll, L. (2010 [1871]) *Alice Through the Looking Glass*. London: Penguin.

CBI/NUS (2011) *Working Towards Your Future: Making the most of your time in higher education*. Available online at *www.nus.org.uk/Global/CBI_NUS_Employability%20 report_May%202011.pdf* (last accessed 11 January 2013).

Claxton, G. (2002) *Building Learning Power: Helping young people become better learners*. Bristol: The Learning Organisation.

Donnelly, K. (2007) 'Australia's adoption of outcomes based education: a critique', *Issues In Educational Research*, 17, 2, pp. 183–206. Available online at *www.iier.org.au/ iier17/donnelly.html* (last accessed 11 January 2013).

Kahn, P. and O'Rourke, K. (2004) *Guide to Curriculum Design: Enquiry-based learning*. Available online at *www.ceebl.manchester.ac.uk/resources/guides/ kahn_2004.pdf* (last accessed 11 January 2013).

Levy, P., Little, S., McKinney, P., Nibbs, A. and Wood, J. (2012) *The Sheffield Companion to Inquiry Based Learning*. Sheffield: CILASS, The University of Sheffield. Available online at *www.shef.ac.uk/ibl/resources/ sheffieldcompanion* (last accessed 11 January 2013).

Morgan, J. Williamson, B., Lee, T. and Facer, K. (2007) *Enquiring Minds Guide*. Bristol: Futurelab. Available online at *www.enquiringminds.org.uk/pdfs/Enquiring_Minds_Guide. pdf* (last accessed 11 January 2013).

Opening Minds website: *www.rsaopeningminds.org.uk* (last accessed 11 January 2013).

Roberts, M. (1998) 'The nature of geographical enquiry at key stage 3', *Teaching Geography*, 23, 4, pp. 164–7.

Roberts, M. (2003) *Learning Through Enquiry: Making sense of geography in the key stage 3 classroom*. Sheffield: The Geographical Association.

Roberts, M. (2012) 'Introducing Margaret Roberts', *GeoBuzz, Journal of Geography Teachers' Association of Singapore*, 2, 1.

Tyler, R. (1949) *Basic Theory of Curriculum and Instruction*. Chicago, IL: University of Chicago.

Wiggins, G. and McTighe, J. (1998) *Understanding by Design*. Alexandria, VA: Association for Supervision and Curriculum Development.

Wiggins, G. and McTighe, J. (2008) 'Reshaping high schools: put understanding first', *Educational Leadership*, 65, 8, pp. 36–41. Available online at *www.ascd.org/publications/ educational-leadership/may08/vol65/num08/Put- Understanding-First.aspx* (last accessed 11 January 2013).

Wiggins, G. and McTighe, J. (2011) *The Understanding by Design Guide to Creating High Quality Units*. Alexandria, VA: Association for Supervision and Curriculum Development (ASCD).

Winter, C. (2011) 'Curriculum knowledge and justice: content, competency and concept', *Curriculum Journal*, 22, 3, pp. 337–64.

Why adopt an enquiry approach?

CHAPTER 02

'*Empowerment: excite, promote and sustain children's agency, empowering them through knowledge, understanding, skill and personal qualities to profit from their learning, to discover and lead rewarding lives, and to manage life and find new meaning in a changing world'* (one of the aims of education, listed in Alexander, 2000, p. 19)

Introduction

An enquiry approach to teaching and learning geography is advocated by national curriculum documents and by examination specifications and is applauded in Ofsted inspection reports. It is presented as a good thing. But why?

The fact that enquiry is required or advocated by external bodies is not in itself a justification, although clearly such requirements cannot be ignored. I think that the judgements we make about classroom practice should not be based on simply meeting requirements or on what works best. Our choices should be underpinned by our professional values, by what we consider to be important. We should then strive to maintain our values and to make what we consider good practice work within whatever external requirements we have to meet.

This chapter sets out my own justifications for advocating an enquiry approach based on how I think about geographical knowledge, what I believe about learning and about how enquiry can meet broader educational aims. It addresses the following questions:

▲ How is geographical knowledge constructed?

▲ What are the implications of a constructivist approach to learning geography?

▲ How can using an enquiry approach contribute to other educational aims?

▲ To what extent is an enquiry approach required by national curriculum documents and public examinations?

How is geographical knowledge constructed?

My first justification for an enquiry approach is related to the subject matter of geography itself. Geographical knowledge is a construction rather than something existing 'out there' simply to be found. What we know about the world geographically has been constructed by geographers in response to questions that have interested them: questions provoked by what they have encountered through experience, discussion and reading. These questions are influenced by thinking at the time, within both the academic subject of geography and the wider cultural and academic context. The questions geographers ask create a lens through which they examine the world and which influences the kind of data collected. When they collect data they already have something in mind. This point was well made by Claud Cockburn, in a discussion with Francis Wheen about a remark that journalists were no longer necessary now that information was freely available through the internet. Cockburn commented:

'*To hear people talking about facts, you would think that they lie about like pieces of gold ore in the Yukon days waiting to be picked up. There are no such facts. Or if there are, they are meaningless and entirely ineffective; they might, in fact, just as well not be lying about at all until the prospector – the journalist – puts them into relation with other facts: presents them in other words. They become as much a part of a pattern created by him as if he were writing a novel. In that sense all stories are written backwards. They are supposed to begin with the facts and develop from there, but in reality they begin with a journalist's point of view, a conception'* (Cockburn, quoted in Wheen, 2002).

This is as true for geography as for journalism. Geographical facts are meaningless unless they are 'put into relation with other facts'. They become part of a pattern created by geographers in their attempt to make sense of the world. They start with a geographer's point of view, a conception; and this influences the questions asked and the data collected.

Over the last 100 years the questions geographers have asked have changed, and so has the geography they have constructed. These changes have been well documented (e.g. Johnston, 2004; Livingstone, 1992; Unwin, 1992; Peet, 1998; Castree, 2005). I would like to use two examples to illustrate some of the changes, the first from my own experience and the second from the career of David M. Smith.

In 1960 I had the opportunity to go to Ghana to carry out research for my undergraduate dissertation. I was investigating factors affecting the development of an area of agricultural land on the coast near Accra, north of the settlement of Nungua. My study was influenced by how I had studied regional geography at school and economic development at university. The unreliable rainfall, the soils, the land tenure, methods of fishing and farming, lack of surfaced roads, were all relevant to my analysis. I examined interrelationships between physical and human features and processes. I associated development mainly with economic growth and wrote my report as a detached observer. Had I been embarking on the study now, it would be different not only because Nungua will have changed, but because my study would be shaped by different questions and informed by different understandings of development issues; I would go to Nungua with, as Cockburn commented, 'a different point of view, a different conception'. I would include an investigation of social and cultural aspects of development and agricultural practice. I would examine the influence of wider political and historical contexts. I would be more aware of different ways of seeing. I would give prominence to the perspectives of local people and would recognise that my view was positioned. I would see Nungua differently and would construct a different geography.

The geographies that David M. Smith constructed through his career also changed considerably. He started his career as a spatial analyst, writing about industrial location and quantitative spatial analysis. Later he wrote about welfare geography (1977) and qualitative methods (1988) and more recently about social justice and ethics (1994, 2000). Johnston quotes Smith 'shifting the focus from how things actually are to the way they ought to be' (Johnston, 2004, p. 277) and attributes the shift partly to Smith's encounters with inequality and social injustice in the USA and South Africa. But Smith was also responding to changes in the academic culture in which he was working. Other geographers were turning their attention in the 1970s and 1980s to the meaning of place, inequalities, social justice and political structures.

The point I want to make is that geographical knowledge is a construction. It is framed by the questions and the imaginations that geographers bring to the task. Whereas traditionally geography was mainly concerned with questions of what, where and why, geographers now ask a much wider range of questions, including 'what ought'. This has had an impact on school geography across the world. Neighbour (1992, p. 15) identified a set of questions that 'have received national and international recognition as the focus for geographical education at high school level':

▲ What is the phenomenon?

▲ Where is it located?

▲ Why is it located there?

▲ What impact does its location have?

▲ What changes should be made?

▲ What ought to be done?

It is notable that this list includes questions about impact, change and decisions, going beyond the what, where and why questions which framed pre-1970 school geography. However, since Neighbour identified these questions in 1992, some academic geographers have turned their attention to additional questions:

▲ What does this place mean to different people (e.g. according to nationality, ethnicity, age, gender, class, sexuality, disability?)

▲ How is this place/situation represented?

▲ Is this situation/policy/decision morally just?

▲ What are the implications of this decision?

▲ Is this development sustainable?

▲ What understanding of key concepts, e.g. development or place, underpin the study?

Geography in the 21st century asks more challenging questions; and this has influenced the types of questions asked in public examinations.

When students are learning geography through enquiry, in addition to extending their knowledge and understanding, they are learning something about the nature of geographical knowledge and how the scope of the subject is changed by the questions that are asked. If they begin to construct geographical knowledge for themselves through their work they will become aware that knowledge cannot be neutral. It depends on the questions and viewpoints that shape it. At the same time, they can learn both to question and respect the procedures through which such knowledge is generated.

What are the implications of a constructivist approach to learning geography?

My second justification for learning through enquiry is related to constructivism, a widely accepted theory of learning developed from the work of Vygotsky, Piaget and Bruner. Its central idea is that we can learn about the world only through actively making sense of it for ourselves; knowledge cannot be transmitted or delivered to us ready-made (Barnes and Todd, 1995).

The central ideas of constructivism are:

▲ How we see and understand the world depends on our existing ways of thinking. We make sense of the world not with empty minds but with assumptions about how things are and how things work. We also have expectations and attitudes. These all influence what we see and hear and the sense we make of that information. We construct meaning in relation to what we already know.

▲ Each individual sees and understands the world differently, as each person has developed knowledge about the world through different experiences and different social and cultural encounters.

▲ In constructing new knowledge we are not adding separate new 'bits' of knowledge to what we already have, like extensions to a building. To make sense of the new information we have to incorporate it into, and reconstruct, what we already know.

▲ Our constructions of the world are not fixed but are being modified continuously as we experience new things and encounter new ways of thinking.

Social constructivists emphasise the role of other people in helping us to make sense of the world. The knowledge we have is not constructed in isolation but through interactions with other people, directly, e.g. in families, with friends and in groups with which we interact, and indirectly, through various media within our culture. We make sense of the world through participating in the world and through sharing, discussing and debating how we understand things with other people. We develop some common understandings, but because individual experiences are different we all see the world differently.

Although the theory of constructivism emphasises the world we have constructed in our minds, this does not mean that any construction of the world is valid or possible. We have to make sense of the

world in relation to the material world as we know it through our senses and perceptions.

If we accept this theory of learning, then we also need to accept that students cannot learn simply by having information and ideas transmitted to them; they have to be actively engaged in the construction of geographical knowledge. We need to:

▲ take account of students' existing knowledge and ways of understanding

▲ allow time for students to explore new information and to relate it to what they already know: making sense is not an instant process

▲ provide opportunities for students to reshape and reconstruct their existing knowledge in the light of new knowledge

▲ make students aware of the way they see things, and of different ways of seeing things.

The work of Russian psychologist Vygotsky (1962) has been influential in the development of the constructivist theory of learning, particularly on the need to support learning. Vygotsky became interested, through his experimental work with young children, in how they could solve problems beyond their existing level of understanding if they were given 'light assistance'. He referred to the difference between what a child could do without help and what he or she could do with support as what has generally been translated as the 'zone of proximal development' (Figure 2.1). Vygotsky's assumption was that children would eventually be able to solve the problems unaided.

Vygotsky's zone of proximal/potential development

In the 1920s and 1930s, Vygotsky carried out a series of studies to investigate how children developed their conceptual thinking. He was interested in the relationship between a child's level of development and the learning of concepts. He used problem-solving tests to find out children's mental ages, i.e. existing levels of development. In previous research the tests were considered invalid if the children had been given any assistance. Vygotsky, however, questioned this and considered that finding out a child's mental age should be the starting point rather than the finishing point of study. In *Thought and Language* (1962), Vygotsky wrote:

'We tried a different approach. Having found that the mental age of two children was, let us say, eight, we gave each of them harder problems than he [sic] could manage on his own and provided some light assistance; the first step in a solution, a leading question, or some other form of help. We discovered that one child could, in co-operation, solve problems designed for 12 year olds, while the other could not go beyond problems intended for 9 year olds. The discrepancy between a child's actual mental age and the level he reaches in solving problems with assistance indicates the zone of his proximal development; in our example, the zone is four for the first child and one for the second. Can we truly say that their mental development is the same?' (p. 103).

Although what Vygotsky wrote has been translated from the Russian as 'zone of proximal development', Alexander (2000, p. 431) refers to Jean Simon, who has translated the works of Vygotsky. She prefers 'next' or 'potential' development instead of 'proximal', which has spatial connotations, whereas 'next' and 'potential' suggest development over time. Alexander himself then refers to the 'zone of potential development' which can also be abbreviated as ZPD. Several key aspects of the zone of potential development can be identified from the above quotation:

▲ The ZPD is ahead of what a child can already achieve unaided.

▲ The ZPD has limits; there is an area beyond it in which problems are too hard for a child to solve even with assistance.

▲ Each individual child has his or her own ZPD in which learning can take place with assistance. There can be big differences in what children can achieve with support.

▲ The present level of achievement does not necessarily indicate what the child is capable of achieving with support.

The concept of the ZPD is significant for learning geography through enquiry:

▲ 'The only good kind of instruction is that which marches ahead of development and leads it'. If students are given things to do that they can already achieve without help then this fails to use the ZPD and they will fail to learn new things. Students are capable of learning new things within the ZPD. Vygotsky describes them as being 'ripe' to learn.

▲ A child can be expected to progress but 'only within the limits set by the stage of his development'. It is important that what students are expected to do is not beyond the ZPD, i.e. beyond what they can achieve with help.

▲ 'With assistance, every child can do more than he can by himself'. A student's conceptual learning is developed in the ZPD in collaboration with an adult or a more competent peer.

▲ 'What the child can do in co-operation today he can do alone tomorrow'. It is important that children should ultimately be able to do the work independently (Vygotsky, 1962, p. 104).

Figure 2.1: Vygotsky's zone of proximal/potential development (ZPD).

How can using an enquiry approach contribute to other educational aims?

Purposes of education

My third justification for adopting an enquiry approach to learning geography is that it can enable students to learn much more than geographical subject knowledge. There is broad agreement that the purpose of schooling is more than acquiring subject knowledge. Students also need to develop skills and capabilities for their present and future lives as individuals, citizens and in the world of work.

The ways in which an enquiry approach in geography might contribute to wider educational aims depends on what the purpose of school education is believed to be, both by teachers and by those with various interests in what education can achieve, e.g. employers, politicians and parents. To what extent is it to serve the economic and social needs of society or to develop an individual's potential? To what extent is it about socialising young people into the existing culture or equipping them to challenge current thinking, policies and practice? Is it more important to equip students with skills or to develop their knowledge and understanding? The purposes of education are always open to debate, as suggested by alternatives in the questions above. Although many would express purposes in a way that combines the above alternatives, the emphasis given to either end of the spectrum reveals underpinning values about education and what kind of society we want. It is useful to apply these questions to policy documents and projects, asking what exactly we want to achieve.

My own view is that school education has to be relevant to the needs of both society and individuals. Students need to be socialised into the culture in which they are growing up and should be able to contribute to it in their work and as citizens. But they should also be able to think critically about it and recognise that people can contribute to developing, challenging and changing it. I believe education should also aim to enhance personal lives through developing new interests and opening students' minds to a wide range of ideas and possibilities.

21st-century skills

There are important generic skills that need to be developed at school, but I think these are best developed in a purposeful context rather than in

isolation. It has long been accepted that schools should develop students' literacy and numeracy. Now there is a widely held belief that a new range of skills is needed in order for people 'to function effectively at work, as citizens and in their leisure time' (Ananiadou and Claro, 2009, p. 6) in the 21st century. These new skills are referred to variously as key skills, competences or capabilities and are promoted by various interest groups including international organisations, policy makers, employers, politicians, teachers and educational researchers. The main arguments used in support of developing these skills are related to changes in society and the economy, the demands of employers and developments in information technologies. Documents listing and explaining what is required for the 21st century include:

▲ Assessment and Teaching of 21st-Century Skills (ATC21S) project, an international project based in Australia (Figure 2.2)

ATC21S

'In a digital world, stu[...] for new technologies [...] Developing these 21s[...] classroom can transf[...] communities' (www.[...]

The Assessment and [...] Skills project (ATC21[...] Melbourne, was esta[...] new ways of assessin[...] were required for the[...] was a response to th[...] of developed countr[...] manufacturing towa[...] to rapid changes in [...] The project was sponsored by Cisco, Intel and Microsoft.

The project has involved over 200 researchers worldwide and has developed work in 10 countries including Australia, Finland, Singapore, the USA, Costa Rica and the Netherlands.

ATC21S identified four broad categories of skills:

1. Ways of thinking: creativity, critical thinking, problem-solving, decision-making and learning

2. Ways of working: communication and collaboration

3. Tools for working: information and communications technology (ICT) and information literacy

4. Skills for living in the world: citizenship, life and career, and personal and social responsibility

Figure 2.3: 21st Century Skills and Competences for New Millennium Learners in OECD Countries.

...ng Paper

*...ts in society and economy require
...tional systems equip young people
...w skills and competencies, which allow
...n to benefit from the emerging new forms of
...cialisation and to contribute actively to economic
development under a system where the main asset
is knowledge'* (Ananiadou and Claro, 2009, p. 5).

The OECD Working Paper 41 (Ananiadou and Claro, 2009) draws on curriculum documents and findings from research into the teaching and assessment of 21st-century skills and competencies in OECD countries. It defined 21st-century skills and competencies as:

'Those skills and competencies young people will be required to have in order to be effective workers and citizens in the knowledge society of the 21st century'.

It categorised the skills and competencies into three dimensions, each with subdivisions:

1. Information dimension
   Typical skills in this dimension are research and problem-solving skills, as they both involve at some point defining, searching for, evaluating, selecting, organising, analysing and interpreting information.
   a. Information as source: searching, selecting, evaluating and organising information.
   b. Information as product: the restructuring and modelling of information and the development of own ideas (knowledge).

2. Communication dimension
   This is about the need to be able to communicate, exchange ideas, criticise and present information and ideas.
   a. Effective communication.
   b. Collaboration and virtual interaction.

3. Ethics and social impact dimension
   Ethical challenges brought about by globalisation, multiculturalism and the increase in use of ICT.
   a. Social responsibility.
   b. Social impact.

▲ 21st Century Skills and Competences for New Millennium Learners in OECD Countries (Figure 2.3)

▲ P21 Framework produced by Partnership for 21st Century Skills, USA (Figure 2.4).

There is no single definition of 21st-century skills or one way of categorising them. What is included in each document has been influenced by who produced it and the purpose for which it was made. For example, ATC21S was set up as a multinational research project involving educational researchers and initially included skills related to the economy and general 'living in the world' skills. As it developed it focused on collaborative problem solving and ICT literacy, perhaps reflecting the interests of its sponsors, Cisco and Microsoft. The OECD report (Ananiadou and Claro, 2009) is also a multinational report and focuses on what 'workers and citizens in the knowledge society of the 21st century' require. The P21 Framework has been produced in the context of USA's 'standards' approach to curriculum planning; both core knowledge and skills are included in the framework.

Although some of these frameworks include skills students need to participate in society, they tend to promote more utilitarian aims related to the needs of the economy and the workplace. Although it is justifiable to take the needs of society and the concerns of employers into account, education should also enable students to make sense of the world for themselves, to be critical of information, to enable them to participate in decision making and to promote their own social and intellectual development so that they can get more out of life and contribute more to society.

The promotion of 21st-century skills has led to projects such as the RSA's Opening Minds (see Chapter 1) and has encouraged interdisciplinary approaches to the school curriculum. The same skills can, in my opinion, be developed equally well in subject contexts. Figure 2.5 illustrates how learning geography through enquiry can contribute to the development of the skills mentioned in the various frameworks.

National curriculum documents and examination syllabuses recognise that learning geography can contribute to developing '21st-century skills'. For example, the Australian national curriculum for geography states that 'each of the seven identified general capabilities should be embedded in the content descriptions and/or elaborations where appropriate', the capabilities being: literacy; numeracy; ICT; ethical behaviour; personal and social responsibility; and inter-cultural understanding. Singapore's O-level geography syllabus states that, 'The inquiry approach to the teaching and learning of geography will play a pivotal pedagogical role in achieving the aims of the syllabus by providing students with the opportunity to develop the different types of competencies needed for the 21st

P21

P21 is a US national organisation that advocates integration of skills into core subjects such as geography. In addition to core subjects there are core themes and 21st-century skills.

Core themes
- Global awareness
- Financial, economic, business and entrepreneurial literacy
- Civic literacy
- Health literacy
- Environmental literacy

21st-century skills

Learning and innovation skills
- Creativity and innovation
- Critical thinking and problem solving
- Communication and collaboration

Information, media and technology skills
- Information literacy
- Media literacy
- ICT literacy

Life and career skills
- Flexibility and adaptability
- Initiative and self direction
- Social and cross-cultural skills
- Productivity and accountability
- Leadership and responsibility

Figure 2.4: P21 Framework produced by The Partnership for 21st-Century Skills.

Literacy skills

Students gradually learn an extended vocabulary: both the specialist vocabulary of geography, and the vocabulary they need to develop reasoned arguments. They learn to interpret and evaluate geographical evidence presented in printed and online materials in a wide variety of reports, articles, advertisements, letters, etc. They learn to write in different ways: composing factual accounts; reporting their investigations; presenting an argument; and analysing viewpoints. Their literacy skills are reinforced through discussion and from listening to ways in which teachers and the media present and explain geographical knowledge.

Numeracy skills

Students learn to apply a variety of mathematical concepts in context: they need to understand a wide variety of units of measurement, scale and distance. They need to understand concepts such as 'average' and 'percentage'. They learn to use numerical data, to interpret them, and to represent them on graphs and maps. They use statistical methods in calculating averages and in using data to investigate relationships.

ICT skills

Students develop and apply generic ICT skills: searching for, accessing, selecting and storing digital information; processing it and presenting it graphically or in text. They also develop ICT skills specifically related to geography: they use geographical information systems (GIS) and global positioning systems (GPS) to manage and represent spatial data. They use 3D visualisations of maps and landscapes, as in Google Earth. They can use smartphones and social networking as sources of data and to communicate. Through geography they can become more aware of the global impact and implications of developments in digital technologies.

Skills required for the world of work

Surveys have shown that employers value, in addition to skills of literacy, numeracy and ICT:

- personal skills: working in teams, communication skills, interpersonal skills
- self-reliance: willingness to learn, ability to prioritise, ability to work independently
- flexibility.

In an enquiry approach to learning geography, students can be given opportunities to plan how they are going to investigate something; produce a project report; work collaboratively with others in small groups; work individually, taking responsibility for their work; use a decision-making exercise; present information or arguments to others in role play or other forms of presentation.

Citizenship skills

Some of the skills identified as 21st-century skills, such as social responsibility, cultural awareness, problem solving and decision making, are related to people's capacity to be involved in issues in their community, their region, their country or even globally. Learning through enquiry can contribute to these skills by expecting students to study controversial issues, to be aware of different viewpoints, to suggest solutions to locational and environmental problems and to be involved in decision-making exercises. Students can also develop the confidence to talk and write about issues and to become aware of what solutions are possible.

Figure 2.5: Ways in which learning geography through enquiry can contribute to 21st-century skills.

Aims of education

The Cambridge Primary Review stated that their set of 12 aims: *'unashamedly reflect values and moral purposes, for that is what education is about. They are designed to empower children to manage life and meaning in the 21st century. They reflect a coherent view of what it takes to become an educated person'* (Alexander, 2009).

The 12 aims are listed under three headings:

The individual

▲ Well being

▲ Engagement

▲ Empowerment

▲ Autonomy

Self, others and the wider world

▲ Encouraging respect and reciprocity

▲ Promoting interdependence and sustainability

▲ Empowering local, national and global citizenship

▲ Celebrating culture and community

Learning, knowing and doing

▲ Exploring, knowing, understanding and making sense

▲ Fostering skills

▲ Exciting imagination

▲ Enacting dialogue

---

century'. The syllabus maps out the content of the syllabus against 21st-century competencies which it has identified as: social–emotional competencies; information and communication skills; critical and inventive thinking; and civic literacy, global awareness and cross-cultural skills.

General educational aims

Whereas the various formulations of 21st-century skills emphasise what is perceived to be needed for the future in terms of skills, other formulations of educational aims are broader than this and include the development of knowledge and understanding. For example, the Cambridge Primary Review (Alexander, 2009), a report of an independent enquiry into the future of primary education in England, identified 12 general aims for primary education (Figure 2.6). Although all are relevant to geographical education in secondary schools I would emphasise two that seem particularly relevant to my thinking about learning geography through enquiry:

1. Exploring, knowing, understanding and making sense:

   'give children the opportunity to encounter, explore and engage with the wealth of human experience and the different ways through which humans make sense of the world and act upon it'.

2. Enacting dialogue:

   'Help children grasp that understanding builds through collaboration between teacher and pupil and among pupils. Enable them to recognise that knowledge is not only transmitted but also negotiated and re-created: and that each of us in the end makes our own sense out of that knowledge. Dialogue is central to pedagogy; between self and others, between personal and collective knowledge, between present and past, between different ways of thinking' (Alexander, 2009, p. 19).

To what extent is an enquiry approach required by national curriculum documents and public examinations?

A fourth justification for adopting an enquiry approach in the classroom is that it is required by the national curriculum and/or by the specifications for public examinations to be taken.

'Enquiry' has been presented differently in successive versions of the geography national curriculum (GNC) for England. In the 1991 GNC, geographical enquiry was mentioned at the beginning of each Programme of Study, but not explained or integrated into either the Programme of Study or the Statements of Attainment. In the 1995 GNC, the process of enquiry was included in paragraph 2 of the Programme of Study for each key stage and as a section in each level description, but the word 'enquiry' was not used. In the 1999 GNC, geographical enquiry was described for each Programme of Study. In the 2008 GNC, geographical enquiry is one of the key processes listed in the Programme of Study:

'Pupils should be able to:

a. *ask geographical questions, thinking critically, constructively and creatively*

b. *collect, record and display information*

c. *identify bias, opinion and abuse of evidence in sources when investigating issues*

d. *analyse and evaluate evidence, presenting findings to draw and justify conclusions*

e. *find creative ways of using and applying geographical skills and understanding to create new interpretations of place and space*

f. *plan geographical enquiries, suggesting appropriate sequences of investigation*

g. *solve problems and make decisions to develop analytical skills and creative thinking about geographical issues'.*

Students are expected to demonstrate achievement related to geographical enquiry at every level. These are the requirements for students to demonstrate that they have achieved level 8:

'Drawing on their knowledge and understanding, they show independence in identifying appropriate geographical questions and issues, and in using an effective sequence of investigation. They select a wide range of skills and use them effectively and accurately. They evaluate sources of evidence critically before using them in their investigations. They present full and coherently argued summaries of their investigations and reach substantiated conclusions'.

At the time of going to press, the national curriculum and GCSE criteria for England are under review, but it is clear from draft proposals that students are expected to develop the skills of learning through enquiry. In developing their knowledge and understanding of real world places, secondary students will be required to:

▲ investigate geographical questions and issues

▲ collect, interpret, analyse, present and evaluate primary and secondary geographical data of all kinds

▲ develop well-evidenced geographical arguments

▲ communicate informed conclusions

▲ think and study like a geographer.

Summary

An enquiry approach to geographical education can be justified in relation to ways of thinking about geographical knowledge, ways of thinking about learning and in relation to the purposes and aims of education. The view of enquiry as developed in this book is underpinned by a view that geographical knowledge is constructed, by a constructivist theory of learning and by the potential of an enquiry approach to contribute to the broader purposes of education.

Suggestions for research

1. What do students already know and understand about a geographical theme or place to be studied? Devise ways of eliciting their prior knowledge (e.g. through use of spider diagrams, concept maps, diagnostic questionnaires, pictorial representations, interviews). Do they have misunderstandings or stereotypical images? How can information about students' prior knowledge and experiences be used in planning and teaching?

2. To what extent could learning geography through enquiry contribute to the broader purposes and aims of education within a school? This could be investigated through a critical study of documents and initiatives influencing school policy.

References

Alexander, R. (2000) *Culture and Pedagogy.* Oxford: Blackwell.

Alexander, R. (ed) (2009) *Introducing the Cambridge Primary Review: Children, their world, their education.* Cambridge: University of Cambridge Faculty of Education. Available online at *www.primaryreview.org.uk/downloads/ CPR_revised_booklet.pdf* (last accessed 11 January 2013).

Ananiadou, K. and Claro, M. (2009) '21st Century Skills and Competences for New Millennium Learners in OECD Countries', *OECD Education Working Papers,* No. 41, OECD Publishing. Available online at *http://dx.doi. org/10.1787/218525261154* (last accessed 11 January 2013).

Barnes, D. and Todd, F. (1995) *Communication and Learning Revisited.* Portsmouth, NH: Boynton/Cook.

Castree, N. (2005) *Questioning Geography: Fundamental debates.* Oxford: Blackwell.

Johnston, R. (2004) 'Disciplinary change and career paths' in Lee, R. and Smith, D. (eds) *Geographies and Moralities.* Oxford: Blackwell.

Livingstone, D. (1992) *The Geographical Tradition: Episodes in the history of a contested enterprise.* Oxford: Blackwell.

Neighbour, B. (1992) 'Enhancing geographical inquiry and learning', *International Research in Geographical and Environmental Education*, 1, 1, pp. 14–23.

Peet, R. (1998) *Modern Geographical Thought.* Oxford: Blackwell.

Smith, D.M. (1977) *Human Geography: A welfare approach.* London: Edward Arnold.

Smith, D.M. (1988) 'Towards an interpretative human geography', in Eyles, J. and Smith, D.M. (eds) *Qualitative Methods in Human Geography.* Cambridge: Polity Press, pp. 255–67.

Smith, D.M. (1994) *Geography and Social Justice.* Oxford: Blackwell Publishing.

Smith, D.M. (2000) *Moral Geographies: Ethics in a world of difference.* Edinburgh: Edinburgh University Press.

Unwin, T. (1992) *The Place of Geography.* Harlow: Longman.

Vygotsky, L. (1962) *Thought and Language.* Cambridge, MA: Massachusetts Institute of Technology Press.

Wheen, F. (2002) *Hoo-Hahs and Passing Frenzies: Collected journalism.* London: Atlantic Books.

CHAPTER 03

The role of the teacher in an enquiry approach

'An important part of the teacher's role is to try to understand how each child's mind works, what makes them "tick" and what changes when learning occurs' (Ghaye and Robinson, 1989, p. 117).

Introduction

Geography teachers, with their considerable geographical subject knowledge and professional expertise in the classroom, are often concerned about the way an enquiry approach might change their role. This is of particular concern to those teachers who associate enquiry entirely with students working relatively independently, deciding what to investigate, finding information, choosing how to analyse it, reaching their own conclusions etc. This concern is misplaced: the teacher has a highly significant role in the classroom even when students work independently. This chapter sets out to address the following questions:

▲ What is the role of teachers in devising the overall framework for units of work?

▲ What is the role of a teacher's subject expertise in planning an enquiry-based curriculum?

▲ What is the role of the teacher in the enquiry classroom?

▲ What different approaches can teachers adopt in implementing an enquiry-based curriculum?

The role of teachers when controversial issues are being investigated is examined in Chapter 12.

What is the role of teachers in devising the overall framework for units of work?

Using questions rather than topics as headings for units of work

If an enquiry approach is to be encouraged, then a good starting point in planning the curriculum is to use questions rather than topics as headings for units of work. Questions suggest that what is to be studied is something to be investigated rather than something simply to be transmitted. Most geography teachers in England and Wales are familiar with this practice as the majority of current examination specifications for geography at both GCSE and A-level use key questions as headings (Figure 3.1). There are guidelines in the form of key ideas or subsidiary questions suggesting the general ideas which need to be addressed as well as information about required content.

Questions are also used as frameworks for the geography curriculum in other countries. The new Singapore O-level geography syllabus, with its emphasis on 'inquiry-based learning', uses questions and sub-questions for each of the six themes (Figure 3.2) and explains the rationale:

'The heading for each of these topics is presented in the form of an overarching geographical question. Each topic is organised around three key questions and these key questions serve as the organisational framework of the syllabus. For each key question, there are associated guiding questions, main ideas, learning outcomes, content and main terms. The syllabus is designed such that the first two key questions guide students to gain an understanding and appreciation of the topic as stated in the overview. The knowledge and skills acquired would subsequently be used by students to apply to the issue studied when they proceed with their enquiry to the third key question. The three key questions and associated guiding questions present an enquiry route through which the main ideas may be explored. At the end of every topic, a case study or an example together with a set of guiding questions reiterates the overarching question and guides students to come to a conclusion or answer the overarching question with reasoned argument'.

The questions differ from those in the English and Welsh specifications in that for each of the six topics there is a progression in types of questions, from two initial questions which focus on the development of knowledge and understanding and a third question which requires students to apply their knowledge to an issue.

What makes a good key question for a unit of work?

Even if questions have been specified by examination boards there are decisions to be made when producing geography schemes of work. The first thing to consider is 'what kind of questions make overarching or key questions?' Riley, in his seminal article 'Into the key stage 3 history garden: choosing and planting your enquiry questions' (2000), discussed the characteristics of a good enquiry question in history (Figure 3.3).

A scheme of work for geography could be framed in a similar way with questions that are rigorous, challenging and intriguing. The titles of the Geographical Association's *Key Stage 3 Geography Teachers' Toolkit* publications adopt the approach of framing a series of lessons with one key enquiry question, for example *A Thorny Issue: Should I buy a Valentine's rose?* (Ellis, 2009) and *British or European: Who do you think you are?* (Brassington, 2008). Such questions satisfy Riley's criteria in that they are intriguing and could lead to challenging and rigorous geography.

How should key questions be used in plans for units of work?

Even if key questions have been prescribed already by a national curriculum or an examinations specification there is still a role for the teacher in deciding how they should be presented to students.

▲ Is there a need or scope for modifying the prescribed question in order to make it a really good enquiry question, using Riley's criteria, to present to students?

▲ Should subsidiary questions be identified and if so should these be presented to students or negotiated with students?

▲ If subsidiary questions are identified, should they be in a sequence as in the Singapore O-level syllabus in which questions serve different purposes?

Examination board	Are there questions?	Example of questions	How developed in specification
AQA GCSE A	no		
AQA GCSE B	yes	Why has industry become increasingly global?	Key ideas Specification of content
EDEXCEL GCSE A	no		
EDEXCEL GCSE B	yes	What is the value of the biosphere?	Key ideas Detailed content
OCR GCSE A (GCSE pilot)	yes	What do we know about mountains and how have they been represented in cultural resources?	Key ideas Content
OCR GCSE B (Bristol Project)	yes	How does river flooding illustrate the interaction between natural processes and human activity?	Key ideas Content
WJEC GCSE A	yes	In what different ways are European city centres being renewed?	Subsidiary enquiry questions Exemplification
WJEC GCSE B (Avery Hill GYSL project)	yes	How effective is international aid in narrowing the economic gap between countries?	Depth of coverage Learning and research opportunities
AQA GCE	no		
EDEXCEL GCE (16–19 project)	yes	How should we tackle the global challenges of increasing risk and vulnerability in a more hazardous world?	What students need to learn Suggested teaching and learning
OCR GCE	yes	What are the environmental issues associated with urban change?	Key ideas Content
WJEC	yes	Can food production be sustainably increased?	Content Opportunities for research and fieldwork Suggested examples

Figure 3.1: The use of enquiry questions in examination specifications (January 2013).

What is the role of a teacher's subject expertise in planning an enquiry-based curriculum?

In traditional models of teaching, the teacher is the source of geographical knowledge and transmits this to students. The teacher's geographical expertise is clearly essential. There is an even greater need for such expertise in an enquiry-based approach. The teacher still has the overall responsibility for what students learn through the geography curriculum, and geography teachers need to have a deep knowledge and understanding of the subject.

Selecting key questions

Teachers need to be able to identify good key questions, preferably intriguing ones. This requires a comprehensive knowledge of what is being investigated. Considering appropriate sub-questions requires an understanding of the essential structure of what is being studied. Many geographical concepts are too difficult or complex for students to understand unaided: the teacher must identify key concepts that need to be understood in studying a particular theme, place or issue and decide how to help students acquire them.

Sources

The teacher must identify sources of appropriate geographical information and ideas and decide whether to provide the information; expect students to search for information themselves; or provide a limited choice of sources from which students can select information, e.g. a few reliable, accessible internet sites. Illustrative case studies or examples relevant to the question being considered must be identified; the teacher must also decide whether students could have a choice of case studies. Students should have access to different viewpoints on a controversial issue.

Tasks and activities

Students need tasks and activities to help them make sense of data, e.g. analysing maps or graphs; annotating text; converting information from one form into another, e.g. text to diagram, photograph

---

Key questions

Theme 1: Our Dynamic Planet (Physical Geography)

Topic 1: Coasts – should coastal environments matter?

▲ How and why are coastal environments different and dynamic?

▲ Why are coastal areas valuable? (Focus is on tropical coasts)

▲ How can we manage coastal areas in a sustainable manner?

Topic 2: Living with tectonic hazards – risk or opportunity?

▲ Why are some areas more prone to tectonic hazards?

▲ What landforms and associated tectonic phenomena are found at plate boundaries?

▲ How do people prepare for and respond to earthquakes?

Topic 3: Variable weather and changing climate – a continuing challenge?

▲ Why do different places experience different weather and climate?

▲ What is happening to the Earth's climate?

▲ Is the weather becoming more extreme?

Theme 2: Our Changing World (Human Geography)

Topic 4: Global tourism – is tourism the way to go?

▲ How does the nature of tourism vary from place to place?

▲ Why has tourism become a global phenomenon?

▲ Developing tourism at what cost?

Topic 5: Food resources – is technology a panacea for food shortage?

▲ How and why have food consumption patterns changed since 1960s?

▲ What are the trends and challenges in production of food crops?

▲ How can the problem of food shortage be addressed?

Topic 6: Health and diseases – are we more vulnerable than before?

▲ What are the global patterns of health and diseases?

▲ What influences the spread and impact of infectious diseases? (Focus is on malaria and HIV/AIDS)

▲ How do we manage the current and future spread of infectious diseases?

Theme 3: Geographical Skills and Investigations

Topic 7: Topographical map reading skills

Topic 8: Geographical data and techniques

Topic 9: Geographical investigations

Figure 3.2: Singapore O-level geography syllabus: content outline and key questions.

to text; writing reports; producing concept maps; discussing issues; analysing different viewpoints.

In short, planning an enquiry approach demands an extensive knowledge of geography.

What is the role of the teacher in the enquiry classroom?

While it might be clear that subject expertise is needed in planning for enquiry, what about the teacher's role in the classroom? Sometimes the teacher is said to be a 'manager' or 'facilitator' of learning. 'Manager' suggests that the teacher oversees what is going on, checking that everyone understands what to do, is getting on with the task, etc. Simply managing could be done by a non-specialist. 'Facilitator of learning' suggests a bit more; that the teacher is focusing on what the student is learning rather than on whether they are simply getting on with their work. But the term undervalues the need for teacher input based on expertise in geography. The role of the teacher in the classroom is more significant than that of a manager or facilitator.

The characteristics of good enquiry questions

Riley's article, 'Into the key stage 3 history garden: choosing and planting your enquiry questions', explored the idea of using a 'carefully-crafted enquiry question' to provide a focus for students' learning throughout a unit of work. In getting teachers to think about what made an enquiry question a good one, he asked them:

'Does each of your enquiry questions:

▲ *Capture the interest and imagination of your pupils?*

▲ *Place an aspect of historical thinking, concept or process at the forefront of pupils' minds?*

▲ *Result in a tangible, lively, substantial, enjoyable "outcome activity" (i.e. at the end of the lesson sequence) through which pupils can genuinely answer the enquiry question?' (p. 8).*

He used the criteria in these questions to examine possible questions related to medieval towns. He thought that the question 'Why did medieval towns grow?' could be rigorous but was probably not exciting. 'What was life like in the towns?' was weak because it was merely descriptive, not intriguing and not rigorous and did not take students into an understanding of how history works. On the other hand 'Did medieval towns make people free?' contained a puzzling element, would appeal to students' interest in fairness and provided a purpose for studying guilds and apprentices.

He used his ideas to construct a series of questions for the whole of key stage 3 history, designed to address the range of skills, knowledge and understanding required at the time by the history national curriculum. He devised the questions below for year 8 students.

During the course of the year there was a range of question types so that collectively they addressed the requirement to develop particular skills and understanding. Some questions encouraged a particular focus on one of the key concepts of the history national curriculum. For example, 'Did life get better for ordinary people?' could be used to increase understanding of 'change and continuity'. 'What lay behind the weaver's riots in Frome?' is an example of a question using a local context to explore the concept of 'cause and consequences'. The question, 'Why was it difficult to find out about changes in the religious beliefs of ordinary people?' focuses on problems related to evidence and its use in history and could be used to increase evidential understanding.

Each of the questions in Riley's scheme of work was designed to act as a key question for a unit of work lasting several lessons. Each would lend itself to being explored through a range of investigative activities using evidence. None of the questions could be answered with a simple 'yes' or 'no'.

	Term 1	Term 2	Term 3
Curriculum content	Change through time: ordinary lives 1300–2000	The French Revolution	Industry, politics and empire, 1815–1960s
Enquiry questions	Did life get better for ordinary people?	How did King Louis XVI lose control of his kingdom?	Why did it take so long for women to get the vote?
	How did people in our locality enjoy themselves?	What made the ideas of the revolution so shocking?	What lay behind the weavers' riots in Frome?
	How much did the treatment of the poor improve?	Does Robespierre deserve his reputation as a bloodthirsty tyrant?	Was the British Empire 'a good thing'?
	Why is it so difficult to find out about changes in the religious beliefs of ordinary people?	Did Napoleon betray the Revolution?	How have interpretations of 20th-century India been changing?

Figure 3.3: The characteristics of good enquiry questions in history. Source: Riley, 2000.

The geography curriculum that students experience is constructed in the classroom, not at the planning stage. It is in the classroom that teachers support students to enable them to move beyond their existing knowledge and understanding, within the 'zone of proximal/potential development' (ZPD: see Chapter 2). Vygotsky recognised that students need help with this: 'With assistance, every child can do more than he can by himself', (Vygotsky, 1962, p. 104). Vygotsky's emphasis on the need for support to take thinking forward within the ZPD suggests a crucial role for teachers in using the enquiry approach. He wrote about providing 'light assistance, the first step in a solution, a leading question or some other form of help' (*ibid.*, p. 103).

This idea was later developed by others into the notion of 'scaffolding'.

Scaffolding

Vygotsky (1962), Wood *et al.* (1976) and Webster *et al.* (1996) identified the kinds of 'scaffolding' that could help students achieve more with assistance than they could unaided (Figure 3.4).

Some scaffolding can be prepared at the planning stage. An investigation can be simplified by breaking down the key question framing a unit of work into a sequence of sub-questions, each to be investigated in one lesson. Students could be

---

Scaffolding

Although Vygotsky did not use the term himself, he was the first to develop the concept of 'scaffolding'. In his experimental work with children, he studied how working in collaboration with adults could develop students' conceptual understanding. Vygotsky (1962) referred to several types of assistance that might be given when children could not complete problem-solving activities on their own:

▲ providing the first step in a solution by asking a leading question

▲ explaining

▲ supplying information

▲ questioning

▲ correcting

▲ making the child explain.

Wood *et al.* (1976) were the first to use the word 'scaffolding' in an educational context. They carried out experimental work with young children to investigate 'the nature of the tutorial process; the means whereby an adult or expert helps somebody who is less adult or less expert' (p. 90). They described as a kind of scaffolding the process that enables a child or novice to solve a problem, carry out a task or achieve a goal which would be beyond their unassisted efforts. They designed a task in which children had to build a pyramid out of building blocks, a task designed to be challenging but not so difficult as to be completely beyond the capability of any of the children and where the learning could potentially be applied to a later activity. In the experiment the tutors allowed the children to do as much as possible themselves and established an 'atmosphere of approval'. They collected data on the interaction of the tutor and the learners and found that scaffolding involved much more than modelling and imitation. They found that tutors scaffolded the activities through dialogue and intervention by:

▲ simplifying the task by reducing the number of steps involved in a task

▲ maintaining the pursuit of the goal and helping the learner to risk a next step

▲ noting inconsistencies between what the child had produced and the ideal solution

▲ controlling frustration and risk during the problem-solving activity but without creating too much dependency on the tutor

▲ demonstrating an idealised version.

Webster *et al.* (1996) investigated and developed ideas about scaffolding as part of a large-scale research project into the development of children's literacy. They collected detailed data of tasks and interaction in year 6 and 7 classrooms (10–12 year olds). Although they recognised the importance of teachers devising tasks appropriate to students' needs, they found that a study of the tasks was insufficient to determine what or how children learnt. Different teachers mediated the tasks in different ways. They found that the most powerful determinant of children's learning, 'the difference which makes the difference' (*ibid.*, p. 151) was how teachers scaffolded the learning process. By scaffolding they meant 'the complex set of interactions through which adults guide and promote children's thinking'. This definition emphasised that scaffolding was much more than teachers simply providing help. It was a collaborative process involving dialogue in which learners had as important a role as teachers. Webster *et al.* concluded that scaffolding was 'the critical link between teacher and child' (*ibid.*, p. 96). From their research data, they identified various components of teaching and learning which enabled these critical interactions and interventions to take place:

▲ getting children involved in the task

▲ helping children to represent tasks in terms they understand

▲ helping children to adapt and develop concepts

▲ helping children externalise their learning

▲ listening to how children are pursuing the learning activities

▲ reviewing the process of learning and its worth.

The research data showed that the nature of the scaffolding varied from teacher to teacher. They concluded that 'in order to be good at scaffolding, teachers must have a precise knowledge of the characteristics and starting point of the learner, together with a thorough knowledge of the field of enquiry' (*ibid.*, p. 151).

Figure 3.4: Scaffolding.

provided with frameworks with headings, e.g. social, economic, environmental, to help them structure their data collection or analysis of text. Some students could be provided with writing frames with starter sentences for each paragraph to give them a structure for writing reports on what they have found out.

However, it is in the classroom that the kind of scaffolding researched by Wood et al. and Webster et al. is crucial. The 'difference that makes the difference', according to Webster, is not the nature of the tasks themselves but the interaction between teachers and students in the classroom. This takes place through classroom talk, both in the whole class but particularly in dialogues between teacher and students when they are working in small groups or individually. It is then that it is possible to listen to what students are saying, to attempt to understand the sense they are making of the activity and of the data and ideas they are grappling with. It is when listening or eavesdropping that the teacher can detect how students understand or misunderstand. In these dialogues of learning, the teacher has to decide how best to intervene to take students' thinking forward geographically. A simple prompt or probing question might be needed. Sometimes, some teaching might be required; it might be necessary to explain a concept, to explain how to analyse data geographically or to respond to students' questions. It is in these interactive dialogues that enquiry teachers need to be able to think on their feet and to draw on subject knowledge and understanding.

Scaffolding has been found to be a useful and powerful metaphor (Verenikina, 2008) but the way it is understood and interpreted in the classroom varies. Where it is associated with strong teacher direction, scaffolding can limit rather than support learning. When the emphasis is put on the role of the teacher as collaborator and co-constructor of knowledge through dialogue with the learner, then scaffolding can provide successful support in the ZPD.

What different approaches can teachers adopt in implementing an enquiry-based curriculum?

In the same way as universities have used EBL and IBL flexibly to apply it in different contexts, it is possible to apply an enquiry-based learning approach to teaching geography in different ways. The teacher's role can vary along a continuum, with strong teacher guidance at one end and less at the other. There is a corresponding change in the role of the student, from less student self-direction at one end and more at the other. A framework devised by Barnes et al. (1987) to evaluate the Technical Vocational Education Initiative (TVEI) transformed the way I see classrooms (Figure 3.5). The framework was used to examine the extent to which teachers enabled learners to participate in the construction of knowledge. Although the 'participation dimension' was seen as a continuum, it was divided into three categories for the purpose of analysing data: closed, framed and negotiated.

	Closed	Framed	Negotiated
Content	Tightly controlled by teacher. Not negotiable	Teacher controls topic, framework of reference and tasks; criteria made explicit	Discussed at each point
Focus	Authoritative knowledge and skills; simplified; monolithic	Stress on empirical testing; processes chosen by the teacher; some legitimation of student ideas	Search for justifications and principles; strong legitimation of student ideas
Students' role	Acceptance; routine performance; little access to principles	Join in teacher's thinking; make hypotheses, set up tests; operate teacher's frame	Discuss goals and methods critically; share responsibility for frame and criteria
Key concepts	'Authority'; the proper procedures and the right answers	'Access' to skills, processes, criteria	'Relevance'; critical discussion of students' priorities
Methods	Exposition; worksheets (closed); note-giving; individual exercises; routine practical work, the teacher evaluates	Exposition, with discussion eliciting suggestions; individual/group problem-solving; lists of tasks given; discussion of outcomes, but teacher adjudicates	Group and class discussion and decision making about goals and criteria; students plan and carry out work, make presentations, evaluate success

Figure 3.5: The participation dimension. Source: Barnes et al., 1987.

Role of teacher	More teacher guidance	Some teacher guidance	Less teacher guidance
Role of student	Less student self-direction	Some student self-direction	More student self-direction
Deciding the focus of the enquiry	Focus of enquiry and questions decided by teacher	Some choice of content; or teacher devises activities to encourage students to identify questions or sub-questions	Students choose focus of enquiry, devise questions and plan how to investigate them
Using geographical sources as evidence	All data chosen by teacher, presented as authoritative evidence	Teacher provides variety of resources from which students select data using explicit criteria. Students encouraged to question data	Students are helped to find own data from sources in and out of school. Students encouraged to be critical of data
Making sense	Activities devised by teacher to achieve predetermined objectives. Students follow instructions	Students introduced to different techniques and conceptual frameworks and learn to use them selectively	Students decide how to interpret and analyse data in consultation with teacher
Reaching conclusions and reflecting on them	Predictable outcomes	Students discuss conclusions they have reached	Students reach own conclusions and evaluate them critically
Summary	The teacher controls the construction of knowledge by making all decisions about content, data, activities and conclusions	Teacher inducts students into ways in which geographical knowledge is constructed. Students are made aware of choices and are encouraged to be critical	Students are enabled, with teacher guidance, to investigate questions of interest to themselves and to evaluate their investigation critically

Figure 3.6: The role of the teacher in learning through enquiry.

I have adapted the original framework so that it relates to key elements of geographical enquiry (Figure 3.6). I can illustrate the categories with examples.

My son's GCSE coursework was at the left-hand end of the continuum. The whole class was investigating the use of shopping centres of different sizes in Sheffield. The teacher devised a questionnaire which students used in groups in different centres. The teacher collated the data and suggested graphs to use. The conclusions were as expected. The teacher made all the key decisions about the enquiry and enabled the students to carry it out.

My son's A-level coursework was at the other end of the continuum. He chose to investigate the role of two action groups, both of which opposed a proposal for a large new supermarket. He devised a questionnaire and collected data from a public meeting and locally. He decided how to present and interpret the data and reached his own conclusions. He took responsibility for all the key decisions.

A teacher with whom I was working developed a unit of work which would fall in Barnes' 'framed' category in the centre of the continuum. The class was studying flooding through a case study of floods in Mozambique which were then in the news. He created a 'need to know' by showing a short TV news report and used it to negotiate with the class a framework of questions. He selected maps, photographs and reports from newspapers and put them into folders on the school's intranet. The students had to search through these to select information for a newspaper report, for which he had provided categories for paragraph headings: physical and human causes and short-term and long-term impacts. The students used the information to write reports and reach their own conclusions. The teacher had provided a framework which helped students select information and make sense of the floods for themselves.

Barnes *et al.*'s categories oversimplify the ways in which a teacher's role can vary. It can vary from one unit of work to another, but it can also vary within a unit of work or even within a lesson (Roberts, 1996). For example a teacher might start a unit of work in a closed way, choosing the focus of the enquiry, the key question and subsidiary questions and the geographical sources to be used, but enable students to make choices about how to present and analyse data. Alternatively, teachers might allow students to choose the focus of the enquiry, e.g. which volcano to study, but provide structured guidelines on how this should be investigated.

It is worth reflecting on when it is appropriate to provide strong guidance and when it is appropriate to give students greater independence, either for a whole unit of work or within a unit of work. Professional judgements have to be made within the constraints of examination specifications, so not all decisions can be made freely. However, the framework draws attention to the effect that the role of the teacher has on the extent to which students can participate fully in the construction of knowledge and become critically engaged in constructing their understanding of the world.

Summary

The teacher's role is crucial in an enquiry approach to the teaching and learning of geography. At the planning stage, the teacher's expert subject knowledge can be used to devise stimulating key questions, to be aware of appropriate resources and to structure a unit of work. In the classroom, the assistance that teachers provide students through various forms of scaffolding helps students develop geographical understanding. Depending on the context in which an enquiry approach is developed, the teacher might provide substantial guidance or offer students considerable freedom.

Suggestions for research

1. Use Riley's ideas to develop a range of key questions to frame units of work in geography. Investigate how you develop the use of one of these questions and how you enable it to become the students' own question.

2. Use the ideas of Vygotsky, Wood *et al.* and Webster *et al.* (Figure 3.4) to produce a framework to investigate the different ways in which you scaffold students' learning, e.g. in prepared materials; in dialogues with the

whole class or with groups and individuals. It would help to record your dialogues for later analysis. What kinds of interventions promote the development of geographical understanding? To what extent do the ways you use scaffolding restrict or enable students' learning?

References

Barnes, D., Johnson, G., Jordan, S., Layton, D., Medway, P. and Yeoman, D. (1987) *The TVEI Curriculum 14–16: An interim report based on case studies in twelve schools.* Leeds: University of Leeds.

Brassington, J. (2008) *British or European? Who do you think you are?* Sheffield: The Geographical Association.

Ellis, L. (2009) *A Thorny Issue: Should I buy a Valentine's Rose?* Sheffield: The Geographical Association.

Ghaye, A. and Robinson, E. (1989) 'Concept maps and children's thinking: a constructivist approach' in Slater, F. (ed) *Language and Learning in the Teaching of Geography.* London: Routledge.

Riley, M. (2000) 'Into the key stage 3 history garden: choosing and planting your enquiry questions', *Teaching History,* 99, pp. 8–13.

Roberts, M. (1996) 'Teaching styles and strategies' in Kent, A., Lambert, D., Naish, M. and Slater, F. (eds) *Geography and Education: Viewpoints on teaching and learning.* Cambridge: Cambridge University Press.

Verenikina, I. (2008) 'Scaffolding and learning: its role in nurturing new learners' in Kell, P., Vialle, W., Konza, D. and Vogl, G. (eds) *Learning and the Learner: Exploring learning for new times.* Wollongong, Australia: University of Wollongong.

Vygotsky, L. (1962) *Thought and Language.* Cambridge, MA: Massachusetts Institute of Technology Press.

Webster, A., Beveridge, M. and Reed, M. (1996) *Managing the Literacy Curriculum.* London: Routledge.

Wood, D., Bruner, J. and Ross, G. (1976) 'The role of tutoring in problem solving', *Journal of Child Psychology and Psychiatry,* 17, 2, pp. 89–100.

CHAPTER 04

Creating a need to know

'Communication is about telling stories. Try to start with something familiar that hooks the audience in; or start with an interesting question or something mysterious that you promise to reveal' (Alice Roberts, TV presenter, quoted in Tickle, 2012)

Introduction

Generally, the content of the geography curriculum is constrained by external requirements. We have to take into account public examination specifications and, if it applies, national curriculum requirements. Students do not generally have any say in what they study in geography. The Young People's Geographies Project (Firth and Biddulph, 2009; Firth *et al.*, 2010; Biddulph, 2011) provided an interesting exception. It was set up to explore ways in which students and teachers, in collaboration, could use the experiences of young people to inform curriculum choices. This kind of practice, however, is extremely rare. This presents a challenge. Students do not necessarily come into the classroom wanting to know about, for example, flood hydrographs or life expectancy in Kenya. Yet, if they are to learn anything, they need to become interested in what is included in the geography curriculum and to engage with the ideas introduced. It is important that we create in students 'a need to know'. This has been expressed in different ways as 'sparking curiosity' or 'providing a hook'.

This chapter is about different ways of doing this and addresses the following questions:

▲ Why is the stance of the teacher important in creating a need to know?

▲ What distinguishes initial stimulus material from 'starters'?

▲ What can we learn from how history teachers use initial stimulus materials?

▲ What different kinds of stimulus or hook are successful?

▲ What kinds of speculation can create a need to know?

▲ Is it feasible to offer students choice?

The chapter explores four ways of creating a need to know: stance, stimulus, speculation and choice.

Why is the stance of the teacher important in creating a need to know?

I came across the concept of 'stance' in Jerome Bruner's book, *Actual Minds, Possible Worlds* (1986). Stance is about the attitude of a teacher towards a subject. Teachers communicate their stance by what they say and by their attitudes towards the subject discipline. Bruner illustrates this by using an example of a science lesson he still could remember years later:

'I recall a teacher, her name was Miss Orcutt, who made a statement in class, "It is a very puzzling thing not that water turns to ice at 32 degrees Fahrenheit, but that it should change from a liquid into a solid". She then went on to give us an intuitive account of Brownian movement and of molecules, expressing a sense of wonder ... She was inviting me to extend my world of wonder to encompass hers. She was not just informing me. She was, rather, negotiating the world of wonder and possibility. Molecules, solids, liquids, movement were not facts; they were to be used in pondering and imagining' (ibid., p. 126).

Bruner commented that this teacher was a rarity. When I read this passage I thought about my own experience of being at school, reflecting on how many teachers I could remember who had this sense of wonder about what we were learning. For me, like Bruner, it was a rarity because I could remember only one, my biology teacher, Miss Page. She was evidently interested in everything she taught us and shared her excitement in every lesson. I remember that in one lesson she mentioned an article she had read about bird migration and about how scientists were trying to understand how birds from Europe could find their way to Africa and back again. She joined in the scientists' wondering and made us wonder too; she made us curious.

In my opinion, of the fours ways of creating a need to know included in this chapter, stance is the most important. It cannot be reduced to a fun activity at the start of a scheme of work. It is not an attitude towards an activity: it is an attitude towards subject matter and learning that permeates everything the teacher does. So what do teachers need to do to have a stance which promotes curiosity? Bruner writes: 'if the teacher wishes to close down the process of wondering by flat declaration of fixed factuality, he or she can do so. The teacher can also open wide a topic ... to speculation and negotiation' (*ibid.*, p. 127).

We can learn about stance by watching the way the best television presenters of documentary programmes present their material. David Attenborough, for example, always conveys his own continuing fascination with the world about him. A stance that encourages curiosity is marked by:

▲ expressing uncertainty and doubt

▲ expressing a sense of puzzlement

▲ expressing a sense of wonder or amazement

▲ indicating the hypothetical nature of knowledge

▲ speculating about information rather than presenting it simply as 'fact'

▲ expecting students to think about something for themselves

▲ conveying an interest in what is being studied.

The importance of stance is evident from the geography PGCE students I taught. In many cases the reason they became interested in geography was because of one special geography teacher. They often described them as being 'so enthusiastic'. Special geography teachers promote curiosity by sharing their excitement in the subject matter with students, making it evident that they are constantly

learning new things and wanting to find out more. Geographical knowledge for these special teachers was not fixed information to be transmitted, but something that was constantly being updated, considered and reconstructed. The stance of geography teachers is about opening up 'the world of wonder and possibility' to students.

What distinguishes initial stimulus material from 'starters'?

An important way of 'creating a need to know' is through the use of some sort of stimulus at the beginning of the study of a new theme and possibly for the sub-questions framing individual lessons. This has been referred to by history teachers as initial stimulus material or ISM (Phillips, 2001) or as a 'hook' to get students curious. The main purpose of ISM is to provoke students' interest in what is to be studied and to get them involved in lines of enquiry to be pursued.

In recent years, teachers in England have developed a repertoire of 'starters' encouraged by guidance from the UK government's National Strategy (DfES, 2004) and supported by books and articles with suggestions for starters. Although a stimulus is used at the start of an investigation and can be made into a lesson 'starter', there are some significant differences between starter activities and using a stimulus.

- ▲ The main purpose of starter activities is to get all students involved in an activity at the start of the lesson; the main purpose of a stimulus is to create interest in what is to be studied. Starters emphasise an activity whereas a stimulus emphasises geography.

- ▲ Starter activities are not necessarily focused on the content of what is to be studied; there may be no obvious link at all. Government guidelines for starters suggested they could also be used to practise skills, test vocabulary or relate to prior knowledge. These are all worthwhile activities, but do not create interest in what is to be studied. Collections of generic starter activities, applicable to any topic, suggest that the relationship to the subject matter is unimportant. In contrast there is always a tight relationship between ISM and the ensuing study.

- ▲ A starter activity is a short discrete activity. Guidance on their use emphasises 'pace' and 'timing'. In contrast, ISM can be used more flexibly, e.g. for a short period or to lead into more prolonged discussion for the entire introductory lesson to a unit of work. Discussion of stimulus material can be slow, calm, gradually unfolding the key issues and questions involved in the topic. In contrast to being discrete, it can be used to provoke questions and establish lines of enquiry. The emphasis of ISM is on stimulating interest to be sustained throughout the study.

- ▲ Starters are usually supplemented with a display of lesson objectives. An Ofsted report (2011) based on inspections of schools in England, stated: 'Students often had to copy objectives into their books at the start of the lesson with little thought about what these meant. In many cases, the activity at the start of the lesson had little relevance to the main task; it added little to the students' learning and used up precious time' (paragraph 51). In an enquiry approach it is more appropriate to introduce what is to be studied as a question than as a list of what is to be learnt; questions open out a topic rather than closing it down. The practice of telling students what they are about to learn can remove the element of surprise and intrigue in what is to follow; it is rather like being given the answer to a puzzle before attempting to solve it. However, as many schools require teachers to present students with objectives at the start of lessons, objectives could be phrased in enquiry terms rather than in terms of learning outcomes, e.g. 'to investigate why some parts of the world experience frequent earthquakes'. Alternatively, it might be an option for objectives to emerge in a more meaningful way during the discussion of ISM.

- ▲ The use of lists of objectives at the start of a lesson rarely includes discussion of the purposes of studying a topic. Discussion of ISM can incorporate discussion of why it is worth investigating this topic. Davidson (2006) commented that the information to be acquired to achieve the objectives is taken for granted, rather than being in response to questions that are worth asking.

- ▲ Although the guidance for starter activities suggests they should be challenging, some starters are closed activities with an emphasis on correct answers, whereas stimulus materials encourage questions and more open and speculative responses.

- ▲ Starter activities emphasise student activity. Although initial stimulus materials can involve student activity, it is also possible that a teacher-dominated introduction to a particular unit of work could be used to spark their curiosity.

Starter activities have become ritualised in many schools and have been used successfully to get students involved in an activity. In an enquiry-based approach it is important to consider what constitutes an effective start to a unit of work or lesson in terms of getting students curious about what they are about to study.

What can we learn from how history teachers use initial stimulus materials?

Phillips (2001), from his research into Initial Stimulus Material (ISM) in history teaching, advocates taking three things into consideration when selecting ISM. First, the material should have an oblique relationship to what is being studied. Second, he advocated starting with something 'concrete' rather than conceptual, using 'concrete' in the Piagetian sense of using examples students could relate to immediately through their senses. Third, referring to Vygotsky, he stressed the importance of using examples that students could connect with their own experience.

Geography teachers could learn from the example he provided to illustrate what he meant by this. He discussed how a year 8 class might be introduced to 17th-century England. A logical starting point might be the causes of the Civil War but Phillips thought that 'this might not be the best way of arousing curiosity' (p. 20). Instead of starting with causes, which are highly conceptual, he suggested starting with a key event or key personality. He had found, through his teaching, that a Dutch print of Charles I's execution was 'an excellent way in to explaining many of the extraordinary events of the seventeenth century.' Instead of telling students that they were to study the 17th century, he showed them the print and simply asked 'What can you see?' He found that the oblique nature of the stimulus immediately aroused curiosity. Through careful pre-planned questions he probed their knowledge and understanding and then asked them, in pairs, to write down questions they wanted to ask. These were then related to the pre-planned key questions and used to establish aims and objectives and lines of enquiry: What were the events that led up to the King being executed? Why was the King executed? What were the results of the execution? Why this event was so significant in British history? The purpose of the ISM was to provoke curiosity and prompt questions. Far from being a discrete part of the lesson, Phillips suggested that the print could be further examined after this initial activity or revisited later in the series of lessons. He stressed the importance of considering what students are likely to know when planning questions and of introducing them to key vocabulary through the use of the ISM.

What different kinds of stimulus or hook are successful?

In selecting ISM the teacher needs to plan how it is going to be used, what questions to ask, what activity students might undertake in response to the stimulus and how to lead from the discussion of the stimulus to investigating the geographical theme or place. Planning can take into account Phillips' advice on using something oblique and working from the concrete to the conceptual. In the same way as people have built up repertoires of starters, it would be useful to build up a repertoire of successful stimulus material related to specific themes.

Figure 4.1 suggests some types of ISM, together with some illustrative examples.

What kinds of speculation can create a need to know?

The power of speculation

Although creating a need to know through speculation usually involves some kind of stimulus, I have given it a separate section because of the power of speculation to get students thinking for themselves. It opens up a topic to uncertainty and it generates questions. It also involves students drawing on their existing knowledge and understanding, giving a teacher the opportunity to elicit prior knowledge and understanding (and also any misunderstandings). Students can be invited to speculate on how something was formed, how something might be investigated or about factual information.

Guessing how something was formed: how did it get to be like this?

I once observed a student teacher's lesson on the formation of sand-spits. Pictures and maps were presented and students were told how they were formed. They were not particularly interested because nothing had been done to spark their curiosity. But sand-spits are extraordinary shapes and students could be invited to speculate on how they got to be like this and – by being shown maps of different examples – why they grow in the direction they do and why they have varied features. This kind of speculation can lead to a need to know and can be rewarding if students are given the opportunity to use their reasoning powers to work out some of the processes for themselves. Guessing how something was formed, from looking

Different types of ISM

Photographs

Photographs, including aerial photographs and aerial views from Google, are readily available and there are many ways of using them. Students can be asked: 'What do you think this is?', 'What is happening here?' and 'How did this get like this?' They can be asked to discuss photographs and jot down questions. Students can be motivated by the familiar as well as by the exotic; I have observed classes responding well to photographs and aerial views of their own locality. Part of a photograph can be shown before revealing the whole (Halocha, 2008; Durbin, 2006). Another possibility is cutting photographs into jigsaw pieces. Emma Rawlings Smith has provided an example of how she used jigsaw photographs for a lesson introducing Beijing (Figure 4.2).

Film and YouTube

Films, DVDs and short extracts from YouTube can all make excellent ISM. Good examples of how they have been used can be found in articles by Richard Bustin (2011a; 2011b) in which he explains how and why he uses a music video and extracts from a film to get students thinking about 'first, second and third space' in Las Vegas and Edinburgh.

Personal anecdotes and stories

A vividly told anecdote or story from personal experience can be more accessible and motivating than a resource. Many geography teachers have travelled widely. Some have experienced earthquakes, have seen volcanoes erupt, have crossed glaciers, have walked in tropical rainforest, have visited or lived in countries being studied etc. By sharing these experiences, we are not only providing a good stimulus, but also conveying to students that geography is not simply something that happens in the classroom but is something that is related to the 'real world' and enhanced through experiences of different places and environments.

Reading extracts from travel writing and fiction

There are many possibilities. I have observed lessons in which students were riveted by being read a short extract from the book *Alive: The story of the Andes survivors* (Piers, 1974) to stimulate interest in tropical rainforests. The book tells the story of a Uruguayan rugby team whose plane crashed in the Andes in 1972 and how 16 of the 45 people on the flight managed to survive. The book was made into the film *Alive* in 1993.

Music and sound

Different kinds of music, with or without lyrics, e.g. classical, folk, jazz, pop, folk, can be used to create an atmosphere of a place or event. A CD that many of my PGCE students used successfully was *Rainforest Requiem: Recordings of wildlife in the Amazon rainforest* (Ranft, 2006). The 29 tracks, all recorded in the Amazon rainforest, take the listener through an imaginary day, and include sounds of the many creatures and the afternoon storm followed by sounds of water dripping off the canopy.

Imagined Facebook page

Owen (2011) describes in an article in *Teaching Geography* how she used the start of a Facebook page for Jerzy Bronowski, a migrant from Poland, using information from another *Teaching Geography* article by Bolton (2008).

Maps

Ordnance Survey and other topographical maps can be used as ISM. Students enjoy doing treasure hunts for particular features on them. Students can speculate on what the landscape/townscape would look like before they see other resources. Atlas maps can be used by students to find out all they can about a particular place or country before investigating it in more detail. Worldmapper maps, in which countries are resized according to the theme being shown, make excellent puzzle maps at the start of a unit (*www.worldmapper.org*). Students can be presented with one or more maps and asked to speculate on what the map shows.

Objects in a bag

Amis (2012) describes how she used what she called 'hot topic bags' which contained a range of objects to stimulate discussion about the Olympic Games. Each bag included: newspaper articles, items purchased from London 2012 shop, foreign currency, medals and cups, and an advert about houses to let in the summer of 2012. The students generated questions, shared and sorted them and discussed which were the big and which the subsidiary questions. As a class they decided on the big question: 'Are the 2012 Games good value?'

I observed a lesson on comparison and convenience goods (NB comparison goods are bought infrequently, e.g. furniture, and shoppers might compare products and prices before buying. Convenience good are bought frequently, e.g. groceries, and often locally). The teacher displayed the definitions and then pulled objects out of the bag. Students were asked to write down to which of the two categories each object belonged. It was amazing how interested they were in the everyday objects that came out of the bag, e.g. a pair of trainers, a bag of potatoes, a magazine, etc.

Objects on a tray

Emma Rawlings Smith used objects on a tray to stimulate curiosity about surviving in polar conditions: *'When starting a mystery about Scott's expedition to the South Pole I had 10 items which were taken to the Pole. Students had to remember them, and later tell me which object I had removed. I did this again as a plenary task. The two items I had removed had never made it into Scott's expedition kit'.*

Food and drink

Plates of food can be used to illustrate different diets or different calorie intakes. Davidson (2006) took a bunch of bananas into the classroom and asked students to guess how much they cost, to provoke curiosity at the start of a lesson investigating the effect of a hurricane on banana prices.

Emma Rawlings Smith often uses everyday items to help students make sense of new knowledge. For example, when teaching about the drop in the water table in India, she demonstrated the amount using bottles of water:

'I use everyday items so that knowledge can be linked to students in a more meaningful way. Teaching about the water table drop in India of 4cm a year and comparing it to the same amount of water in water bottle, a second bigger bottle with 40cm of water gone to get students to think about sustainability.'

Rubbish

To stimulate interest in sustainability, students can be asked to guess whether items in a collection of rubbish can be recycled or not and why. The items can then be placed into two separate bins.

Twitter feed

'A Twitter feed is a great starter as students still see "their technology" as being separate from what goes on in class. In this case I was recapping climate change with my GCSE group and I showed the tweet. They all then needed to know the answer.' (Emma Rawlings Smith)

Figure 4.1: Different types of initial stimulus material.

at maps and/or photographs, can be used for many landscape features or for the impact of processes on environment, for example:

- ▲ sand-spit
- ▲ longshore drift
- ▲ a waterfall
- ▲ a delta
- ▲ destruction caused by a tornado or a tsunami
- ▲ an area of soil erosion.

Students are asked, 'How did it get to be like this?' or 'What do you think has happened here?' Through discussion, students raise questions and sometimes suggest their own hypotheses.

Speculating on how something might be investigated

I once visited a PGCE student who was teaching a lesson on glaciers. She mentioned that they moved slowly. A student asked how this could be measured. She was flummoxed, thought on her feet and suggested they thought about this in pairs for a few minutes. This unplanned part of the lesson provoked a lot of interest and debate and everyone was interested in the discussion. She had stumbled, by chance, on something that makes students curious: speculation.

Students could be invited to speculate on:

- ▲ How could we measure how fast a river is flowing or how much water is flowing?
- ▲ How could we find out where water which disappears underground in limestone areas reappears?

- ▲ How could we find out if glaciers are getting smaller?
- ▲ How could we know if the world is getting warmer? How would we measure world temperature? (this could provoke interest in world maps of temperature change and how they were produced)
- ▲ How could people find out views about building new nuclear power plants?
- ▲ How could people find out which were the most popular tourist destinations in the UK?

Speculating by guessing facts and figures

This is a more limited type of speculation and can only be used when students might be expected to make reasonable guesses based on their existing knowledge. It can be used to introduce the key concepts and questions of a unit. Students can be invited to speculate on, for example:

- ▲ The number of earthquakes in the world on the previous day. Students could be invited to write down their guesses. Some might write down 0 if there hadn't been news of any. The number they guessed could be checked against a list from the United States Geological Survey (USGS) website of earthquakes greater than 2.5 on the Richter scale. Discussion of responses could introduce the concept of earthquakes – what counts as an earthquake – and the Richter scale, and could raise questions relevant to an enquiry into earthquakes.
- ▲ Which country (in the Europe or the world) is the most popular destination for UK tourists?

Contrasting images

Resources

- As many nine-piece jigsaws of images about the place you are studying as you have tables in your classroom. I used five for an introduction to Beijing. I had images of the city centre, National Stadium, National Grand Theatre, Botanical Gardens, Dahuisi South Road and the street market. These jigsaw pieces can be laminated so you can write on the back and reuse them.
- Non-permanent pens
- Layers of meaning grid printed on A3 (see below)

Procedure

Opener

Introduce students to the idea that images can be used to paint a picture of a place and that in this lesson they will be focusing on Beijing.

Activities

Give each group a mixture of nine jigsaw pieces from different puzzles. Tell the class that they have to speculate about what they think the images represent. They can note down ideas on the reverse of the images.

Students move around the class to recreate one nine-piece jigsaw on each table. This is placed in the centre of a 'layers of meaning' grid. Students can then use their ideas from the back of jigsaw pieces, and any more they can think of, to build a picture of what Beijing is like: what they can generalise about the city; what they do not know; what other images would be useful; and what they want to find out about Beijing.

Now introduce students to a different source of images of Beijing, focusing on a different aspect of the city on each table. I used:

- Geog.3 textbook double page spread
- a laptop with the *visitbeijing.com* website loaded up
- four images of historical Beijing
- four images of haze/people with face masks/traffic jams and rubbish
- four images of iconic buildings in Beijing.

Revisit the 'layers of meaning' grid with the different sources of information to build up quality enquiry questions. Using the command words shown on the left side of the layers of meaning grid, have an interim discussion to prompt the development of questions which reach beyond the 5Ws.

For the next task, give each student on a table a card marked with the letters A, B, C, D or E and ask them to regroup onto tables A–E. There should now be five student experts from the different image source groups working together; they can discuss the enquiry questions in more detail and a class discussion can refine ideas about good enquiry questions. Finally, ask students to choose four independent enquiry questions to answer using the suggested websites on laptops.

Summary

Display one image from the lesson on the IWB and debrief the class using a sequence of questions which delve deeper: Can we tell how reliable an image is by looking at it? What other information do we need to know? Describe the alternative images you found for Beijing. Identify features of the new images which were surprising.

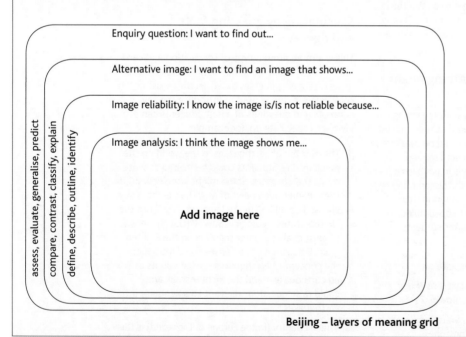

Enquiry question: I want to find out…

Alternative image: I want to find an image that shows…

Image reliability: I know the image is/is not reliable because…

Image analysis: I think the image shows me…

Add image here

assess, evaluate, generalise, predict
compare, contrast, classify, explain
define, describe, outline, identify

Beijing – layers of meaning grid

Figure 4.2: Contrasting images: using different image sources to find out 'What is a place really like?' Source: Emma Rawlings Smith.

The suggestions could be listed together with reasons why students thought these were the most popular. The countries suggested could be located on a map of Europe or the world and the discussion could lead into key questions to be investigated.

Is it feasible to offer students choice?

Over a long career as teacher educator and researcher I rarely came across examples, either in the classroom or in plans for the geography curriculum, which gave students the opportunity to choose what they studied. The few examples I did encounter demonstrated to me the motivating power of allowing students choice. Three examples I came across were: Pole to Pole, studying volcanoes and the Big Project.

Pole to Pole

Pole to Pole was a unit of work for a year 7 class designed to introduce them to the use of the school library. The stimulus at the start of the unit was a clip from the BBC *Pole to Pole* video (1992) showing Michael Palin at the North Pole wondering which line of longitude to choose. Students were given the instructions in Figure 4.3.

Although this unit of work was designed for students to learn library research skills, it was the choice element that was so motivating. Some students chose the countries of origin of themselves or their parents, e.g. one student chose South Korea. Some chose countries they were interested in, e.g. Brazil because of football, and some chose countries they knew nothing about because that would be interesting. Although the enquiry element was geographically limited, in that what they set out to investigate about each country was basic information, it was a very motivating start to a year 7 geography course.

Studying volcanoes

I observed a year 9 class completing their project folders of a study of 'their' volcano. The class had studied one example of a volcano together, using a framework of questions to apply to various sources, e.g. atlases, photographs, maps and accounts of its eruption. Students then had to use the same framework to find out about a volcano of their choice. The students had learnt how to investigate volcanoes, what questions to ask and what kinds of data to use. They were very motivated by being able to choose their volcano. Depending on the ability of students to search for information for themselves and depending on how the work is to be assessed,

Pole to Pole

Imagine you are making a journey from the North Pole to the South Pole. You have to choose a line of longitude to travel along. It must be a line that passes through at least three countries.

Use the lessons in the library to find out about three countries you will be travelling through. You could also find out information from the internet and travel brochures, and use information from your own experience of the countries.

You must then write about the places you saw and the people you met. You could send home a postcard from each country, write an email about each country, write a diary or make a podcast. You could collect souvenirs of your travels and include them in your work. You must include a map of your journey.

it might be advisable for students to be offered a limited choice of volcanoes, with recommended books and websites.

The Big Project

In *Learning Through Enquiry* (Roberts, 2003), I described a project devised by Steve Wilson, in which students investigated natural hazards which took place over a period of several months. Before starting their investigation, they discussed what questions they would focus on, what kind of evidence to collect and how it might be presented. Then each student produced, mostly during homework time, a folder of what they had found out. In this project, students selected natural hazards that were in the news. This motivated students and they also involved parents and relations in the collection of data. Students began talking about 'their volcano' or 'their earthquake'.

Other possibilities

The website for the Young People's Geographies Project provides examples of students choosing what to they want to study. There are also possibilities for student choice within a curriculum even when the themes have been decided by external requirements or by geography departments. Given support it would be feasible for students to investigate for themselves an example of:

▲ a glacier

▲ a river or river basin

▲ a tropical cyclone/hurricane

▲ an earthquake

▲ a coral reef

▲ a tourist destination – a country or a particular attraction

▲ a commodity chain – from raw material, through processing or production, to sale

▲ a national park

▲ an example of ecotourism.

There are some issues related to students having a completely open choice. They might choose an example which does not illustrate key characteristics and could be misleading. They might choose examples where the information available is not easily accessible to them because of complex language, tables of statistics, etc. It is more difficult for teachers to check the accuracy of the work if many different choices are made. These issues could be resolved by providing a list of examples from which choices are made, together with advice about where information could be found easily.

Summary

If students are to learn anything in geography then they must have a certain curiosity about what they are studying. Teachers can create 'a need to know' in different ways. Of crucial importance is the teacher's stance: the attitude towards the subject and subject knowledge. Students' interest can be engaged at the start of a unit of work through the use of various kinds of stimulus or through speculation. Students are motivated by being given some choice in what they study.

Suggestions for research

1. Apply Phillips' history teaching research to geography and investigate the extent to which ISM can be used to stimulate curiosity initially and throughout a unit of work.

2. Investigate the extent to which inviting students to speculate about something can create a need to know and can inform the teacher about their prior knowledge and understanding.

3. Experiment with four ways of creating a need to know: stance, speculation, stimulus and choice. Decide how to collect data to illustrate if and how students become more curious.

References

Amis, K. (2012) 'Finding the big questions', *Teaching Geography*, 37, 1, pp. 10–11.

BBC (1992) *Pole to Pole* (DVD). London: BBC Publications.

Biddulph, M. (2011) 'Articulating student voice and facilitating curriculum agency', *Curriculum Journal*, 22, 3, pp. 381–99.

Bolton, P. (2008) 'Should I stay or should I go? An enquiry investigating Polish migration to the UK', *Teaching Geography*, 33, 3, pp. 125–32.

Bruner, J. (1986) *Actual Minds, Possible Worlds*. Cambridge, MA: Harvard University Press.

Bustin, R. (2011a) 'Thirdspace: exploring the "lived space" of cultural "others"', *Teaching Geography*, 36, 2, pp. 55–7.

Bustin, R. (2011b) 'The living city: Thirdspace and the contemporary geography curriculum', *Geography*, 96, 2, pp. 60–8.

Davidson, G. (2006) 'Start at the beginning', *Teaching Geography*, 31, 3, pp. 105–8.

DfES (2004) *Pedagogy and Practice: Teaching and learning in secondary schools, unit 5: starters and plenaries*. London: Department for Education and Skills.

Durbin, C. (2006) 'Media literacy and geographical imaginations', in Balderstone, D. (ed) *Secondary Geography Handbook*. Sheffield: The Geographical Association.

Firth, R., Biddulph, M., Riley, H., Gaunt, I. and Buxton, C. (2010) 'How can young people take an active role in the geography curriculum?', *Teaching Geography*, 35, 2, pp. 49–51.

Firth, R. and Biddulph, M. (2009) 'Young people's geographies', *Teaching Geography*, 34, 1, pp. 32–4.

Halocha, J. (2008) 'Geography in the frame: using photographs', *Teaching Geography*, 33, 1, pp. 19–21.

Ofsted (2011) *Geography: Learning to make a world of difference*. Available online at www.ofsted.gov.uk/resources/geography-learning-make-world-of-difference (last accessed 1 August 2012).

Owen, C. (2011) 'Should Jerzy stay or should he go?', *Teaching Geography*, 36, 2, p. 74.

Phillips, R. (2001) 'Making history curious: using initial stimulus material (ISM) to promote enquiry, thinking and literacy', *Teaching History*, 105, pp. 19–24.

Piers, P. (1974) *Alive: The story of the Andes survivors*. Philadelphia, PA: J.B. Lippencott Company.

Ranft, R. (2006) Audio CD: *Rainforest Requiem: Recordings of Wildlife in the Amazon Rainforest*. London: British Library.

Roberts, M. (2003) *Learning Through Enquiry: Making sense of geography in the key stage 3 classroom*. Sheffield: The Geographical Association.

Tickle, L. (2012) 'So you want to be the new Brian Cox? How to become a celebrity academic', *The Guardian*, 15 May. Available online at www.guardian.co.uk/education/2012/may/14/celebrity-academic-radio-tv-funding (last accessed 7 May 2013).

US Geological Survey (USGS) 'Real time earthquake map'. Available online at http://earthquake.usgs.gov/earthquakes/map (last accessed 14 January 2013).

Worldmapper website: www.worldmapper.org (last accessed 14 January 2013).

Young People's Geographies website: www.youngpeoplesgeographies.co.uk (last accessed 14 January 2013).

 05 Encouraging students' questions

'Constant and frequent questioning is the first key to wisdom ... For through doubting we are led to inquire, and by inquiry we perceive the truth' (Peter Abelard, 1079–1142)

Introduction

An enquiry approach to learning geography requires a questioning attitude towards knowledge and a pedagogy which encourages students to ask questions. This chapter addresses the following questions:

▲ How can students be involved if the key questions are predetermined?

▲ What are the advantages and disadvantages of commonly used frameworks for generating students' questions?

▲ In what other ways can students' questions be generated?

▲ Which is the best framework to use for an enquiry-based approach?

▲ How can students' questions be used?

▲ How can the use of frameworks to generate students' questions be evaluated?

How can students be involved if the key questions are predetermined?

It is all very well for units of work to have predetermined key questions as headings, but these are the teacher's or the examination board's questions. If students are to be engaged in the process of enquiry then it is important that these questions become their own.

Students need to be aware of the key question that frames a unit of work; they need to understand what exactly they are investigating. It is not enough simply to state the question or to display it in the routine way that objectives are sometimes displayed at the start of lessons. It is important that students have a need to know and this can be

created through the strategies suggested in Chapter 4. I would suggest that before the key question is revealed one or more of the following activities are used:

▲ Some sort of stimulus is provided to introduce students to the topic, e.g. a photograph, a film, an anecdote, an object.

▲ Students are given the title of the theme to be investigated, and their prior knowledge and experience of this theme is elicited through discussion or an activity.

▲ Students are given the title of the theme to be investigated and they generate their own questions about the topic, possibly using one of the frameworks below. These are then related to the key question.

If the key question has not been predetermined, students could generate it through discussion. The freedom they are given in doing so would depend on the extent to which individual students can choose what they study, and the extent to which the teacher wants to influence how a theme is investigated, which concepts are to be developed and what evidence is to be studied.

What are the advantages and disadvantages of commonly used frameworks for generating students' questions?

Students are often asked to generate questions in geography lessons and three frameworks are commonly used to guide their thinking: KWL, the 5Ws and the Compass Rose.

KWL framework and variations

The KWL framework, based on the questions 'What do I **K**now?', 'What do I **W**ant to know?' and 'What have I **L**earned?', was developed by Ogle (1986) to help students read for understanding. KWL has been used widely ever since and publicised through the work of Wray and Lewis (1997). It has also been modified and extended:

▲ KWFL includes an additional column, headed 'Where will I **F**ind the information?'

▲ THC (What do you **T**hink? **H**ow can we find out? What can we **C**onclude?) was adapted from KWL to support students' science projects (Crowther and Cannon, 2004). The first question uses 'think' rather than 'know' as this was considered less daunting for students. The second and third questions emphasise the enquiry process, encouraging speculation about how we get to know things and emphasising the process of reaching conclusions rather than simply finding out answers.

▲ The QUADS (Question, Answer, Detail, Source) extension provides a framework for listing questions and recording findings.

The advantage of the KWL and THC frameworks is that they are straightforward to use and provide opportunities for students to record prior knowledge or experience. KWFL and THC suggest an enquiry framework in which sources will be used to investigate the questions. The QUADS framework provides a simple means of recording findings from sources.

If, however, students have limited prior knowledge of a topic, it is unreasonable to expect them to generate many questions. I once observed a year 7 lesson on shanty towns in which a PGCE student used a KWL framework for the first time. At the very start of the lesson, students were asked to write in the first column what they knew about shanty towns. All the students near me wrote down that they knew nothing. So in the second column (what they wanted to know) they wrote, 'What is a shanty town?' One wrote 'Where is a shanty town?' They had nothing in their minds to generate further questions. They then watched a film on YouTube which consisted of a succession of still photographs interspersed with pieces of factual information. This proved to be a powerful stimulus and provoked a lot of interest. They were sitting in groups and could have generated a lot of questions and written them down in the W column. The class could have shared their questions and discussed the YouTube resource as evidence. But another activity was introduced. It was a lost opportunity. This use of KWL illustrated to us both that students cannot ask worthwhile questions if they have limited prior knowledge and that it would have been better to use the stimulus first.

Another limitation of these generic frameworks is that they do not necessarily encourage geographical questions. I remember being asked by a PGCE student to answer year 7 students' questions on South Africa which I had recently visited. One girl asked 'What is South Africa like?' At the time this

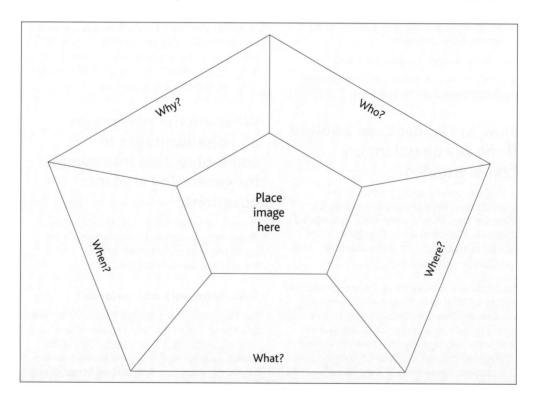

Figure 5.1: The 5Ws.
Source: Nichols and Kinninment, 2000.

seemed a childish question, but on reflection it is the kind of question that adults ask each other if someone has visited a new place or country: 'What is it like?' But we would hope as geography teachers to enable students to generate questions that probe the geography of what is being studied and are more specific.

The 5Ws

The 5Ws template (developed by Nichols and Kinninment, 2000) shown in Figure 5.1 is widely used. It has the advantage of simplicity, in that the starter words for each question are easily understood. It is most frequently used with a photograph placed centrally, but it can also be used to generate questions related to any form of source material, including film, graphs, etc., or to generate questions for a questionnaire. The 5Ws template has the advantage of encouraging different kinds of questions, including questions that seek descriptive or factual responses and ones that seek explanation.

The main limitation of the 5Ws framework is that it does not explicitly encourage questions focusing on different aspects of geography. For example

it would be possible to use the 5Ws but ignore questions probing aspects of geography relevant to the study, e.g. climate or physical geography. It does not explicitly encourage questions related to decision-making (what ought to happen?). It would be simple to modify the 5Ws template by adding additional questions to draw attention to processes ('How?'), to a futures dimension ('What might happen if...?') or an ethical dimension ('What ought...?') Using these questions would produce an octagon framework: 7Ws and an H (Figure 5.2).

The Compass Rose

The Compass Rose (Birmingham DEC, 1995) shown in Figure 5.3 is also widely used. Instead of starter words for questions it presents four categories within which questions can be generated. It has the advantage that it is specifically geographical, focusing attention on different aspects of the subject: environmental, social, economic and political. Because it uses the initial letters of the cardinal points of the compass, the framework is easily remembered.

Like all frameworks, the Compass Rose has limitations. It is initially more difficult for

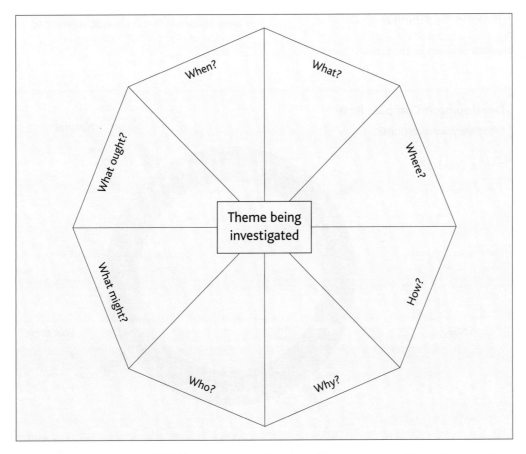

Figure 5.2: 7Ws and an H.

students to use than the 5Ws because it requires an understanding of the distinctions between environmental, social, economic and political aspects of geography. However, these are distinctions that students need to be able to make if they are to progress in geography, so frequent use of the Compass Rose helps students understand these terms. The categories of questions might not be suitable for all units of work but like all frameworks it could be modified, by limiting or making more specific what might be included under each cardinal point. N could be limited to the natural environment. For particular enquiries S could be limited to diversity, e.g. variations according to gender, ethnicity, class or disability. The Compass Rose, unlike the other frameworks, encourages questions about power relationships, but does not explicitly encourage questions about the future or about what ought to happen, although these dimensions could be included in the guidance provided for each cardinal point of the compass.

In what other ways can students' questions be generated?

The route for enquiry

Figure 5.4 is based on the route for enquiry originally designed for the Schools Council 16–19 Geography Project to support students' investigation of questions, problems and issues. This framework has the advantage that, like the 5Ws framework, the starter words are simple. However, it has a greater range of questions than the 5Ws and includes questions that are particularly suitable for investigating issues, e.g. 'what decision', 'what might?' and 'with what impact?' The route for enquiry adds an ethical dimension by including the question 'what do I think?'.

Big questions, little questions

Getting students to distinguish between big questions and little questions is a strategy that has been used in history. Burnham (2007) had found that her year 12 students had difficulties in identifying appropriate questions. She decided that learning to ask good questions should begin in year 7 and that she would use two lessons to get them to devise their own questions to frame a unit of work on the Islamic Empire. Figure 5.5 provides an outline of these lessons.

The strategies that Burnham used could be applied to geography. She enabled year 7 students to generate questions to frame a unit of work by:

▲ focusing on only three aspects of the theme being studied so that the questions generated could be used to produce a coherent unit of work

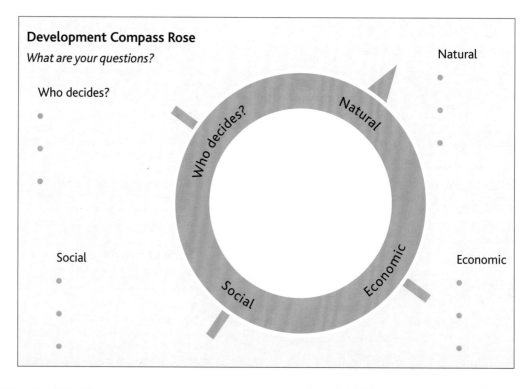

Figure 5.3: Compass Rose. Source: Birmingham DEC, 1995.

Questions	Enquiry skills involved
What?	Observation and perception
What and where?	Definition Description
How and why?	Analysis Explanation
What might happen? What impact? What decision?	Evaluation Prediction Decision making
What do I think? Why? What will I do next?	Personal evaluation Response

Figure 5.4: The route for enquiry. Source: Rawling, 2007.

▲ selecting different types of source materials on the theme: maps; a painting; text; a photograph; and a role-play

▲ introducing students to the distinction between big questions and little questions

▲ using whole class, individual and paired activities to generate questions

▲ asking students to reflect on the questions they had generated and to select and sequence appropriate ones.

Encouraging critical enquiry

When students generate their own questions using any of the frameworks above, they do not necessarily ask questions which probe the data or the issue critically. In order to encourage critical thinking, students need to be made aware of a range of probing questions that it is possible to ask in geography. Students are more likely to ask such questions about evidence and issues if the teacher does so frequently themselves.

Questions on geographical source material that encourage critical thinking include:

▲ How reliable is this evidence?

▲ What is the source of this evidence?

▲ Why was this data produced?

▲ Who funded the production of the data and why?

▲ What does the data not show?

Questions on issues that encourage critical thinking include:

▲ Why is this an issue?

▲ What are the causes of this issue?

▲ Who are the interested parties?

▲ What is the reason for their interest?

▲ Who might gain from this issue?

▲ Who might lose?

▲ Who has the power to decide?

▲ What would be a just solution?

▲ What are the implications of this issue for the future?

▲ What would be the consequences of different decisions?

Brainstorming for questions without an initial framework

Given sufficient stimulus students are capable of generating questions without the help of a supporting framework and this has some advantages. If students are not constrained by categories they might produce more genuine questions arising out of their own curiosity. The disadvantage of not having a framework is that the range of questions might be limited or they might not be particularly geographical. However, discussion could refine the students' questions and this could be used to explore the nature of geographical questions and generate questions appropriate to the resource or theme being investigated. Alternatively students could brainstorm questions freely before being given one of the frameworks above.

Using frameworks to categorise questions provided by the teacher

Students could be introduced to any of the frameworks above by being presented with appropriate questions devised by the teacher. These could be subsidiary questions for discussion at the start of a unit of work, possible questions for a questionnaire, or questions to be used to analyse

Big and little questions

Burnham (2007) used two lessons with her year 7 history class to generate questions to frame a unit of work on 'The Islamic Empire 600–1600'

Lesson 1

In order to make the unit of work coherent, Burnham decided to focus on three aspects of the Islamic Empire at the start of the unit:

▲ the spread of Islam

▲ Islamic medicine (leading to questioning about Islamic scholars and knowledge)

▲ the Ottoman sultans.

She selected a series of historical sources to use as stimulus material to generate questions on these three aspects.

Activity 1: Distinguishing between big and little questions

To clarify what she meant by 'big' and 'little' questions Burnham used questions on the medieval course they had just studied.

Big question	Little question
Why did William win the Battle of Hastings?	What happened to Harold Godwinsson's body?
Why could no one ignore the Church in the Middle Ages?	Why was swearing a sin?
How did the Black Death change people's lives?	How big were the buboes?
How accurate is the Disney interpretation of King John?	Why was King John called Softsword and Lackland?

She displayed the questions randomly and asked students to raise two hands if they thought a question was big and a little finger it was little. They then discussed the difference between big and little questions and decided that big questions took a lot of time to answer, possibly several lessons, whereas little questions were interesting but could be answered quickly.

Activity 2: The spread of Islam

Burnham showed students a series of maps and asked them to write down questions. Although this generated some good questions, some students were unsure of what the maps were showing. She reflected after the lesson that it would be

preferable to have a less abstract focus for the first question-generating activity.

Activity 3: Islamic medicine

Burnham adapted a role play, in which she acted the doctor and the classroom assistant the patient. This was much more accessible to the students than the maps and generated a lot of questions.

Activity 4: The Ottoman sultans

Students were given copies of a portrait of Sultan Mehmed II painted in 1480 and annotated them with lots of questions. Burnham also showed the class a picture of the Topkapi Palace and asked students to add questions to their lists.

Activity 5: Generating further questions

From a variety of different source materials Burnham gave pairs of students one picture and one piece of text to use to generate further questions.

Lesson 2

In the second lesson students worked in groups to categorise the questions they had produced as big or little questions. They then selected a few big questions and put them into sequence to frame a series of lessons, listing them in a grid with one column for the questions and another for notes. One group produced the following questions:

▲ Why was Muhammad so important?

▲ Why did Islam spread so fast?

▲ What did Muslim scholars study?

▲ How powerful were the Ottoman sultans?

▲ Why was the army so successful?

▲ How friendly were Muslims and non-Muslims?

Through discussion, one list of big questions was agreed for the whole class. Burnham, in her role as teacher, decided which skills and concepts students could develop while addressing these questions and what the activities would be for the unit of work.

Burnham was pleased with the unit of work she developed from their questions and felt the process had given students ownership of the unit of work. She commented that although it would be easy to teach the same scheme of work the following year, the process of developing the scheme was too valuable not to be repeated. She decided to use the same procedure the following year, using enquiry questions devised by the new year 7 students. She also planned to use the procedure with other age groups.

Figure 5.5: Generating big questions and little questions in history.

a resource. The task for students would be to categorise the questions provided and write them in the framework chosen by the teacher. This could be helpful for students who are inexperienced in asking good geographical questions; it could model the kinds of questions geographers ask and could be used to develop understanding of the different categories within the frameworks.

Which is the best framework to use for an enquiry-based approach?

The frameworks are not neutral; they generate different kinds of questions and would lead to a different type of enquiry and to students learning a different geography. Each framework has advantages and limitations, so the choice of framework is a matter of professional judgement. The choice should be influenced by the capabilities of the students, what is being investigated and what use is to be made of students' questions once they have identified them. If students are to have the opportunity to generate subsidiary questions for a topic, then it is important to choose a framework that will encourage the kinds of questions that need to be addressed in answering the key question of the unit and through which the key concepts can be developed. If the students are using a framework to produce questions for a questionnaire, the framework needs to encourage questions related to the purpose of the survey.

How can students' questions be used?

It is crucially important to recognise that the frameworks in themselves do not generate curiosity; the teacher has to do this through the use of a stimulus and through interaction with students. The frameworks should not be simply handed out like worksheets to be completed as exercises. Students might write down questions because that is what they have been asked to do, rather than because they have any genuine interest in them. If the use of any of the frameworks is to have value and meaning then it is important that students know that their questions will be taken seriously. If what they write down is ignored then the task of completing the framework could seem routine and pointless. Students' questions could be used in several ways:

▲ If a framework is used to question a particular resource, e.g. a film, a photograph, a graph, a map, the questions could be shared and addressed immediately through discussion. I remember one of my PGCE students being concerned that students would write down questions which he couldn't answer. It is important that likely questions related to a resource can be answered and that the teacher is as informed as possible about the resource being used, e.g. photographs found on the internet or a film from YouTube.

▲ If questions are being generated for a questionnaire, students' questions can be shared and discussed with the aim of negotiating good survey questions (see Chapter 20).

▲ If a framework is being used to generate subsidiary questions to a key enquiry question, students' questions can be shared and discussed and related to the investigation to follow. Students could group the questions they had

devised into categories, sequence the categories and select or negotiate as a class the best question in each category. The best questions could be used to frame individual lessons in a unit of work.

Snowballing

Wood (2006; 2008) suggests using the 'snowballing' procedure for generating and using students' questions. After being provided with a stimulus, students work individually to devise three questions each; then they work in pairs to discuss their questions and decide on the best three; then they join in groups of four or six to choose the best three. The groups feed back their questions to the whole class, and the class chooses the best five or six and uses them in their enquiry work.

A year 10 class who used snowballing to generate questions on volcanoes finally decided on the following:

▲ What is the tectonic setting of the volcanoes?

▲ What were the characteristics of each volcano?

▲ What were the warning signs of the eruptions?

▲ What were the primary and secondary effects of the eruptions?

▲ How do the differences in effects correspond with the development of the affected areas?

By sharing and discussing questions they were focusing on the theme and also learning to ask geographical questions.

How can the use of frameworks to generate students' questions be evaluated?

If the completion of any of the frameworks is rushed, with the emphasis on getting something written down and then moving onto the next activity, and if no attention is paid to what students write down, then what is their value? In evaluating the use of these frameworks and activities it is worth considering the following questions:

▲ Did students generate genuine questions of their own?

▲ Are they more interested in and curious about what they are going to study?

▲ Has their understanding of the kinds of questions geographers ask increased?

▲ Were their questions respected, by being answered or by being discussed in the following enquiry work?

Summary

An enquiry approach to learning geography should promote students' curiosity and their need to ask questions, preferably spontaneously and throughout a unit of work. Students can learn to ask geographical questions through the use of various frameworks. The frameworks are not neutral, in that they ask different kinds of questions which would produce different geographies, so choosing between them is a matter of professional judgement. The frameworks in themselves do not promote curiosity, nor do they specifically encourage a critical attitude towards data and towards issues, so their use needs to be evaluated carefully.

Suggestions for research

1. Investigate the types of questions generated by the use of different frameworks, either using different frameworks within the same class or by using different frameworks applied to the same theme or place with different classes.

2. Develop Burnham's ideas to explore the distinction between big and little questions in geography.

References

Abelard, P. (1121) 'Sic et Non, Prologus' (quotation from translation) in Graves, F. (2004) *A History of Education During the Middle Ages and the Transition to Modern Times*. Whitefish, MT: Kessinger Publishing, p. 53.

Birmingham DEC (1995) *The Development Compass Rose*. Birmingham: Development Education Centre. Available online at *www.tidec.org/sites/default/files/uploads/compass%20rose%20text_2.pdf* (last accessed 14 January 2013).

Burnham, S. (2007) 'Getting year 7 to set their own questions about the Islamic Empire, 600–1600', *Teaching History*, 128, pp. 11–15.

Crowther, D. and Cannon, J. (2004) 'Strategy makeover: K-W-L to T-H-C'. Available online at *www.nsta.org/publications/news/story.aspx?id=49675* (last accessed 14 January 2013).

Nichols, A. and Kinninment, D. (2000) *More Thinking Through Geography*. Cambridge: Chris Kington Publishing.

Ogle, D. (1986) 'K-W-L: A teaching model that develops active reading of expository text', *The Reading Teacher*, 39, 6, pp. 564–70.

Rawling, E. (2007) *Planning your Key Stage 3 Geography Curriculum*. Sheffield: The Geographical Association.

Wood, P. (2006) 'Developing enquiry through questioning', *Teaching Geography*, 31, 2, pp. 76–8.

Wood, P. (2008) 'GTIP Think Piece: Questioning'. Available online at *www.geography.org.uk/gtip/thinkpieces/questioning* (last accessed 14 January 2013).

Wray, D. and Lewis, M. (1997) *Extending Literacy: Children reading and writing non-fiction*. London: Routledge.

Using source materials: an evidence-based approach

'Maps are just one means of representation of world views, and all maps necessarily present a particular understanding of the world. But many other things too – from tourist brochures to the news to travel programmes on the television – contribute to the formation of our geographical imaginations. Being able to interpret these sources is important because the nature of geographical imaginations – our views of the shape of the world – can be of fundamental importance to how we act within it' (Massey, 1995, p. 41).

Introduction

This chapter focuses on issues related to the wide range of resources that can be used in the geography classroom and how they can provide evidence for investigations (Figure 6.1). Here, I am referring to resources containing geographical information as 'sources', which is the term commonly used in history. This chapter addresses the following questions:

▲ What are the advantages and disadvantages of using primary and secondary sources?

▲ What can students learn from using geographical sources?

▲ What general problems are associated with the use of sources?

▲ Is VAK learning theory applicable to learning through enquiry?

▲ Are some forms of data more accessible than others?

▲ What needs to be taken into account in using the printed word, numerical data and maps as evidence?

▲ How can critical examination of geographical sources be encouraged?

Issues related to selection of geographical sources and misrepresentation will be discussed in Chapter 7. Specific issues related to using online resources are discussed in Chapter 21.

Figure 6.1:
Various forms of
representation and
sources of geographical
information.

Sources of information

Images

- Photographs
- Paintings and drawings
- Film
- Diagrams
- Cartoons
- TV advertisements
- Satellite images
- Google Street View

Words

- Textbook descriptions and accounts
- Magazine and journal articles
- Newspaper articles
- Letters
- Advertisements
- Fiction
- Poetry and lyrics of songs
- Non-fiction, e.g. travel writing
- Brochures
- Twitter

Sound

- Commentaries on film
- Recorded interviews
- Music
- Natural sounds, e.g. the Amazon rainforest soundscape

Multimedia

- Incorporating several forms of representation e.g. text, still images, animation, film, audio

Statistical data

- Tables of statistics
- Graphs (bar, pie, line, flood hydrographs, population pyramids, climate)
- Choropleth maps
- Flow line maps
- Gapminder

Maps

- Street maps, Google maps
- Topographical maps, e.g. OS maps
- Atlas maps (political, physical, thematic)
- Worldmapper
- Weather maps
- Gapminder
- Non-educational maps, e.g. in brochures, newspapers, football programmes etc.
- GIS maps

Personal knowledge

- Memories of place, including remembered images and events
- Mental maps
- Affective maps – mapping feelings about places

Objects

- Rocks
- Vegetation
- Artefacts and objects from other places
- Bags of rubbish
- Food

What are the advantages and disadvantages of using primary and secondary sources?

Primary data and primary data sources

Primary data are collected first-hand for the purpose of investigating particular questions. In schools, students might have opportunities to collect quantitative data through observation and measurements during fieldwork or through questionnaire surveys. They might collect non-numerical qualitative data through field-sketches, photographs, open-ended surveys or interviews. There are advantages and disadvantages in students collecting and using their own primary data (Figure 6.2).

Sometimes it might be possible for students to use primary sources, i.e. data collected by geographers and published in articles written by those who devised the research questions and collected the data. Some academics have published their research in journals such as *Teaching Geography* or *Geography*, e.g. Scott (2007) on labour migration to the UK from Eastern Europe.

Secondary data and secondary data sources

Secondary data are collected by a researcher or organisation for their own purposes but used by other people for different purposes. Secondary school students are more likely to use secondary than primary sources in the classroom. Secondary data include: climate data; census data; large data sets of economic and social indicators collected by governments and organisations such as the World Bank and the United Nations. They also include archive collections of photographs, film and satellite images and some interview data (e.g. the British Library's food stories project). Secondary sources would include websites where secondary data can be accessed, articles that have made use of other people's primary data and a wide range of resources, e.g. photographs, satellite images, advertisements, brochures, maps, which were produced for other purposes but can be used as sources of geographical information.

Secondary data and secondary sources have advantages and disadvantages (see Figure 6.3).

What can students learn from using geographical sources?

The widespread use of sources began in the 1970s and 1980s when Schools Council projects encouraged geography and history teachers to use source materials as evidence to be interpreted rather than simply as information to be learnt. In geography the influential projects were Geography for the Young School Leaver Project (also known as the Avery Hill Project), the 14–18 Geography Project (also known as the Bristol Project) and the 16–19 Geography Project. Before the 1970s, 'sample studies' and primary sources had been used in geography and history but the emphasis had been on establishing facts and generalisations about place and about the past. The inclusion of data-response questions in the public examinations based on the Schools Council projects shifted the emphasis from testing the ability of students to reproduce and use remembered information towards testing skills of data interpretation in relation to topics and concepts in the syllabus.

From the 1970s geography textbooks began to include pictures, tables of statistics, graphs and maps not merely as illustrations but as data to be studied. The innovative Oxford Geography Project textbooks (Rolfe *et al.*, 1974) devoted 80% of its space to pictures, diagrams and work activities rather than text (Walford, 2001). For the geography examinations based on the Schools Council projects, publishers produced textbooks and ring-binders containing secondary data of all kinds, e.g. census data, newspaper reports, extracts from large-scale maps, photographs and cartoons.

The aim of Schools Council projects was for students to develop skills of data analysis and interpretation at the same time as they were increasing their subject knowledge and developing conceptual understanding through their study of places, themes and issues; developing skills and understanding were both seen as important. In recent years, however, there has been a shift towards an emphasis on using resources to learn skills with a corresponding downgrading of knowledge and understanding. Many schools in England, influenced by initiatives such as 'Learning to learn' promoted by the Campaign for Learning and RSA's Opening Minds, implement a skills-based curriculum in year 7. The focus on either skills or knowledge is a false dichotomy, a point recognised by the panel that was asked to give advice to the UK government in their review of the national curriculum:

'Some educationalists emphasise subject knowledge and discount the significance of more developmental aspects of education. There are also many who foreground the development of skills, competencies and dispositions whilst asserting that contemporary knowledge changes so fast that "learning how to learn" should be prioritised. We do not believe that these are either/or questions. Indeed, it is impossible

Advantages	Disadvantages
Data are collected to answer the particular questions students are investigating.	Data sets are likely to be small and possibilities of sampling limited. It is therefore unlikely that such data can be used to reach reliable conclusions.
Students know exactly what the data refer to in the 'real' world.	
Students are aware of decisions made before data were collected, e.g. the choice of variables to measure, numerical categories, interview questions or the focus of photographs. They are therefore aware of the subjectivities involved in data collection and could discuss the extent to which data are likely to be reliable.	Students are likely to collect data at limited times of day or week and cannot build up data sets to include variations over time, e.g. of traffic flows, or volume of water in a river.
Students can become aware of how geographical knowledge is constructed through the collection and interpretation of data.	It is not feasible for students to collect their own data for most questions they are investigating.
Students can develop skills of data gathering, processing, analysis and interpretation in a context which has meaning for them.	

Figure 6.2: Advantages and disadvantages of primary data and sources.

Figure 6.3: Advantages
and disadvantages of
secondary data and
sources.

Advantages	Disadvantages
Students can access large reliable data sets which would be impossible for them to collect themselves. Many data-sets available online are updated regularly so it is possible to get the most up-to-date data. Secondary data are available for all themes and places studied in geography. Some secondary sources, in which primary data or secondary data are presented in reports, are more easily accessible to school students than primary sources such as research articles.	Many data sets are large and complicated to use. The decisions which have influenced how, when or why the data were collected are not always explicit. The subjectivities involved in the collection of data, which influence what the data show, are therefore hidden. The purposes for which many sources were produced, e.g. photographs, advertisements, brochures, maps, are often very different from the purposes of geographical education so the information found in them might be limited or biased; this needs to be taken into account when interpreting them.

to conceptualise "learning to learn" independently of learning "something". Our position is therefore that both elements, knowledge and development, are essential and that policy instruments need to be deployed carefully to ensure that these are provided for within education' (DfES, 2011, p. 20).

This view is also supported by a ten-year programme of educational research, the Teaching and Learning Research Programme (TLRP, 2011), which used insights from over 100 projects to devise 10 principles of effective pedagogy, the second of which was:

'Effective pedagogy engages with valued forms of knowledge. Pedagogy should engage learners with the big ideas, key skills and processes, modes of discourse, ways of thinking and practising, attitudes and relationships which are the most valued learning processes and outcomes in particular contexts. They need to understand what constitutes quality, standards and expertise in different settings' (James and Pollard, 2011, p. 284).

I would endorse this principle: learning geography through enquiry can enable students to engage with the big ideas of geography and its ways of thinking at the same time as developing the range of skills involved in investigating, analysing and interpreting geographical sources.

What general problems are associated with the use of sources?

McAleavy (1998) identified problems that secondary school students had when they used sources in history. Each of the problems has a parallel issue related to the use of data in geography (Figure 6.4).

An additional problem was encountered by my eldest daughter, who had accumulated notes in a ring binder for her O-level Avery Hill geography course. I was helping her revise and we looked at a resource sheet listing development indices for about 30 countries. I commented that she obviously didn't need to memorise all these. She threw the binder down in despair and asked 'How do I know what I have to learn and what I don't?' She did need to memorise detailed information about case studies but not data provided to help her to develop skills of analysis and generalisation. It is important that students are made aware of what they need to remember and which sources are used for other purposes.

If, as I believe, the main purpose of geographical education is to increase understanding, then I would suggest some principles of practice arising from the issues identified above.

1. In order to provide the context for purposeful study, sources should be studied in relation to the question framing the enquiry, not as an exercise to develop skills.

2. In order to provide a context for understanding, sources should be supplemented with an appropriate amount of selected background information provided by the teacher or through the use of other resources, e.g. atlases.

3. Students should be encouraged to make connections between information in sources and other information, including their own prior knowledge.

4. Even when the focus is on developing skills of presenting, analysing and interpreting data, attention should also be paid to the meaning of the data.

5. Students are entitled to know how much, for examination purposes, they need to remember of the factual information presented in the sources they use.

Is VAK learning theory applicable to learning through enquiry?

Learning style theorists make claims that people learn in different ways. A large research study (Coffield *et al.*, 2004a, 2004b) identified and investigated 71 different learning style theories. There are theories, for example, about divergent and convergent thinkers, globalists versus analysts, concrete versus abstract learners and deep versus surface learners. The learning style theory that has most impact in the geography classroom has been related to the identification of visual, audio and kinaesthetic learners (VAK). The central claim of VAK theory is that visual learners learn best from visual information, audio learners learn best from listening and kinaesthetic learners learn best through body movement. The theory has strong intuitive appeal as we all have individual preferences in the way we learn and because teachers are aware of differences between students. VAK has been promoted in England through the National Strategy and encouraged through the commercial interests of publishers.

Some criticisms of VAK theory

VAK theory has generally been accepted without question and applied widely in primary and secondary schools. However, there have been some serious criticisms.

The reliability and validity of the questionnaires used to determine learning styles have been questioned (Sharp *et al.*, 2008; Coffield *et al.*, 2004a). Too much is claimed for simple, self-reporting questionnaires, and the questionnaires assume that the same preferences apply to learning different kinds of things. There are also disagreements about whether the style of teaching should match the learning style or not. Empirical studies have been small-scale and contradictory; e.g. nine studies showed that learning was more effective where there was a match and nine that it was more effective when there was a mismatch (Coffield *et al.*, 2004b, p. 45).

Some critics fear that if teachers categorise students according to preferred learning style it 'might lead to simplistic conclusions about best practice' (*ibid.*, p. 31). Preferences are interpreted as fixed; but from their research into the use of VAK in primary schools, Sharp *et al.* (2008) concluded that 'the labelling of children in schools as visual, auditory or kinaesthetic learners is not only unforgivable, it is potentially damaging' (p. 20).

Problem identified through research into use of sources in history	What needs to be considered in geography?
Students did not understand the different status of what was presented to them so accepted, uncritically, everything as true. They needed to be able to make inferences about the sources and in their thinking go beyond the information given.	Are students helped to understand the nature of data provided, e.g. its origins and reliability, and use it as evidence rather than as fact and information to be learnt?
Students did not understand the distinction between sources and evidence. Not all sources were useful as evidence; it depended on what question was being investigated and whether the source contributed to understanding.	Are students encouraged to evaluate the extent to which any piece of data provides good evidence for a particular investigation?
Witnesses of events were assumed to be correct.	Are local people always reliable sources of geographical information? To what extent is information provided in speech bubbles based on genuine sources?
Some students could not interpret sources because of their lack of awareness of the wider context; making sense depended on wider contextual knowledge.	Do students have enough regional and/or national contextual information to make sense of local case studies?
Many historical sources had been reduced to 'small gobbets' of information in order to provide poor readers with source materials. Many mini-gobbets were too small and presented out of context.	To what extent does geography provide 'small gobbets' of information which are too small to be used as evidence?
Some history teachers put too much emphasis on detecting bias rather than on developing historical understanding.	Is more emphasis put on the skills of representing and analysing data, rather than on the geographical knowledge they represent?

Figure 6.4: Problems of using sources in history and their parallels in geography. Source: based on McAleavy, 1998.

VAK theory encourages self-labelling by students and this may limit how they feel able to learn. Coffield *et al.* (2004b) quote a student saying 'I learned that I was a low auditory, kinaesthetic learner. So there's no point in me reading a book or listening to anyone for more than a few minutes' (p. 55).

Another criticism, about the way VAK is used in geography, is the use of the word 'kinaesthetic'. According to the glossary in Coffield *et al.* (2004a) it means: 'perceiving through an awareness of body movements' (p. 171). Kinaesthetic learning might be relevant to sport, dance or learning to play a musical instrument, but has little relevance to learning geography. I have seen many activities identified as 'kinaesthetic' on lesson plans but none of them were related to awareness of body movement. The word kinaesthetic was being misused to mean 'active', sometimes involving movement around the classroom but more often something like sorting cards or another practical activity. There are advantages of using practical activities in geography but to categorise them as 'kinaesthetic' is nonsense.

Applying VAK in geography could limit what students are expected to do, and it is preferable to increase students' ability to use data and sources by:

▲ helping develop the ability of all students' to analyse and interpret all forms of data

▲ being aware of differences between students in terms of their preferences and what they can do and providing appropriate guidance when they use data they find difficult

▲ using a variety of forms of geographical information in every unit of work and being aware of how accessible this information is to different students.

Are some forms of data more accessible than others?

What Jerome Bruner wrote about the accessibility of different forms of data is far more useful and relevant to teachers of geography than the VAK learning styles theory. In his book *Towards a Theory of Instruction* (1966) Bruner claimed that any child of any age could be taught any concept in some intellectually honest form; it depended on how the concept was presented. He distinguished between three forms of representation:

▲ Enactive: representing the concept through action. This is the most accessible form of representation.

▲ Iconic: representing the concept visually. This is the next most accessible form of representation.

▲ Symbolic: representing the concept through words or mathematical symbols; the least accessible form of representation.

He illustrated his ideas through the example of a see-saw. Young children could learn to understand the concept of balance enactively through their experience of being on a see-saw and what happens if more or heavier children sit on one end. But to work with the concept of balance requires highly symbolic mathematical forms of representation. Bruner's ideas can be applied to geography and can be illustrated by different ways of representing the concept of longshore drift (Figure 6.5).

Although Bruner's forms of representation might seem remarkably similar to VAK learning styles theory, there is a crucial difference. VAK labels students. Bruner labels the forms of representation. Also, Bruner suggested that enactive learning was the most accessible for all students, followed by iconic; symbolic representation was more difficult for all students because of the higher levels of abstraction. Bruner's ideas relate to what geography teachers know through experience. Students find it easiest to understand complex ideas through being actively involved in fieldwork. In the classroom students find learning from films and photographs easier than learning from the printed word or from using numerical data (tables, graphs, statistical maps). In short, information represented symbolically in words and numbers is the least accessible.

What needs to be taken into account in using the printed word, numerical data and maps as evidence?

The printed word

Geographical data presented mainly through the printed word is difficult for many students because:

▲ Geography uses specialist vocabulary which is either not encountered in everyday life, e.g. precipitation, or is used with different meanings or connotations, e.g. relief.

▲ Geography often uses multi-syllabic words and long sentences which require higher reading ages.

▲ Geography textbooks are usually written in a formal style.

▲ Useful articles for geography that can be found in newspapers and on the internet are often written for adult readers and demand high reading ages.

Enactive: through activity during fieldwork.
Photo: Ruth Totterdell.

Iconic: through images. Photo: Richard Allaway.

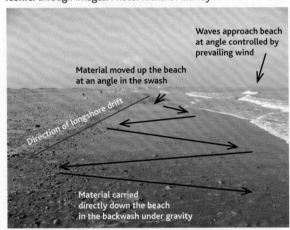

Waves approach beach at angle controlled by prevailing wind

Material moved up the beach at an angle in the swash

Direction of longshore drift

Material carried directly down the beach in the backwash under gravity

Symbolic: through words and numerals

Printed word (Wikipedia)

Longshore drift consists of the transportation of sediments (clay, silt and sand) along a coast at an angle to the shoreline, which is dependent on prevailing wind direction, swash and backwash. This process occurs in the littoral zone, and in or within close proximity to the surf zone. The process is also known as longshore transport or littoral drift.

Longshore drift is influenced by numerous aspects of the coastal system, with processes that occur within the surf zone largely influencing the deposition and erosion of sediments. Longshore currents can generate oblique breaking waves which result in longshore transport.

Statistics

This is the CERC formula with the K-coefficient calibrated for shingle beaches as 0.0527. It takes the form of

$$Q_{ls} = K \left(\frac{(1+e)}{(p_s - p)} \right) \left(\frac{1}{16} \, pgH_{sb}^{2} \, C_{nb} \, sin2\theta_b \right)$$

where all the factors and values are the same as in (1), g is the acceleration of gravity $9.81ms^{-2}$ and C_{nb} is the wave group velocity at breaking ($10ms^{-1}$). Using these values, the resulting transport rate is $246kg^{-s}$ or $2400m^3$ for the 7 hours of wave action.

Source: *www.sussex.ac.uk/geography/researchprojects/BAR/publish/Phase-1-final-drift%20experiments.pdf*

Figure 6.5: Bruner's different forms of representation applied to longshore drift.

Bruner's ideas suggest that because information presented symbolically, in words, is difficult, teachers should supplement this information with iconic (visual) information which is more accessible. Television programmes and news reports do this all the time, supplementing talking heads with photographs, film and diagrams. This is not because some viewers are 'visual' learners but because words on their own are more difficult for everyone.

Before using a piece of text teachers might need to provide support by reading the text out loud, by editing it, by checking that the vocabulary is known and by encouraging students to compile their own glossaries of specialist vocabulary. They can draw attention to any visual information that is provided to support the text. They can also help by making connections between what is in the text and the everyday experiences of students in the class.

Numerical data

Sources based on numerical data, including tables of statistics, graphs and some maps, can be difficult for students to use. Not all students have a good understanding of number as required in geography; for example, they might have difficulties with decimals, percentages and negative numbers, or with the meaning of units of measurement, e.g. hectares, degrees Celsius, isobars.

Some students have difficulty with some mathematical concepts, e.g. ratio, density, volume, correlation. Some sources use metric measurements and others imperial measurements: students need to understand both types of measurement. Students do not always check the unit of measurement and consequently misinterpret the data; for example, they might not notice that a figure is in thousands,

Key question being investigated
Type of source material, e.g. printed word, graph, atlas map, photograph, etc.
Source of material a) Author, organisation b) Where was this source found, e.g. details of book, article or website c) When was this source produced? d) I know this source is reliable/might not be reliable because … e) Is this source likely to be biased? Why or why not? f) What assumptions are made about the way the world works? (related to market forces, role of government, role of local communities)
The source provides the following evidence which helps to answer the key question:
Are there any queries you have about this source? Is there anything in this source that you do not fully understand?
Is there other information you need to find out?

with the additional noughts omitted, or that a rate is per thousand and not per hundred.

Graphs which display relationships between items on different axes are difficult, especially if both axes present figures which are themselves the result of mathematical calculations, e.g. percentages of something related to density.

It is important to be aware of these kinds of difficulties and provide the necessary support for students when they are using numerical data. Teachers need to be aware of what students have studied in mathematics and the different mathematical capabilities of students in the class. It is useful to draw attention to the units of measurement, to check that students understand the mathematical concepts required, and to relate any numerical data to figures which have meaning to students in their everyday lives. Bruner's ideas on representation suggest that tables of statistics and abstract formulae are more difficult to understand than visual representation of statistics on graphs or maps.

Maps

For most themes and places investigated in geography, maps of various kinds can be used as sources: topographical maps at various scales; the variety of maps found in atlases; weather maps; and maps found in brochures. Many geography courses devote a lot of time when students start secondary school teaching the map skills required to use topographic maps and atlases. What I find astonishing is that they emphasise the importance of these skills but then fail to make much use of them when investigating themes and places. In my experience as external examiner for PGCE courses I have only rarely seen information on maps used as evidence, in spite of their relevance to what was being studied and in spite of wall maps, globes and atlases being readily available for use. If the skills are not used for several years, e.g. using six-figure grid references, then students will forget how to use them. If skills are not applied in meaningful contexts students are less likely to perceive their value.

Maps are, however, quite complex to use as sources of information. Issues involved in their use include:

▲ The information on maps is highly processed; it is the result of many decisions about what to include, what to exclude and how to represent something symbolically. Some of the decisions might be made explicit in keys, e.g. decisions on symbols for different sized settlements in atlases. Most decisions about what is included and excluded, however, are not explicit, so the subjectivities involved in map-making are concealed (Wiegand, 2006, 2007).

▲ The selection of information to be included on a map depends on the scale of the map, who made it, and for what purpose. Students may encounter difficulties, therefore, not only in relation to the skills required to read a map but also the understanding necessary to interpret it.

▲ Although maps present information iconically they are highly symbolic, so could fall into Bruner's symbolic form of representation. Apart from pictorial maps, everything included on them is represented by symbols, so students need to know what the symbols represent in the real world. For instance, it is not enough for a student to know that a symbol represents a canal or deciduous forest if they do not know what a canal or a deciduous forest is.

▲ Students need to be aware that some maps are drawn to scale whereas others are not, e.g. world maps using Mercator's and Peter's projection.

▲ If a map is drawn to scale, then students need to be able to use the scale, and relate it to their existing knowledge of distances and understand its significance.

How can critical examination of geographical sources be encouraged?

The layers of inference (or layers of meaning) framework, commonly used in history lessons, encourages students to examine sources closely and to consider the extent to which a source provides evidence for an enquiry. Examples of how it has been used in history and geography are shown in Chapter 17.

Figure 6.6 shows a framework for making notes from a geographical source designed to encourage critical scrutiny of the source as evidence.

Summary

An enquiry approach uses a wide variety of sources of geographical information as evidence in investigating key questions. There are advantages and disadvantages of using both primary and secondary data sources. It is important to take account of the accessibility of source materials to students in the class and any difficulties students might have with specific types of source material.

Suggestions for research

1. Develop the ideas presented in McAleavy's article to investigate issues related to the use of source materials in geography. Use annotated source materials, questionnaires, interviews or learned journals to investigate any problems students have with the different types of source materials used in geography lessons, encouraging students to identify misunderstandings, confusions, etc. as well as what they do understand.

2. Use Wiegand (2007) to devise ways of investigating students' understanding of atlas and/or topographical maps.

3. Investigate the numeracy skills required for activities in a scheme of work. Liaise with the mathematics department about when these skills are developed in maths, issues related to developing them and differences between students in that year group. Review the scheme of work and its activities in light of the research.

References

Bruner, J. (1966) *Towards a Theory of Instruction.* New York: W.W. Norton and Company.

Coffield, F., Moseley, D., Hall, E. and Ecclestone, K. (2004a) *Learning Styles and Pedagogy in Post-16 Learning: A systematic and critical review.* London: Learning and Skills Development Agency. Available online at *www. leerbeleving.nl/wp-content/uploads/2011/09/learning-styles.pdf* (last accessed 14 January 2013).

Coffield, F., Moseley, D., Hall, E. and Ecclestone, K. (2004b) *Should We Be Using Learning Styles? What research has to say to practice.* London: Learning and Skills Research Centre. Available online at *http:// itslifejimbutnotasweknowit.org.uk/files/LSRC_ LearningStyles.pdf* (last accessed 14 January 2013).

DfES (2011) *The Framework for the National Curriculum: A report by the expert panel for the national curriculum review.* London: Department for Education and Skills. Available online at *www.education.gov.uk/publications/ eOrderingDownload/NCR-Expert%20Panel%20Report.pdf* (last accessed 14 January 2013).

James, M. and Pollard, A. (2011) 'TLRP's ten principles for effective pedagogy: rationale, development, evidence, argument and impact', *Research Papers in Education*, 26, 3, pp. 275–328.

Massey, D. (1995) 'Imagining the world' in Allen, J. and Massey, D. (eds) *Geographical Worlds.* Oxford: Oxford University Press.

McAleavy, T. (1998) 'The use of sources in school history 1910–1998: a critical perspective', *Teaching History,* 91, pp. 10–16.

Rolfe, J., Kent, A., Rowe, C., Grenyer, N. and Dearden, R. (1974) *The Oxford Geography Project.* Oxford: Oxford University Press.

Scott, S. (2007) 'Coming in from the cold: transition in Eastern Europe and labour migration to the UK', *Teaching Geography,* 32, 3, pp. 116–120.

Sharp, J., Bowker, R. and Byrne, J. (2008) 'VAK or VAK-uous? Towards the trivialisation of learning and the death of scholarship', *Research Papers in Education*, 23, 3, pp. 293–314.

Teaching and Learning Research Programme (TLRP) (2011) 'TLRP's evidence-informed pedagogic principles'. Available online at *www.tlrp.org/themes/themes/tenprinciples.html* (last accessed 14 January 2013).

Walford, R. (2001) *Geography in British Schools 1850–2000.* London: Woburn Press.

Wiegand, P. (2006) *Learning and Teaching with Maps.* London: Routledge.

Wiegand, P. (2007) 'GTIP Think Piece: Using Maps and Atlases'. Available online at *www.geography.org.uk/gtip/ thinkpieces/usingmapsatlases/#4691* (last accessed 14 January 2013).

Representation and misrepresentation

'When we reject the single story, when we realize that there is never a single story about any place, we regain a kind of paradise' (Adichie, 2009).

Introduction

The geographer in Saint-Exupéry's book *The Little Prince* (1974) suggests that the books of the geographer, unless furnished with 'proofs' or evidence, would tell 'lies' and that this would be disastrous (Figure 7.1). No publisher or geography teacher sets out to bring this kind of 'disaster' to the geography classroom. Yet students are nevertheless exposed to various kinds of misrepresentations of the world through what is included in the geography curriculum; stereotyping; bias and 'othering' (see page 68). This might suggest that there is a truth, as opposed to lies, that could be conveyed about the world. Representing the world, however, is not as simple as distinguishing between truth and lies.

This chapter examines the following questions:

▲ How does geography represent the world?

▲ How does the curriculum represent the world?

▲ What is stereotyping?

▲ How can the use of case studies be misleading?

▲ What is bias?

▲ What is 'othering'?

> **Geographer:** The geographer is much too important to go loafing about. He does not leave his desk. But he receives the explorers in his study. He asks them questions and he notes down what they recall of their travels. And if the recollections of any among them seem interesting to him the geographer offers an enquiry into that explorer's moral character.
>
> **Little Prince:** Why is that?
>
> **Geographer:** Because an explorer who told lies would bring disaster on the books of the geographer. One requires the explorer to furnish proofs.

Figure 7.1: Extracts from *The Little Prince* by Antoine de Saint-Exupéry (translated from French by Katherine Woods).

How does geography represent the world?

There are two ways of thinking about representing the world. We can think of trying to reflect it accurately in the way that a mirror reflects an image. This is sometimes referred to as mimetic representation or mimesis, described by Duncan and Ley (1993) as 'the belief that we should strive to produce as accurate a reflection of the world as possible' (p. 2). Duncan and Ley argue that 'a perfect copy of the world is impossible' (p. 3) and that 'For a society to maintain the illusion that its representations are natural representations it must conceal its historic specificity' (p. 4).

Although representing the world as accurately as possible seems to be common sense, social scientists, since the 1970s, have questioned the possibility of mimetic representation. Disciplinary knowledge is constructed at a particular time in the history of the discipline. Many geographers have emphasised this.

'Human geography is not a direct reflection of a straightforward reality that is "out there" but a social construction. In other words, although certain experiences, beliefs and values systems are shared, these also vary and interpretations of the world differ from different vantage points in time and place' (Daniels et al., 2012, p. 2).

'Our knowledge of the world is always from a certain standpoint, a certain location. We see it from here, rather than from there' (Allen and Massey, 1995, p. 2).

'The representation of nature is not a neutral process that simply produces a mirror image of a fixed external reality, like a photocopy. Rather it is instrumental in constituting our sense of what the natural world is like' (Whatmore, 2005, p. 9).

Geographers, instead of seeing the world as if reflected in a mirror, see the world as if through a series of lenses, shaped by the academic and cultural thinking of the time and through their positionality and personal interests. They represent what they see through these lenses in words and images and it is through these that they create geographical meaning. As Hall (1997) wrote, we give things meaning:

'... by how we represent them, the words we use about them, the stories we tell about them, the images of them we produce and the emotions we associate with them, the ways we classify and conceptualise them, the values we place on them' (p. 3).

Representations are 'related to our way of thinking' (Taylor, 2004, p. 2) and our ways of thinking are shaped by our culture, through our positionality. If we accept that how we see the world is more like looking through various lenses than looking in a mirror, then representations cannot be neutral; 'each representation (each geographical imagination) necessarily has a particular perspective' (Massey, 1995, p. 34). I think it is important for students to become aware of the lenses through which the world is investigated and portrayed and that what they study in the geography classroom is not the world itself but representations of it. Only then can they look critically at sources of geographical information.

How does the curriculum represent the world?

It is as impossible for the geography curriculum to represent the world without distortions of some kind as it is to represent the whole world on a flat piece of paper. The scope of geography is unbelievably vast, so not everything can be studied in a school geography course; it is impossible to study in a meaningful way all the countries in the world, all possible themes and all issues. At the macro-scale of curriculum planning, the way a scheme of work is structured, e.g. by themes, issues, regions or a combination of these, conveys messages about what geography is about and contributes to ways in which students know, understand and perceive the world. At the more detailed level of planning, choices have to be made about which themes, places and issues are studied. For example, should students develop a detailed knowledge of particular places and if so, which ones? Should all students in England learn about glaciation? Should the major issues facing the world in the 21st century, e.g. population growth, water supply, climate change, national and global inequalities, be studied by all students? The world is inevitably misrepresented in some way by what is selected for inclusion in the geography curriculum.

The key curriculum questions for geography are:

▲ What should be studied and why?
▲ Who should decide and why?

These questions beg many further questions. If governments and examination boards make decisions about content, how prescriptive should they be about the places and examples to be studied? What are the criteria by which such choices about content should be made? Should the debate be about relevance to students' present lives or to their future working lives? Is studying an issue in a local context always more relevant than the study of distant places? Should the significance of an issue be an important criterion and if so who should determine its significance? Is it important for all students to study countries such as USA and China because of their economic and political importance in the world? The answers to these questions will be influenced by thinking about the purposes of education generally and about geographical education in particular. They will always be a matter of debate. But the choices made will influence the way students encounter and learn to think about the world.

My own research in 2005 into countries studied in the lower secondary school geography curriculum in England showed that the world students studied was extremely distorted (Roberts, 2006). One lasting legacy of the 1991 and 1995 versions of geography national curriculum in England was that textbooks focused on the study of a few countries. Although there had been other options, I found that the majority of students studied in detail two of what I termed 'the big four': Japan or Italy and Brazil or Kenya. Other parts of the world were studied only as case studies and often for only one topic so at that time there was very limited attention to the USA, China, Russia, and limited attention to any other countries in Europe, Africa, South America or Asia apart from the 'big four'. When the places studied by individual students were plotted on a world map, the map was far more distorted than Mercator's projection which many schools thought too distorted to use. Advocacy of equal area world maps was undermined by the shape of the world constructed through the curriculum.

Since my research, there has been a shift in what has been studied, with more attention, for example, being given to the study of China. Different choices will result in different worlds: hopefully, none of them will be inaccurate, but all of them will be distorted by what the curriculum includes and excludes and how it is structured. There cannot be a neutral geography curriculum.

What is stereotyping?

Hall (1997) wrote about how stereotypes produce misleading representations:

'Stereotypes, while classifying people in a similar manner, reduce the person to those simplified and exaggerated characteristics, admit no possibility of change, and insist that these characteristics are natural. Any complexity is ignored and denied, and it is implied that everything that is necessary to know about the person can be known by referring to the traits of the stereotype. In essence a stereotype declares "this is what you are, and this is all you are"' (p. 258).

What Hall wrote about people applies also to places. Of course, we need to categorise things to make sense of the world and to be able to relate our experiences to new information. The point about stereotyping is that it reduces a person or place to a few 'simplified and exaggerated characteristics'. It is not that stereotypes are untrue; they have elements of truth in them. It is that they ignore complexity. They are misrepresentations that can influence our thinking and inform our attitudes. If they are negative they can be dangerous.

We do not set out deliberately to convey stereotyped representations of peoples or of countries. Yet we need to take into account the stereotypical images students might already have of places and examine how places are represented in the resources we use. Most students have some stereotypical images of various parts of the world. I am using Africa as an example, but it is worth examining students' perceptions of other parts of the world before they study them. Students typically associate Africa with jungles, drought, safaris, tribal cultures, famine, poverty and disease (Borowski and Plastow, 2012). These images come from what children and young people encounter in the media.

Stories and television programmes about Africa, including those for the very young, are very often about jungles and wild animals, and travel programmes, advertisements and brochures tend to emphasise the exotic – safaris and traditional ways of living. Charity programmes and advertisements, e.g. Comic Relief, Oxfam, emphasise poverty and the need for outside help. News reports in the press or on TV tend to include news of Africa only when it is related to disasters of various kinds, e.g. famine or conflict.

As with all stereotypical images of places, these images are based on reality, but they misrepresent Africa by:

▲ focusing on a few characteristics

▲ emphasising ways in which people and places in Africa are different from places in the UK, e.g. emphasising the exotic

▲ emphasising catastrophes

▲ ignoring diversity within the continent as a whole and within individual countries

▲ ignoring ways which people and places in Africa are similar to places in the UK

▲ ignoring positive aspects of African places and societies.

The Nigerian novelist, Chimamanda Adichie, has warned of 'The danger of a single story' (2009). When she went from her home country, Nigeria, to university in the USA at the age of 19, she was struck by the attitude of her room-mate. 'Her default position towards me was a kind of patronising, well-meaning pity. My room-mate had a single story of Africa: a single story of catastrophe'. Adichie argues that 'The single story creates stereotypes, and the problem with stereotypes is not that they are untrue, but that they are incomplete. They make one story become the only story'.

Borowski (2011) has written about how fundraising events such as Red Nose Day can, through the images they present, have 'a hidden cost on how we perceive people in distant countries' (p. 18). A by-product of charities' fundraising work is to present a single story of Africa: the story of a continent needing help from the West.

Stereotypical images of Africa have a long history, dating back to the days of early explorers. Africa used to be referred to as 'the Dark Continent' and the 'White Man's Grave'. Accounts of explorers' expeditions to Africa often depicted Africans as 'savage', 'primitive' and 'uncivilised'. Such powerful images can shape the way we think and our expectations. Tony Binns (1995) in his presidential address for the Geographical Association, described how he set out to do his doctoral studies in the 'Dark Continent', with a 'baggage of myths and stereotypes' and 'intellectual baggage' provided by texts such as Gourou's *The Tropical World* (1966) 'with its heavy emphasis on "problems" of climate, disease and soils' (Binns, p. 316). Although he was aware of positive achievements of Ghanaian farmers from his reading, it was his field research in West Africa that dispelled the myths. Drawing on his experiences he commented on the 'vibrancy and friendliness of the people' of Sierra Leone and entrepreneurial farmers who had a good understanding of price variations and market opportunities. He commented on Fulani pastoralists in Northern Nigeria who were well aware of the need to sustain environmental resources. He commented on the resilience of both the land and the people of Mali in their capacity to recover from drought. It is clear that Binns, while acknowledging that poverty and problems exist, now has a very positive attitude towards Africa.

My experience of working with PGCE students confirms what Binns found: that living or studying in tropical Africa is a powerful force for dispelling myths. I taught students who had been brought up in Africa, who had studied there, had spent a gap year teaching there or who had been on a school exchange to Zanzibar. All had very positive feelings towards the countries they had lived in and were aware of diversity and complexity.

It is only rarely that secondary school students have had the opportunity to dispel myths by spending time in Africa or other distant parts of the world yet it is important that the stereotypes are tackled. So what can be done? I would suggest the following:

▲ Start by eliciting students' existing perceptions and where they think these come from, and decide how to address any stereotypes.

▲ Look for opportunities to invite people from other countries into the classroom. Borowski (2011) used African students studying at Leeds University to run lessons in primary schools and this changed children's perceptions. Sheffield University PGCE course invited university students from other countries to accompany PGCE students to their classrooms to answer students' questions.

▲ Look for opportunities to use teachers and student teachers who have lived in the places being studied (and who would be likely to counteract, rather than reinforce, stereotypical images).

▲ Look for opportunities to put students in contact with young people in other places being studied, through setting up email or video links.

▲ Use resources which enable people in other countries to speak for themselves, through their writing or through photographs they have taken.

▲ Use resources that show diversity within places studied. Taylor (2011) has pointed out that this is not achieved by simply providing a binary contrast, e.g. rich and poor Brazil or north and south Italy, as these can lead to further stereotyping.

▲ Use activities that probe stereotypical images (Figure 7.2).

How can the use of case studies be misleading?

Case studies are used in geography for very good reasons. They provide illustrative examples of human and physical processes and of the interplay of geographical factors. The detail, at a human and local scale, which they provide can be more accessible to students than broad generalisations. By using current events, e.g. the 2011 tsunami in Japan or the Olympic Games, they show the relevance of geography to understanding what is happening in the world.

However, because many places in case studies are studied in relation to only one topic, they can unintentionally stereotype those places. A good example of this is using Bangladesh as a case study of large-scale flooding. For many years I have run a workshop activity, intelligent guesswork (see Chapter 13), which is designed partly as a strategy for 'creating a need to know' and partly to demonstrate a way of eliciting prior knowledge. I now use it with the additional purpose of exposing stereotypes. I use a list of between 15 and 20 countries, including South Africa and Bangladesh, and ensure that there are at least three countries with lower life expectancy than Bangladesh.

Participants, in pairs or small groups, 'guess' life expectancy rates for each country. I ask for their guesses for the top three and bottom three countries. Bangladesh is always listed in the bottom three. Their reason: flooding. When this is probed they mention deaths from drowning, damage to crops and disease. Although all participants in this activity have been trainee or experienced geography teachers, they had insufficient additional knowledge to suggest that Bangladesh's life expectancy could be higher. They were surprised that Bangladesh's life expectancy is 65, whereas South Africa's, which they invariably think is higher, was only 54. It becomes clear from discussion that they had studied Bangladesh only as an example of flooding and the textbooks they used never mentioned Bangladesh in any other context. Furthermore, Bangladesh rarely features in news reports except when there are disastrous floods. These images are not untrue, but they present a fixed stereotypical view of Bangladesh which influenced their reasoning about life expectancy. As Adichie (2009) has argued, if you 'show a people as one thing, as only one thing, over and over again, that is what they become'.

Case studies have shown Bangladesh as one thing and Bangladesh has become a single story. Other commonly used case studies present 'single stories'. School geography often represents Mexico by the

Activities to counteract stereotyping

The following activities can be used to challenge stereotypical views of places. They would all work best if they are used not as a quick starter activity but are developed into a discussion in which stereotypes can be exposed and which could be an integral part of an investigation into a place or theme.

Where in the world?

▲ Find between six and 20 varied photographs to illustrate one place that is to be studied, choosing some which are stereotypical and others which present alternative images. The number chosen depends on the time available and how you want to make use of the activity.

▲ Present them to students.

▲ Number the photographs and ask students to guess and write down the name of the country in which the photograph was taken. If students work in pairs or groups, the discussion between them might produce interesting reasoning on which to draw.

▲ Show the photographs again and find out what students have guessed. Their guesses could be jotted down for use in discussion.

▲ Probe their answers using a selection of Socratic questions, e.g. What are you assuming? What are your reasons for saying that? What information are you basing that on?

▲ Look again at the photographs for which their answers were correct and discuss why.

▲ Look again at some photographs for which their answers were incorrect and discuss why.

▲ This activity could be consolidated by writing about photographs that surprised them and why.

Amazon or not? (and variations)

This activity was suggested by Taylor (2011) as a variation on an activity such as 'India or not?' which is a variation on 'Where in the world?'

▲ Find varied photographs of tropical rainforests.

▲ Present them to students.

▲ Ask students to guess whether they are in the Amazon basin or not.

▲ Find out what students have guessed and probe their answers as in the 'Where in the world?' activity.

▲ Use their guesses to develop an understanding of the concept of diversity within the Amazon rainforest and diversity between the Amazon rainforest and other rainforests.

For younger students photographs of other forest areas of the world could be included so that they could learn to distinguish the characteristic features of rainforests.

Variation: China or not?

Taylor based this activity on the more usual version which asks students to say whether photographs are taken in a particular country or not, e.g. China or not? India or not?

Variation: Less economically developed country or not?

Hopkirk (1998) used photographs he had taken in India for this activity, asking students to decide whether they were taken in an LEDC or not. They were all taken in India. He used this to counteract stereotypical images of India. Today, it is difficult to divide the world into LEDC and MEDC as for almost any indicator of development countries could be arranged along a continuum. So this activity would need to be developed through discussion and related to data e.g. Gapminder, that showed countries arranged along a continuum rather than in two distinct groups.

Photo editor

Students are provided with a scenario, real or hypothetical, in which they have to choose a limited number of photographs to represent a place. Scenarios could include:

▲ Photographs for a school website or brochure.

▲ Photographs of the local area for newcomers to the area or to send to a pen-friend in another country.

▲ Photographs for a tourist leaflet for a town.

▲ Photographs for a tourist leaflet about a country.

▲ Photographs for an Oxfam advert.

▲ Photographs for an article in a geography magazine such as WideWorld (no more than three per article).

The scenarios would be real if students were actually going to advise on photographs to represent the school or if their choices were going to be compared with actual photographs used for any of the above. They would be hypothetical if they were not going to make such a comparison.

▲ Find varied photographs which present different aspects of what is being shown.

▲ Explain the scenario. The criteria for selection could be discussed at this stage, or the implicit criteria they have used could emerge from discussion following their choices.

▲ Students choose a limited number of photographs, e.g. two or three from 10 photographs, or a maximum of six to represent the local area.

▲ After they have made their choices, each photograph is discussed in turn with students explaining why they have or have not selected it. There could be an attempt to reach consensus among a class, through students arguing the pros and cons of each picture.

▲ A general discussion could follow on what messages the chosen pictures convey about the place and the extent to which these are 'accurate' or misleading representations.

An alternative to this would be to invite students to select photographs, or take them, to show a place negatively and positively. By constructing their own representations of place students will be helped to understand stereotyping.

Figure 7.2: Activities to counteract stereotyping.

single story of migration to the USA and China by its 'one-child policy'.

Definitive stories of places limit understanding. This can be avoided by:

▲ using the same country/town for case studies of different themes so that contrasting images of the same place would be encountered during the course. This has the disadvantage, however, that fewer places in the world are studied, which in itself is distorting

▲ locating every case study in a wider context so that students become aware of other aspects of the place being studied

▲ showing Adichie's lecture 'The danger of a single story' (2009), or excerpts from it, to make students aware of the issue.

What is bias?

To be biased has been defined by the online Oxford Dictionary as: 'to feel or show inclination or prejudice for or against someone or something' (*http://oxforddictionaries.com/definition/english/ bias*). Students encounter bias in the geography classroom when they investigate controversial issues (discussed in Chapter 12) and through the sources of geographical information they use.

As Lang (1993) wrote in relation to history sources, 'All sources have an inbuilt bias, some more marked than others, and some more obvious than others, but none are exempt from it. The historian's task is to discover that bias' (p. 13). He argues that the question to ask is not 'is this source biased?' but 'what is this source's bias and how does it add to our picture of the past?' (p. 10). The same argument can be used about sources in geography; all representations of the world are positioned and to various degrees biased. The question students should ask therefore is not 'is this representation biased' but 'what is its bias?' They should be encouraged to be aware of the origin of source materials they use, who produced it and why.

There is a difference between bias, representing a point of view or positionality or arguing a particular case, and conveying a false view of a situation. For example, the way some textbooks represent agriculture in southern Italy is not biased but inaccurate.

The representation of southern Italy in textbooks

In 2006 I set out to compare the representation of southern Italy in three geography textbooks used

Photo: © brunosan (Creative Common License)

Photo: © dougsyme (Creative Common License)

Mexico and Bangladesh have become 'single stories' in many case studies – for Mexico the story of migration to the USA, and for Bangladesh the story of large-scale flooding.

in lower secondary schools in England (Bowen and Pallister, 2005; Hillary *et al.*, 2001; Waugh and Bushell, 2006) with an atlas produced for Italian primary schools (IGA, 2006). The study focused on settlement, agriculture and industry as these were included in all four publications, represented through text, illustrations and activities.

What is meant by southern Italy can vary: Campania, Calabria, Puglia, Basilicata, Sicily and Sardinia are usually included. This study included, in addition, the regions of Abruzzo and Molise because the one textbook which did define what it meant by 'the south' included these.

I focused on particular aspects of othering: stereotyping; developmental comparison; marginalisation.

Stereotyping

The textbooks stereotyped southern Italy through simplification, exaggeration and omission. They simplified it by making generalisations about it as an undifferentiated area. Very few examples of variations within it were given.

Exaggeration of a few characteristics was common. The textbooks exaggerated the significance of hill towns. Eight of the nine textbook illustrations of settlements were of inland hill towns. Only one showed a coastal settlement. The atlas had nine illustrations of settlements only two of which were hill towns. The atlas included photographs of coastal settlements in Campania, Puglia, Calabria, Sicily and Sardinia. In fact, the majority of the population lives in settlements on the coast, not in hill towns.

Two of the books exaggerated the importance of subsistence farming by representing it as the dominant form of agriculture: 'Farming is at subsistence level.' A speech bubble contained this sentence: 'In southern Italy many farms are small and produce enough food to feed my family.' The books exaggerated the problems of agriculture which were identified as: 'summer drought'; 'fierce heat'; 'much of the land is high and steep' and 'little soil on the hills'. Activities asked students to describe the 'problems' of agriculture. The atlas representation of agriculture told a different story. For each region there was a map showing a wide variety of crops. The photographs showed production, not problems, e.g. olives and vines in Puglia, oranges in Sicily, tomatoes in Campania. The atlas text referred to advantages for agriculture: the fertility of the plains and the gentleness of the climate in Campania and the good climate and the lack of mountains in Puglia. An exercise in the atlas based on information about agricultural production revealed that three of the six most productive regions in Italy were Campania, Sicily and Puglia.

References to industry in the textbooks exaggerated the paucity of industrial development in the south and the problems: 'Limited skills'; 'isolated'; and 'lack of power supplies such as coal'. Again the atlas told a different story. Maps for each region, supported by further information in the text, showed the variety of industries including oil refining, textiles, engineering, ceramics, food and tobacco processing, chemical, and electrical. The books did not mention the huge FIAT car plant at Melfi in Abruzzo.

Developmental comparison

Each of the textbooks represented the south of Italy in relation to the north. There were explicit comparisons, e.g. 'the south is the poorest region in Italy', explicit headings, e.g. 'the north/south divide' and comparative statistics on Lombardy and Campania. All three textbooks mentioned differences between north and south. None mentioned similarities. The textbooks constructed the south through a northern lens, presenting it as apart and different. In contrast, there were no comparisons in the Italian atlas. Each Italian region was represented separately.

The textbooks suggested that the south was not only different but also behind the north and inferior to it. Agriculture was presented as 'still traditional', 'using animals instead of modern machinery, with outdated methods and little money to buy fertilizers'.

The textbooks presented the south as a problem that could be improved only with outside help. One activity asked students to imagine they work in a new *Cassa per il Mezzogiorno* ('Fund for the South') to identify problems and suggest improvements. There was no mention of the involvement of local communities in determining and managing the use of EU funding. (NB *The Cassa per il Mezzogiorno* ceased operating in 1986.) This activity has been now been replaced by one in which students are asked to list six problems facing farmers in the south.

Marginalisation

The textbooks marginalised the south, describing it as being 'isolated from the rest of Europe, far away from urban markets in northern Italy and NW Europe and remote'. The atlas referred to remoteness only in relation to Calabria and Basilicata and included maps of rail, road and air communications in Italy, showing the south to be well connected to the north. At a time of increasing globalisation, when food products are flown daily around the world and many industries are footloose it is misleading to represent the south of Italy as marginal. Agricultural and industrial products from southern Italy can be found all over Europe.

Some general comments

The textbooks I examined imposed particular meanings on the south of Italy; they told a single negative story. In constructing this story they have found statistics, photographs and information to support the story and have ignored information which tells a different story of the south, e.g. the high life expectancy figures, the well developed motorway network, a climate that permits a long cultivation season, the large coastal settlements, the successful exports of food and industrial products. Othering was achieved by looking at the south through a negative lens that highlighted problems and ignored anything positive. The textbooks encouraged students to see Italy in binary terms (Taylor, 2011) with a rich north and poor south, to see diversity between north and south rather than diversity within the north and the south.

I was concerned by two other aspects of the textbooks. First, the books not only 'othered' the Italian south by distortion and omission: they were also inaccurate. One book, which is still being sold and used, states that in the south, 'farming is at subsistence level'. Yet, at the same time as students are learning this, it is possible to go into any large supermarket in England and fill a trolley with agricultural produce from southern Italy, e.g. tinned tomatoes, citrus fruit, pasta, olive oil, wine (Figure 7.3). What kind of subsistence farming can supply the shelves of every supermarket in England? Although everything in textbooks is a selection, they should aim to convey accurate, verifiable information rather than presenting an image fixed in the past.

The second worrying aspect was that the exercises required students to reproduce the information presented, not to examine, interpret and evaluate it. The authors have presented an authoritative image of the Italian south which students are expected to accept and reproduce. I am not concerned simply because they are being asked to reproduce distorted inaccurate information. I think that textbook activities should expect students to examine critically what they present rather than simply reproduce it.

The textbook representations of southern Italy have been powerful in influencing how this part of Italy is perceived, on what has been taught and what has found its way onto various websites. As Adichie has said, the single story has become the definitive story. Cosgrove and Domosh wrote, 'When we write our geographies we are creating artefacts that impose meaning on the world' (1993, p. 37).

We need to be aware of the meanings we create through othering, through seeing other parts of the world through negative lenses which obliterate anything positive.

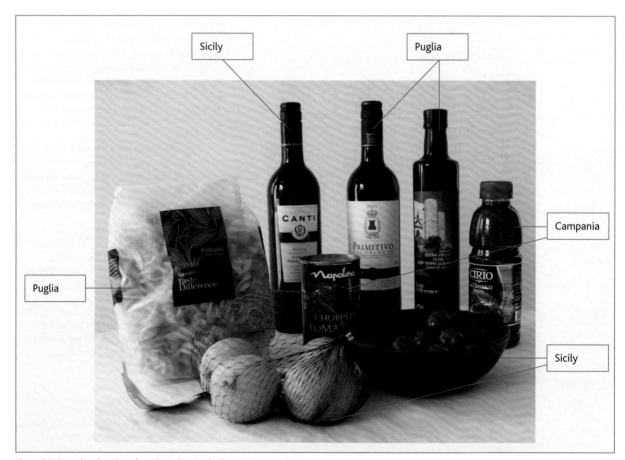

Figure 7.3: Examples of products from the Italian South. Photo: Margaret Roberts.

What is 'othering'?

Another way in which places can be misrepresented in geography is through the process of 'othering'. Throughout history different places have been represented as something 'other'. Ancient Greeks contrasted their 'civilised' world with a world of barbarians. Edward Said's influential book, *Orientalism* (1978), explored ways in which the West had constructed the Orient as something 'other' to bolster the West's sense of superiority. In the othering process one group or place is seen as 'us' and the other as 'them', with the other seen as inferior. Othering is achieved in various ways:

▲ The other area is named and is treated as an undifferentiated entity.

▲ The other area is stereotyped by exaggerating a few characteristics.

▲ The relationship between us and the other is expressed in developmental terms, often with an associated vocabulary of backward/modern; primitive/advanced; underdeveloped/developed.

▲ The other is represented as what we once were and as inferior.

▲ The other is marginalised through the language of core and periphery.

In the past geography textbooks tended to other what were variously termed 'underdeveloped countries', 'developing countries', 'the third world' and 'the poor south'. These areas were presented as inferior through both the words and illustrations used to describe them. Massey has commented on accounts suggesting places such as Nicaragua and Mozambique are 'merely at an earlier stage'. She says that this narrative suggests that 'we are not to imagine them as having their own trajectories, their own particular histories, and the potential for their own, perhaps different, futures' (Massey, 2005, p. 5).

Another part of the world that has been othered in geography textbooks is the Italian south (Roberts, 2008). The history of the Italian south, the *Mezzogiorno*, being perceived as 'other' dates back to the 19th century, before the unification of Italy. In northern Italy, anti-southern feelings, known as *meridionalismo*, produced a set of negative attitudes through which northerners perceived the south. The south has been considered by the north at various times to be barbaric, ignorant, primitive, underdeveloped and lacking the qualities of the north. Some stereotypical attitudes persist in Italy. The perception of the Italian south as a problem is being challenged by historians, who think it is important to understand the south without needing to see it through northern eyes (Lumley

and Morris, 1997). The *Mezzogiorno* needs to be understood, using Massey's phrase, through its own particular histories. The contrast between my own experiences of the Italian south and its presentation in geography textbooks prompted me to research the issue (see above).

Geographers are centrally involved in presenting 'other' places and peoples so have particular responsibilities in relation to the construction of difference. 'Othering' hinders and damages our understanding of other places. We have a responsibility to take the 'other' seriously and attempt to understand it rather than judge it.

Summary

Although we cannot represent the world accurately in geography it is possible to misrepresent it through selection, stereotyping and othering. Students get to know the world partly through what is presented to them in school geography so we need to be critically aware of how we represent it.

Suggestions for research

1. Analyse the shape of the world as studied through the school geography curriculum. What parts of the world and which countries are studied in detail, which are studied as case studies and which are not studied at all? Why were the places to be studied selected? To what extent is the world misrepresented and does it matter?

2. Analyse the case studies used as part of the geography course. What messages are conveyed about the countries/regions/continents in which these case studies are located? Could the use of these case studies lead to misrepresentation of places?

3. Investigate students' perceptions of particular countries or continents, e.g. India or Africa. What is the origin of their views? Can studying geography change these perceptions?

4. Analyse the way a country, region or part of the world is represented in sources and activities used in a unit of work or in textbooks. To what extent are places stereotyped or 'othered'?

References

Adichie, C. (2009) 'The danger of a single story', Technology, Entertainment and Design Conference, Palm Springs, USA. Available online at *www.ted.com/talks/ chimamanda_adichie_the_danger_of_a_single_story. html* (last accessed 14 January 2013). Transcript available at *http://dotsub.com/view/63ef5d28-6607-4fec-b906-aaae6cff7dbe/viewTranscript/eng* (last accessed 14 January 2013).

Allen, J. and Massey, D. (eds) (1995) *The Shape of the World: Explorations in human geography.* Oxford: Oxford University Press.

Binns, T. (1995) 'Geography in development: development in geography', *Geography,* 80, 4, pp. 303–22.

Borowski, R. (2011) 'The hidden cost of a Red Nose', *Primary Geography*, 75, pp. 18–20.

Borowski, R. and Plastow, J. (2012) 'Africans don't use mobile phones: a critical discussion of issues arising from the Leeds University Centre for African Studies (LUCAS) "African Voices" project'. Available online at *www.polis.leeds.ac.uk/assets/files/research/lucas/Galway%20Paper.pdf* (last accessed 14 January 2013).

Bowen, A. and Pallister, J. (2005) *Geography 360 degrees: Core book 2.* Oxford: Heinemann.

Cosgrove, D. and Domosh, M. (1993) 'Author and authority: writing the new cultural geography' in Duncan, J. and Ley, D. (eds) *Place/Culture/Representation*. London: Routledge.

Daniels, P., Sidaway, J., Bradshore, M. and Shaw, D. (2012) *An Introduction to Human Geography.* Harlow: Pearson Education.

Duncan, J. and Ley, D. (1993) *Place, Culture and Representation*. Abingdon: Routledge.

Gourou, P. (1966) *The Tropical World* (4th edition). London: Longman (first published in French in 1947).

Hall, S. (1997) *Representation: Cultural representations and signifying practices.* London: Sage.

Hillary, J., Mickelburgh, J. and Stanfield, J. (2001) *Think Through Geography 2.* London: Longman.

Hopkirk, G. (1998) 'Challenging images of the developing world using slide photographs', *Teaching Geography*, 23, 1, pp. 34–5.

Istituto Geografico de Agostini (IGA) (2006) *Atlante Geografico di Base de Agostini per la Scuola Primaria.* Novara: Istituto Geografico de Agostini.

Lang, S. (1993) 'What is bias?', *Teaching History,* 73, pp. 9–13.

Lumley, R. and Morris, J. (eds) (1997) *The New History of the Italian South.* Exeter: University of Exeter Press.

Massey, D. (1995) 'Geographical imaginations' in Allen, J. and Massey, D. (eds) *The Shape of the World: Explorations in human geography.* Oxford: Oxford University Press.

Massey, D. (2005) *For Space.* London: Sage.

Roberts, M. (2006) 'Shaping students' understanding of the world in the geography classroom' in Purnell, K., Lidstone, J. and Hodgson, S. (eds) *Changes in Geographical Education: Past, present and future. Proceedings of the International Geographical Union Commission on Geographical Education 2006 Symposium.* Brisbane, Australia: IGU-CGE and Royal Geographical Society of Queensland.

Roberts, M. (2008) 'La rappresentazione del sud d'Italia' (Representations of the south of Italy). Paper presented at IGU Conference, Università degli Studi di Milano-Bicocca (published in conference proceedings).

Said, E. (1978) *Orientalism*. Harmondsworth: Penguin.

Saint-Exupéry, A. de (1974) *The Little Prince.* Translated by Katherine Woods. London: Pan Books. (First published in French as *Le Petit Prince* in 1943).

Taylor, L. (2004) *Re-presenting Geography.* Cambridge: Chris Kington Publishing.

Taylor, L. (2011) 'The negotiation of diversity', *Teaching Geography,* 36, 2, pp. 49–51.

Waugh, D. and Bushell, T. (2006) *Key Geography: New interactions.* Cheltenham: Nelson Thornes.

Whatmore, S. (2005) 'Culture-nature' in Cloke, P., Crang, P. and Goodwin, M. (eds) *Introducing Human Geographies.* London: Hodder.

CHAPTER 08

Making sense of geography through reasoning and argumentation

'The ability engage in argument is what makes learning exciting. To feel comfortable with debate changes your relationship with education and just about everything else. It transforms you from a passive and bored receptacle of another's wisdom into a participant; into someone who is neither scared by, nor indifferent to, the society around them but actively involved in its interpretation and transformation' (Bonnett, 2008, p. 1).

Introduction

Learning geography through enquiry does not mean simply finding out answers to questions. In order to develop geographical understanding it is important for students to make sense of the information they encounter by making connections of all sorts: between their existing understanding and new knowledge and between different pieces of information. Making sense is at the heart of learning any discipline. It involves being able to reason and to develop and evaluate arguments.

This chapter focuses on the nature of geographical arguments and examines the following questions:

▲ What is an 'argument' and what is not an 'argument'?

▲ Why is argument important in learning geography through enquiry?

▲ What kinds of reasoning are used by geographers and how can they be developed in the classroom?

▲ What is argumentation and how can arguments be analysed?

▲ What is structured academic controversy (SAC)?

▲ What kinds of reasoning are required by the various command words used in examinations?

What is an 'argument' and what is not an 'argument'?

The word 'argument' is used in different ways:

▲ A quarrel or an exchange of views that might become heated or fierce; e.g. 'she had an argument with someone about...'

▲ A reason or set of reasons given in support of, or against, an idea or a proposal, e.g. 'There are strong arguments for building a bypass'; or 'He rejected the argument that...'

▲ A discussion or debate about different viewpoints, e.g. 'they had an argument about whether there should be more taxes on air fares' or 'do you want to hear about both sides of the argument?'

▲ A reason or set of reasons aimed at persuading, e.g. in a court of law, 'the prosecutor presents arguments based on evidence.'

▲ As a basis for reasoning, e.g. 'For the sake of argument...'

In this chapter I am interested in 'argument' as a reason or set of reasons. These reasons might be used in a discussion or debate or might be used to persuade but I want to focus mainly on the process of reasoning and arguing, the kind of academic argument referred to by Bonnett (2008):

'An academic argument is a tool of learning and understanding. It is a form of intellectual engagement. It is a type of exchange based on the sharing of knowledge, a pooling of facts and opinions. It is, or at least it should be, restless, unsettled, always trying to move forward. Such ideals are diametrically opposed to the notion that the point of arguments is to win them' (p. 2).

One way of introducing students to the concept of argument as a set of reasons rather than as a quarrel is by acting out or showing extracts from the entertaining 'Argument Clinic Sketch' from Monty Python's Flying Circus, episode 29 (BBC, 1972) various versions of which can be found on YouTube. As can be seen from Figure 8.1, the sketch makes some important points which could be elicited and discussed:

▲ argument is not abuse

▲ argument is not contradiction ('the automatic gainsaying of anything the other person says')

▲ 'argument is a connected series of statements intended to establish a proposition'

▲ 'argument is an intellectual process'.

A man (Michael Palin) has paid to have an argument. He first goes into the wrong room where there is an angry and abusive man. He eventually goes into Room 12A where he meets other man (John Cleese)			

A man (Michael Palin) has paid to have an argument. He first goes into the wrong room where there is an angry and abusive man. He eventually goes into Room 12A where he meets other man (John Cleese)

Outside Room 12A   The man knocks on door

Other man	Come in
Man	Is this the right room for an argument?
Other man	I've told you once
Man	No you haven't!
Other man	Yes I have.
Man	When?
Other man	Just now
Man	No you didn't!
Other man	Yes I did!
Man	You most certainly did not.
Other man	Now let's get one thing quite clear. I most definitely told you!
Man	You did not
Other man	Yes I did
Man	Look, this isn't an argument!
Other man	Yes it is!
Man	No it isn't! It's just contradiction!
Other man	No it isn't!
Man	I came here for a good argument.
Other man	No you didn't, you came here for an argument.
Man	Well, an 'argument' is not the same as contradiction.
Other man	It can be.
Man	No it can't. An argument is a connected series of statements to establish a definite proposition.
Other man	No it isn't.
Man	Yes it is. It isn't just contradiction.
Other man	Look, if I argue with you, I must take up a contrary position.
Man	But it isn't just saying 'No it isn't'.
Other man	Yes it is.
Man	No it isn't. Argument is an intellectual process... contradiction is just the automatic gainsaying of anything the other person says.
Other man	No it isn't.
Man	Yes it is.

NB This extract is much shortened from the original which lasts nearly four minutes.

Figure 8.1: Extracts from Monty Python's Flying Circus Argument Clinic Sketch. Source: BBC, 1972

Bonnett (2008) makes a useful distinction between what he calls 'so what' arguments and substantive arguments. 'So what' arguments are descriptive and might, if used in written work, prompt the reaction 'so what?' Bonnett writes that:

'Without a framework with which to interpret them, facts do not constitute an argument. Facts do not speak for themselves. They need to be analysed, explained and provided with a context. Otherwise they are, quite literally, meaningless' (p. 7).

Substantive arguments are based on ideas in a subject and are focused and precise. Substantive arguments tend to be qualified and contextualised and suggest an idea, an explanation or a way in which information might be linked. Two of the geographical examples Bonnett gave to illustrate the characteristics of 'so what' and substantive arguments (which he says might not be accurate but need to be argued) are shown in Figure 8.2.

Why is argument important in learning geography through enquiry?

Argument is central to the construction of geographical knowledge. It is through reasoned argument that geographers develop ideas, relate them to evidence, make claims about the world and justify their interpretations. Arguments are influenced by when and where they take place and the positionality of the researchers. However, this does not mean that claims are completely relative. All claims need to be consistent with the

'So what' arguments	Substantive arguments
The population of the world is increasing rapidly	Neo-Malthusianism remains a viable and accurate model of world population growth
There are 16 ways to prevent desertification	The utility of two principal techniques currently employed to ameliorate or prevent desertification can only be fully exploited when they are allied to a range of other supplementary measures.

Figure 8.2: Examples of 'so what' arguments and substantive arguments. Source: Bonnett, 2008, p. 9.

material world and they need to survive academic critique before being published and accepted. So, although there are different understandings and interpretations of aspects of geography it is not a case of 'anything goes'. Geographers need to defend their claims through reasoned argument.

In traditional approaches to teaching geography in schools, claims are transmitted as fact, as right and wrong answers; students are provided with authoritative explanations. An enquiry approach to learning geography inducts students into geographical ways of thinking, so it seems important that students become aware that geographical knowledge has been developed through debate, disagreement and reasoned argument. Students need to be able to evaluate the arguments they encounter in geographical sources. In addition, it is important in a democratic society to be able to evaluate arguments presented in the media and to present coherent arguments and reason with others.

The significant amount of research into science education (Osborne, 2010) demonstrates that teaching students to reason, argue and think critically improves their scientific reasoning. Their scores in tests of conceptual understanding improved, and the collaborative approaches used were better at engaging them in ideas.

What kinds of reasoning are used by geographers and how can they be developed in the classroom?

The book *How to Argue* was written by a geographer, Alistair Bonnett, to help undergraduates of all subjects develop reasoned arguments in essays and presentations (Bonnett, 2008). Although intended for a different audience, the six categories of argument that he identified are relevant to the geography classroom. Below, I summarise what is included in each of his categories. In Figure 8.3 I suggest ways in which each type of reasoning might be developed in secondary school geography.

Argument 1: Identifying tensions

The words and place names used in geography are not always as straightforward as they might seem from glossaries and atlases; there can be conflicting meanings. Bonnett identified two approaches to reasoning about these kinds of tensions.

▲ There is a contradiction when two statements directly oppose one another or when there are

contradictions in the terminology itself, e.g. sustainable development. This kind of reasoning identifies and explains the conflict.

▲ Deconstruction attempts to expose the way knowledge is constructed and to examine the meaning of terms. Instead of taking things for granted the categories are broken open and scrutinised.

Argument 2: Cause and effect

Reasoning about cause and effect in geography needs to be considered in relation to evidence:

'To say that one thing causes another can be a statement of fact. But it is always also a claim, an assertion that we can take issue with or revise. Indeed, as a general rule, it is better to think of claims of causation as something to be considered in the light of supporting evidence rather than as "obvious" or "common sense"' (Bonnett, 2008, p. 17).

Arguments about cause and effect based on qualitative data attempt to understand and explain relationships between events, policies and processes.

Arguments about cause and effect based on quantitative data look for statistical relationships between two or more sets of data. Rather than provide explanations, they measure the strength and nature of the relationship between sets of data. Two types of analysis commonly used in school geography are correlation and regression analysis.

Correlation analysis indicates the strength of relationship between two things. Correlation coefficients vary between 1 (a perfect positive correlation) and -1 (a perfect negative correlation) but care has to be taken interpreting them. The fact that there might be a strong correlation between two sets of data does not necessarily indicate a cause/effect relationship between the two. Rogerson (2001) wrote about a strong correlation that had been found between British coal production and the death of penguins in the Antarctic and commented that it would be 'a stretch of the imagination to connect the two in any direct way' (p. 88).

Regression analysis presents two sets of data plotted against each other on a graph. If a 'best fit' line can be plotted it can indicate whether there might be a positive relationship, in which both data sets increase and decrease together, or a negative relationship, in which one data set increases while the other decreases. Regression analysis can be used to suggest a cause/effect relationship or to refute one, to expose exceptions and to make predictions.

Argument 3: Starting with observation or starting with hypothesis testing

The process of starting with observations and reaching conclusions from empirical data is known as induction. It is not possible to generate universal laws by starting with observation, but it can be used to make limited claims, which might indicate general patterns.

The process of testing a hypothesis against the facts to establish its truth or falsity is known as deduction. A hypothesis is a speculative, provisional statement, which provides a starting point for an investigation, although the inspiration for a hypothesis may well have come from observation. Two competing claims are used to test a hypothesis:

▲ A null hypothesis, which assumes that there is no support for the speculative statement.

▲ An alternative hypothesis, which is the speculative statement that the investigation sets out to establish.

Data are collected to support or refute the null hypothesis. If the null hypothesis is not supported by the data, the investigation accepts the alternative hypothesis.

In science the aim is to produce universal laws about how things work which are accepted until they are refuted by contradictory evidence. In geography, few processes are deterministic because they operate differently in different locational contexts, so the process of hypothesis testing often leads to the formulation of generalisations about physical and environmental processes rather than universal laws. The scientific method, with the use of hypotheses and statistical methods at its core, is less suitable for studying and developing arguments about the complexities of human interactions and social processes.

Argument 4: Arguing about words: meanings and classifications

Some words used in geography, e.g. globalisation, sustainable development, nature, are used differently by different writers, so it is important to understand how they have been used and applied. Because of different usage, such words cannot be reduced to one simple glossary definition. If students are to understand what they hear and read they need to discuss the meaning of terminology and how it has been used in their textbooks.

Geography classifies things into categories, e.g. deserts, Mediterranean climate, less/more economically developed. What is or is not included in a category is based on reasoned argument. If students are to understand the meaning of the classification they need to understand the reasons behind what is and is not included in a category and learn to use these arguments themselves.

Argument 5: Contributions and impacts

Explaining the contribution of an event, action, policy or decision to something involves assessing the strength of the contribution and might include comparing it with other contributions. For example, reasoned arguments could be developed about the contribution of European countries to carbon reduction compared with other countries in the world.

Explaining the impact of an event, policy or decision on a place or situation is the kind of argument commonly needed in geography. Arguing about impact is not simply a case of presenting facts; it is about examining and explaining the processes that change situations. There is a danger of oversimplification so it is important to examine the strength of the impact.

Argument 6: Comparison

Comparisons are common in geography. It is important to justify the choice of comparison and to consider:

▲ Why are these two places or phenomena being compared?

▲ Which aspects of them are being compared and why?

▲ Are similar kinds of data available: is it possible to compare them?

▲ Is the purpose to see how things they have in common vary in different contexts?

▲ In what ways are these places/situations similar and why?

▲ In what ways are these places/situations different and why?

What is argumentation and how can arguments be analysed?

Argumentation is the process of arguing, i.e. reasoning and using evidence to support what is claimed to be true. Toulmin (1958) developed a model that showed the component parts of argumentation and the relationship between them and advocated its use in educational contexts. This model, sometimes referred to as TAP (Toulmin's

Developing argument in the classroom

Argument 1: Identifying tensions

Contradiction: e.g. sustainable development

There are contradictions in the term 'sustainable development' which can be investigated by looking at different frameworks and applying them to particular cases, e.g. sustainable cities; sustainable tourism. What kinds of development might be sustainable or unsustainable?

Students could examine one or more the following tensions related to the concept of 'sustainable development' identified and exemplified in Gough and Scott (2003) and listed on page 80 in Morgan (2010):

▲ change versus continuity

▲ empowerment versus prescription

▲ me versus we

▲ present generations versus future generations

▲ humans versus nature

▲ local versus global

▲ rich, poor and very poor

▲ disconnected lumps of joined-up thinking.

A related term worth examining is 'greenwashing' which is when an organisation or company claims in its advertising to be green, but in fact is not as green as it claims. Suggestions of how students could examine advertisements can be found online at *www.greenwashingindex.com/about-greenwashing* (last accessed 5 December 2012).

Deconstruction: e.g. Europe and European

It is worth examining the meanings of 'Europe' and 'European' instead of taking them for granted. The meaning of 'Europe' is confused. Its eastern geographical boundary is unclear but includes parts of Russia and Turkey. Sometimes 'Europe' is used to mean the European Union (EU), but as membership has increased this usage has changed. There are interesting oddities, e.g. Réunion, in the Indian Ocean, is one of the 27 departments of France and therefore a member of the EU. Not all countries in Europe are members of the EU. EU countries relate differently to European legislation. Different countries are eligible to play European football and to enter the Eurovision song contest.

The meaning of 'European' is equally confusing. Do students in England feel English, British or European or all three, and why? What meanings do they attach to these terms? What do they think are the characteristics of being European? What does being European mean in a multi-ethnic Europe?

Argument 2: Cause and effect

Reasoning from qualitative data: e.g. Polish migration to the UK in the last 10 years

The evidence for this enquiry would include information about the expansion of the EU, as well as migrants' personal accounts of comparative opportunities in Poland and the UK. Qualitative data might be supplemented by quantitative data.

Useful phrases: 'in part explained by'; 'to some extent'; 'the data suggest that ...'; 'several factors have contributed to ...'

Reasoning from quantitative data: Correlation and regression analysis: e.g. development indices

How do different indices relate to either GDP or to the Human Development Index? It would be preferable to use a computer to calculate correlation coefficients and to draw regression analysis graphs, so that time could be spent discussing the significance of the analysis and whether it suggests a possible causal connection.

Useful phrases: 'there seems to be a significant relationship between ...'; 'There is no significant relationship between ...'

Argument 3: Hypothesis testing

Example: Is the local weather becoming more extreme?

▲ Null hypothesis: there is no significant difference between the pattern of weather in X in the last 10 years and the previous 20 years.

▲ Alternative hypothesis: there is a significant difference between the pattern of weather in X in the last 10 years and the previous 20 years.

Data could be obtained from local weather stations and examined.

Useful phrases: 'the data indicate that ...'; 'the data support the idea that ...'; 'the data do not support the idea that ...'

Argument 4: Arguing about words: meanings and classifications

Example 1: What is globalisation and how does it affect the place where I live?

Students could examine and discuss different definitions of globalisation (see Figure 9.9) and apply them to information about the geography of the local area.

Example 2: Can countries of the world be classified according to levels of development?

Students could examine different ways in which countries of the world have been classified according to levels of economic development and according to the Human Development Index. They could examine the meaning of 'less economically developed' and 'more economically developed', possibly by using Gapminder, and consider what categories the data suggest.

Figure 8.3: Developing Bonnett's six categories of argument in the classroom.

Argument 5: Contributions and impacts

Example 1: What is the contribution of wind power to the UK's total energy production?

Students could compare the present and future potential of wind power with other contributions to the UK energy supply.

Example 2: What has been the impact of the 2012 Olympic and Paralympic Games on London?

Useful phrases: 'the contribution of X is significant because …'; 'the principal impact of X is … because …'

Argument 6: Comparison

Example: How do the road traffic congestion zones of London and Singapore compare?

Students could identify similarities and differences in the history of the congestion zones; why they were set up; the areas they cover; how they operate; the extent to which they are considered successful.

---

argumentation pattern), shows the constituent elements of argumentation as identified by Toulmin:

▲ A claim: a statement (proposition or assertion) about what is believed to be true. In some ways it is both the starting point and the conclusion of an argument. It states the point to be argued at the start but it is also where the argument, if the merits of the claim have been established, ends up.

▲ A warrant: reasons (rules, principles, etc.) that are proposed to justify the connections between the data and the knowledge claim, or conclusion. The warrant provides the link between the claim and the data.

▲ Data (facts, evidence) to support the reasons given in the warrant.

▲ Backing: these are basic assumptions, based on generalisations about what is known within a discipline, which support the reasoning of the warrants.

▲ Qualifiers: these specify the conditions under which the claim can be taken as true; they represent limitations on the claim, or on the strength or reliability of the claim.

▲ Rebuttal: reasons that might be used against the claim being true. The reasons given in rebuttals can be supported with further data.

Figure 8.4 shows how TAP has been applied to an argument related to global warming. Although the use of Toulmin's framework has been promoted in geography through projects and CPD courses organised by the GA (Morgan, 2006), science education has taken the lead in researching its use. Several projects were set up to enhance the quality of argument in school science, with the aim of investigating the impact of interventions on both teachers and students (Driver *et al.*, 2000; Osborne *et al.*, 2004; Erduran *et al.*, 2004; Simon, 2008; Osborne, 2010).

Findings from the projects indicated that:

▲ Explicit teaching of specific strategies and a knowledge of the features of arguments (e.g. claims, reasons, evidence, etc.) improves students' reasoning.

▲ Teaching students to reason, argue and think critically enhances their conceptual learning.

▲ Working collaboratively with teachers to produce curriculum materials and activities to support argumentation played a key role in the projects.

▲ Teachers were able, with the support of the projects, to change their practice and encourage more discussion, but the change was gradual over a year.

▲ Developing the ability to understand and implement argumentation depended on the ability of teachers to reflect on previous experience, to focus on the importance of talking and listening and to convey the meaning of argument through modelling.

Erduran *et al.* (2004) developed an analytical framework to assess the quality of argumentation used in the classroom (Figure 8.5). This focused on the process of argumentation rather than on the content of the arguments.

Although there were positive findings, there were also some problematic aspects of using TAP in science education. When researchers were analysing transcripts of small group discussions, they had difficulties in distinguishing between different elements, e.g. between warrants and backing. Some teachers also found the categories confusing. Also, although Toulmin's framework can be used to assess the structure and process of argumentation, e.g. by using the levels suggested in Figure 8.5, it cannot assess the quality of the subject knowledge needed to support the argument and the students' ability to use it well to support claims (Driver *et al.*, 2000).

Figure 8.4: Using Toulmin's framework to analyse an argument about global warming. Source: Morgan, 2008.

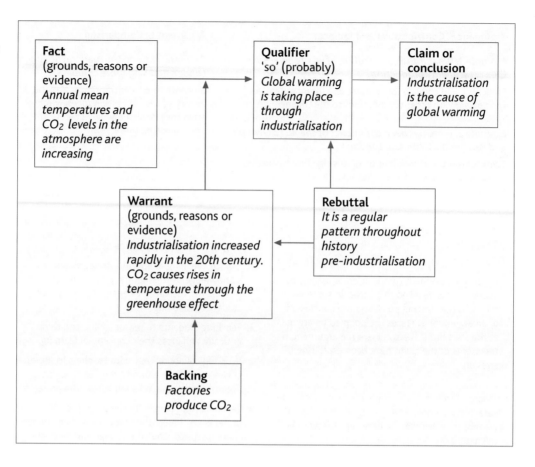

There are lessons for geographical education in this. TAP is useful in identifying the component parts of argumentation but Toulmin's categories are useful only if they clarify rather than confuse thinking.

Figure 8.5: Analytical framework used to assess quality of argumentation. Source: Erduran *et al.*, 2004.

Assessing argumentation quality

Level 1: argumentation consists of arguments that are a simple claim v a counter claim, or a claim v a claim

Level 2: argumentation has arguments which consist of claims with either data, warrants or backings but do not contain any rebuttals.

Level 3: argumentation has arguments with a series of claims or counter claims with either data, warrants or backings with the occasional weak rebuttal.

Level 4: argumentation has arguments with a claim and a clearly identifiable rebuttal. Such an argument may have several claims and counter claims as well but this is not necessary.

Level 5: argumentation displays an extended argument with more than one rebuttal.

The emphasis in geography should be on developing good reasoned arguments rather than on necessarily being able to distinguish between 'warrant' and 'backing' or being able to ascribe statements to appropriate categories.

The research recognises that for students to argue well they need both skills in the process of arguing and also subject knowledge and understanding on which to draw. Yet, research in science education has focused more on the process of argumentation and its mechanics, measuring how many elements are used etc. If we want to assess the quality of students' reasoning in geography, we must put the emphasis instead on students' ability to use geographical evidence and draw on their existing knowledge and understanding of geography to substantiate their claims.

The research does suggest that students benefit from having opportunities to engage in arguments in lessons. Figure 8.6 provides a writing frame to support argumentation in geography which has been completed from a newspaper article on coral reefs.

Figure 8.6: Example of a completed argumentation writing frame.

What is the key enquiry question you are investigating? Are the world's coral reefs under threat?
What is the argument (claim)? Write this as a statement. 'Caribbean coral reefs face collapse.'
Who made this claim? Did you read it in an article or did you hear it on a film? Headline in the *Guardian* 10/09/12, accessed 7/11/12 at *www.guardian.co.uk/environment/2012/sep/10/caribbean-coral-reefs-collapse-environment* (Based on detailed research report published by the International Union for the Conservation of Nature accessible at: *https://cmsdata.iucn.org/downloads/caribbean_coral_report_jbcj_030912.pdf*)
What are the reasons (warrant) given for this statement? Coral reefs are being damaged by: ▲ Pollution ▲ Overfishing ▲ Bleaching because of higher temperatures ▲ Higher levels of acidity in the water
Is there any geographical evidence to support the argument? Give details (data, facts, evidence). Less than 10% of reef area showing live coral compared with 50% in 1970.
What do you know about the geographical processes that support this argument? The amount of carbon dioxide in the atmosphere is increasing and this leads to an increase in sea temperature and higher levels of acidity.
Are there any counter-arguments (rebuttals)? What are they and who is making them? The decline is not uniform. In some areas, e.g. the Cayman Islands, 30% of reefs show live coral. Coral reefs are resilient and do recover from pressures.
In view of the reasons and the evidence does the claim need to be qualified? Yes. The article refers only to the Caribbean and not all areas are affected and some coral reefs recover. It could be qualified with statements such as: 'Evidence from the Caribbean suggests that … '; 'In most parts of the Caribbean … '; 'From the evidence it seems likely that … '; 'But there is evidence that … '
In view of the reasons, evidence and counter-arguments, what is your conclusion? Evidence from the Caribbean suggests that coral reefs are in danger, but there are some areas where coral reefs are not in decline and coral reefs have been known to recover.
What further things do you need to investigate or try to find out? ▲ Are coral reefs are in danger in other parts of the world? ▲ How much have sea temperatures and levels of acidity risen? ▲ What does overfishing mean in the Caribbean? ▲ How is the Caribbean (and/or other areas of coral reefs) being polluted?

What is structured academic controversy?

One way of encouraging students to engage in reasoned argument is through the use of structured academic controversy (SAC), a classroom strategy developed in the United States by Johnson *et al.* (1996) to help students discuss issues. The strategy can be used for issues where two opposing viewpoints can be identified (e.g. for or against onshore wind farms; GM crops; expansion of Heathrow Airport) and for which there are suitable resources. Students work initially in pairs, then in fours and then discuss the issue as a whole class. The purpose of the strategy is to increase students' knowledge and understanding of an issue and to help them examine arguments; the focus is on understanding the issue rather than on winning an argument.

The six stages of SAC

Students need access to sources of information (online or on resource sheets) on each of two viewpoints (viewpoint 1 and viewpoint 2) on an issue. SAC is implemented in six stages.

1. Students are introduced to the issue, expressed as a question or statement. The teacher explains the purpose of the activity, creates an interest in it and, if necessary, provides some initial background information. If the students are not familiar with the strategy, the teacher gives information about the stages, the time allowed for each stage and the ground rules (see below). The teacher provides the students with information to support their viewpoint or with guidance on where to obtain it. The students are allocated to groups of four, divided into two pairs. In each group of four one pair will focus on viewpoint 1 and the other pair on viewpoint 2.

2. Students prepare their presentations. Working in pairs initially, students study information that provides evidence for their viewpoint. They identify the key arguments and supporting evidence.

3. Students make their presentations. The groups of four get together. Each pair, in turn, advocates their viewpoint. The other pair listens carefully, probing what is said, asking questions to make sure they understand. They take notes.

4. Students switch groups and viewpoints and make presentations. The groups are reformed so that the new groups are made up of one pair that advocated viewpoint 1 and one pair that advocated viewpoint 2. Each pair now presents the opposite viewpoint from the one they presented, based on what they can remember and on their notes.

5. Students discuss all the arguments and evidence. Students work in groups of four, either in their new or their original groups. The group discusses the strength of the arguments for viewpoints 1 and 2. They try to form their own opinion and reach consensus supported by evidence.

6. The teacher debriefs the discussion by eliciting feedback on:

▲ The best arguments and evidence for viewpoint 1.

▲ The best arguments and evidence for viewpoint 2.

▲ What conclusions the groups reached and why.

▲ Whether anything was not clear or well understood.

▲ Whether they want to ask any questions about the issue.

Debriefing can be achieved through asking one group to feedback on one of these points and then to see if any other group has anything to add. Then a different group could be asked for feedback on another point, etc.

Suggested ground rules of structured controversial debate:

▲ Listen to everyone's presentations respectfully.

▲ You can probe arguments and ask questions of the other pair.

▲ Try to understand both sides of the issue.

▲ Use evidence to support what you say.

▲ Try to reach agreement within your group about what you think about the issue and why.

▲ Focus on understanding as much as you can, not on winning the argument.

During SAC students engage in all aspects of geographical enquiry: they investigate an issue, ask questions, use data to find evidence, make sense of an issue through discussion and reach conclusions based on evidence. Debriefing can help them reflect on what they have learnt. The six stages of the strategy are shown in Figure 8.7.

What kinds of reasoning are required by the various command words used in examinations?

Students need to be able to reason well in order to answer many of the questions in geography public examinations. Figure 8.8 provides a list of some of the command words that require ability to reason.

Summary

Making sense and exercising reasoning is at the heart of learning geography through enquiry. In order to make sense of geography and to develop understanding, students need to be able to think geographically. Students need to learn how to reason and how to argue; they need to understand how geographical knowledge claims are related to explanation and evidence.

Command words	Reasoning required
Account for	Give reasons for
Analyse	Break down into component parts
Assess	Decide on the significance of something Discuss advantages and disadvantages
Classify	Divide into categories
Compare	Identify similarities and differences using comparative adjectives (not two separate accounts)
Contrast	Identify difference using comparative adjectives (not two separate accounts)
Define	Explain the meaning of a word or term
Discuss	Identify different viewpoints and assess their arguments
Distinguish	Identify the differences between two or more set of information or concepts
Evaluate	Make a judgement based on the strengths and weaknesses of a case or argument
Examine	Consider a case study or an argument to reveal its complexity and underlying assumptions
Explain	Give an account of why or how something happens
Justify	Give reasons to support a conclusion, a decision or a point of view
Predict	Use evidence to suggest what might happen
To what extent	Consider strengths and weaknesses of an argument
Why	Provide reasons for or causes of

Figure 8.8: Command words demanding reasoning used in geography examinations.

Suggestions for research

1. Follow up the research carried out in science education into the use of Toulmin's argumentation pattern (TAP). Investigate how it might be used in geography and the extent to which it can enable students to improve the quality of their arguments.

2. Investigate the use of the structured academic controversy (SAC) strategy in geography through recording group work discussions, through questionnaires and through interviews.

3. Use Bonnett's categories to analyse the types of reasoning students are expected to use in a geography course (from schemes of work and lesson plans or in examination specifications).

References

BBC (1972) *Monty Python's Flying Circus:* Episode 29. Transcript available online at *www.ibras.dk/montypython/ episode29.htm#11* (last accessed 16 January 2013).

Bonnett, A. (2008) *How to Argue* (2nd edition). Harlow: Pearson Education Limited.

Driver, R., Newton, P. and Osborne, J. (2000) 'Establishing the norms of scientific argumentation in classrooms', *Science Education,* 84, 3, pp. 287–312.

Erduran, S., Simon, S. and Osborne, J. (2004) 'TAPping into argumentation: developments in the application of Toulmin's argument pattern for studying science discourse', *Science Education,* 88, 6, pp. 915–33.

Gough, S. and Scott, W. (2003) *Sustainable Development and Learning: Framing the issues.* London: RoutledgeFalmer.

Johnson, D., Johnson, R. and Smith, K. (1996) 'Academic controversy: enriching college instruction through intellectual conflict', *SHE-ERIC Higher Education Reports,* 25, 3, pp. 1–157. Available online at *http://eric.ed.gov/ PDFS/ED409829.pdf* (last accessed 16 January 2013).

Morgan, A. (2006) 'Argumentation, geography education and ICT', *Geography,* 91, 2, pp. 126–40.

Morgan, A. (2008) 'GTIP Think Piece: Global Warming'. Available online at *www.geography.org.uk/gtip/thinkpieces/ globalwarming* (last accessed 16 January 2013).

Morgan, A. (2010) 'Education for sustainable development and geography education' in Brooks, C. (ed) *Studying PGCE Geography at M level.* London: Routledge.

Osborne, J.F., Erduran, S. and Simon, S. (2004) 'Enhancing the quality of argument in school science', *Journal of Research in Science Teaching,* 41, 10, pp. 994–1020.

Osborne, J. (2010) 'Arguing to learn in science: the role of collaborative, critical discourse', *Science,* 328, pp. 463–7.

Rogerson, P. (2001) *Statistical Methods for Geography.* London: Sage.

Simon, S. (2008) 'Using Toulmin's argument pattern in the evaluation of argumentation in school science', *International Journal of Research & Method in Education,* 31, 3, pp. 277–89.

Toulmin, S. (1958) *The Uses of Argument.* Cambridge: Cambridge University Press.

09 Developing conceptual understanding through geographical enquiry

'Practical experience shows that direct teaching of concepts is impossible and fruitless. A teacher who tries to do this usually accomplishes nothing but empty verbalism, a parrot-like repetition of words by the child, simulating a knowledge of the corresponding concept but actually covering up a vacuum' (Vygotsky, 1962, p. 83).

Introduction

Unless care is taken at the planning stage, one of the casualties of adopting an enquiry approach to geography could be the development of conceptual understanding. In order to understand geography, rather than simply accumulate factual knowledge, students need to acquire a wide range of concepts which geographers use to help them think about the world and communicate their ideas. They need to realise that geography is not a fact-based subject but a conceptual discipline which has developed, through its key concepts, 'a powerful way of seeing the world' (Jackson, 2006, p. 203). This chapter is about addressing that challenge and considers the following questions:

▲ What is a concept?

▲ Why is it important to develop conceptual understanding?

▲ Why is developing geographical conceptual understanding difficult?

▲ Are threshold concepts and associated ideas useful for school geography?

▲ What can be done within an enquiry approach to support conceptual development?

▲ What activities can promote conceptual understanding?

What is a concept?

Facts and concepts

Geographical facts are specific; they are about particular places, features, statistics and patterns: e.g. 'Paris is the capital of France'; 'a tsunami devastated parts of Japan in 2011'. To make sense

of facts we need to relate them to one another, to explain and interpret them. As soon as we go beyond specific facts and start to generalise we need to use concepts. As Naish (1982) wrote:

'Humans have the capacity to organise their experiences by categorising them so that a whole fund of varied experience can be subsumed under one concept that is named. In this way we can make sense of our bewildering and multifarious environment, classifying our experiences and slotting them into our growing conceptual filing system' (p. 35).

Concepts are labels we give to categories of things, situations and ideas. They are the way we represent the world to ourselves in language. But concepts are not simply words. Implicit in the word used to represent a concept is an array of background knowledge and ideas. Concepts are related to their attributes, to the contexts in which they are applicable, contexts in which they are not applicable, to the ways in which this concept developed and is used and they way they are associated with other concepts. Implicit in every concept is a complex cluster of knowledge and understanding. Even apparently simple concrete concepts such as 'street' are related to an array of ideas. What are the characteristics of a street? What does it include? Is it the same as a road? What kinds of roads are not streets? What wider uses of the word 'street' are there and what connotations does it have? Is the word 'street' used in the same way in different parts of the world?

Concepts have been classified in various ways: spontaneous and scientific; concrete and abstract; substantive and organising; and as nested hierarchies.

Spontaneous and scientific concepts

Vygotsky (1962) distinguished between 'spontaneous' concepts, and 'scientific' concepts. Spontaneous concepts, sometimes referred to as everyday concepts, are derived from people's direct experience of the world through their everyday lives. They are not taught explicitly but are acquired through recognising patterns and through reasoning.

Children show from an early age that they have the capacity to categorise their experiences and begin to understand concepts such as hill, road, shop and park, although not all hills, roads, shops and parks are the same. Young children often show by the way they misuse words that they do not at first understand the concept in the same way as adults do; developing conceptual understanding takes time. We continue to acquire spontaneous concepts throughout our life. Many of these spontaneous concepts are relevant to geography because we experience our personal geographies in our everyday lives. Marsden (1995) refers to spontaneous concepts as 'vernacular' concepts.

Vygotsky used the term 'scientific' concepts to refer to the range of concepts developed by subject disciplines through education. Scientific concepts have also been referred to as 'technical' and 'theoretical' concepts.

In this chapter I will use the terms 'everyday' and 'theoretical' to refer to spontaneous and scientific concepts.

Concrete and abstract concepts

A distinction can also be made between concrete and abstract concepts. Concrete concepts relate to things/events/phenomena etc. that we can experience through our senses; we can see, hear or feel them, e.g. street, wind, etc. Some concrete concepts are easier to perceive through our senses than others, e.g. street is easier to visualise than conurbation.

Abstract concepts are related to things we cannot experience through our senses; they are represented in our minds as words related to ideas. Some concepts are more abstract than others: 'interdependence' is more abstract than 'trade' and 'social justice' is more abstract than 'inequality'. Although it is possible to categorise concepts as concrete or abstract, it might be more helpful to think of a range of concepts along a continuum of increasing generalisation, ranging from simple concrete to extremely abstract.

Both concrete and abstract concepts can be defined by their attributes, but not all definitions are clear cut. What a concept includes and excludes can be a matter of debate. For example, what exactly are the distinctions between village, town and city? Whereas some abstract concepts have accepted definitions within an area of study, e.g. 'energy' in science, other abstract concepts do not have tight definitions but have definitions and meanings which are contested, e.g. nature (Castree, 2005).

Substantive and organising (or second order) concepts

Taylor (2008; 2009) distinguishes between 'substantive' concepts, related to the substance or content of geography, e.g. lake, climate, and 'organising concepts' which shape the discipline, e.g. place, space, scale. Curriculum development in school history has been influenced for many years by the identification of organising concepts which it refers to as 'second order concepts'. History's second order concepts, e.g. change and continuity; chronology; cause and consequence, are its big ideas, intellectual categories used to shape the questions that historians ask and to structure their thinking (Counsell, 2011). In history one or more of its organising concepts are often used in medium-term planning, influencing both the key question framing a unit of work and the outcome activity. Taylor (2008) has adapted this approach to geography (Figure 9.1) showing how the use of different organising concepts could influence a unit of work on the Amazon rainforest.

There have been various attempts to identify geography's key concepts (Figure 9.2). What is included in any list will always be open to debate. Some people have included concepts which are important to geography but are shared with other disciplines, e.g. pattern, interdependence, while others have attempted to identify geography's defining concepts. A Geographical Association paper, 'Thinking Geographically' (GA, 2012), reduced the list to three main 'organising' concepts: place, space and environment, recognising that each of these encompasses other concepts such as scale and location.

Perhaps it is because I am not a historian that history's organising concepts, e.g. chronology, change and continuity, seem simpler to define and more useful for medium-term planning than those identified for geography. Students in history can develop a consistent understanding of, for example, chronology, and apply it to all their work. Concepts such place, space and environment are difficult to use as organising concepts because of their complex and multiple meanings.

'Place is among the most complex of geographical ideas' (Clifford et al., 2009, p. 153)

'As a concept, "place" is both simple and complicated' (Lambert and Morgan, 2010, p. 83)

'Space has been written about in lots of ways' (Clifford et al., 2009, p. 86)

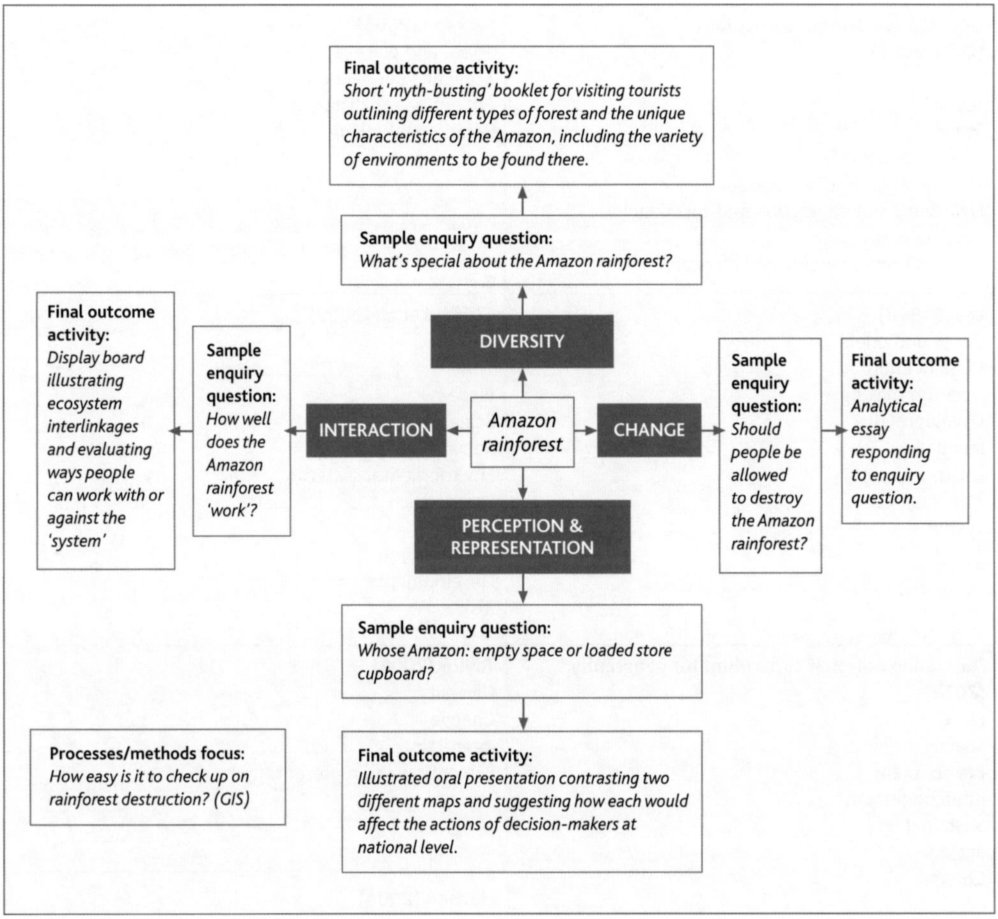

Figure 9.1: How different organising concepts could influence the key enquiry question and outcome activity. Source: Taylor, 2009.

'Sorting out what we mean by space is no easy task' (Lambert and Morgan, 2010, p. 82)

'Yesterday's "truths" about nature often seem absurd to us in the here and now. Nature continues to be understood in a multitude of ways many of them incompatible' (Castree, 2005, p. xvii)

So rather than thinking of 'place', 'space' and 'environment' as 'organising' concepts for which students could develop consistent understandings, I think it is preferable to consider them as permeating key concepts which can vary in meaning (Figure 9.3). Each way of thinking about the concept would lead to different ways of investigating a theme or issue. Each way could help students develop new ways of seeing and understanding the world.

Rawling (2008) outlines the kinds of interest academic geographers have in the concepts identified in the 2007 geography national curriculum (including place, space and environmental interaction) and suggests a range of experiences that would help to deepen students' understanding of them.

Nested concepts

A nested hierarchy of concepts is one in which sets of concepts are contained one within another, in a similar way to a set of Russian dolls. An address is an example of a nested hierarchy: house number; street; town; county; country; continent; world; universe.

Why is it important to develop conceptual understanding?

The most important reason why we need to acquire concepts is that we cannot think or communicate with each other without them. We need concepts to:

▲ generalise

▲ relate facts and ideas to each other

▲ develop explanations

▲ think abstractly.

Developing conceptual understanding in geography enables students to go beyond their own personal

Figure 9.2: Different views on geography's big concepts, key concepts or organising concepts. Sources: ACARA, 2012; Clifford et al., 2009; Hanson, 2004; Jackson, 2006; Leat, 1998; QCA, 2007; Taylor, 2008.

Geography national curriculum (QCA, 2007) Place Space Scale Interdependence Physical and human processes Environmental interaction and sustainable development Cultural understanding and diversity	**Jackson (2006)** Space and place Scale and connection Proximity and distance Relational thinking
Leat (1998) Cause and effect Classification Decision making Development Inequality Location Planning Systems	**Clifford et al. (2009)** Space Time Place Scale Social systems Environmental systems Landscape Nature Globalisation Development Risk
Australian national curriculum for geography (2012) Place Space Environment Interconnection Sustainability Scale Change	**Taylor (2008)** Diversity Change Interaction Perception and representation
	Hanson (2004) Relationships between people and environment Spatial variability Processes operating at multiple and interlocking scales Integration of spatial and temporal analysis

geographies by giving them access to different ways of seeing and interpreting the world. It can enable them to think in more general and abstract ways. The development of geographical concepts is a two-way process in which everyday and theoretical concepts constantly influence each other. Students can make sense of theoretical concepts by connecting them with their everyday concepts. In their advice to geography undergraduates, Cloke et al. (2005) emphasise the importance of making this connection:

'Start with your own experiences and then work outwards from that. Be aware of the human geographies wrapped up in and represented by the food you eat, the news you read, the films you watch, the music you listen to, the television you gaze at. Be aware of the places you live in or travel to or see images of. Be aware of the person you are, the company you keep, the society you live in, the nature of your and others' living, working and play spaces. And in your being aware, take note of what or who is being omitted, marginalised or othered ... Think about how what you read in books and articles

Place, space and environment

The concepts of place, space and environment could be developed in different ways in different units of work.

Place

Places as distinct but unbounded territories
Characteristics of place; how multiple connections of places with other places (economic, social, political) influence them and make them unique and distinct (linked to concepts of interdependence, globalisation, space).

People's attachment to place
Personal geographies of place and affective geographies of place (differentiated by gender, age, ethnicity, disability) (linked to concepts of diversity, identity); the meanings we give to place.

Changing places
Development of places; issues related to change; future of places (linked to concepts of development, sustainability, continuity, change).

Space

Spatial distributions
Patterns of production and consumption, commodity chains, GIS (linked to concepts of trade, uneven development and inequality, production, consumption, sustainability).

Flow space
Movement across space; transport and communication systems; policies related to flows of capital, goods, people and information (linked to concepts of trade, free trade, trading groups, migration, diasporas, tourism).

Spatial inequalities
Uneven distribution of population, resources, wealth, power, etc. (linked to concepts of inequality, social justice, othering); spaces of inclusion and exclusion.

Spatial representations
Maps as selective representations; visual representations; photographs, films, paintings; media representations of space.

Digital space
Interconnections through the internet, social networking, satellites, mobile technologies.

Environment (living and non-living surroundings): physical, natural, built, social

Environmental systems
The physical and biological systems in which we live: ecosystems; ocean currents; atmospheric systems; the water-cycle.

People–environment relationships
Influence of environment on people; influence of people on environment; managing the environment, issues related to change.

Environmental quality
Sustaining the environment: conservation, biodiversity, environmental policy.

Environmental hazards
Floods, droughts, hurricanes, earthquakes, volcanoes, hostile environments (linked with concepts of risk).

---

connects, or doesn't, to your everyday life and if so, why?' (p. 602)

The theoretical concepts acquired through learning geography can transform students' everyday concepts by enlarging their understanding of them and enhancing the way they make sense of the world in their everyday lives. Bennetts (2005) represented this two-way process in a diagram (Figure 9.4) which showed how experience and geographical ideas need to be worked on by various mental processes in order for understanding to develop.

Why is developing geographical conceptual understanding difficult?

Acquiring or developing understanding of a concept is much more difficult than learning a fact. A fact can be memorised; students can demonstrate that they know the fact by recalling it. In contrast, a student might learn and repeat a definition of a concept, or pick it out from a multiple choice list, without necessarily having any understanding of it. They might learn that a symbol on a map represents a canal or a parish boundary without having any understanding of the concept of canal or parish boundary. Knowing a word or remembering a definition is not the same as understanding a concept.

To understand a concept students needs to be able to relate the word to what it represents in the real world, to know what is included within the concept and what is not included, to be able to relate it and apply it to different examples or case studies. Students need to get the word representing the concept into their minds so that they can use it and think with it. Understanding of a concept, particularly geography's key concepts, can continue to deepen as students extend the cluster of background knowledge and ideas that support

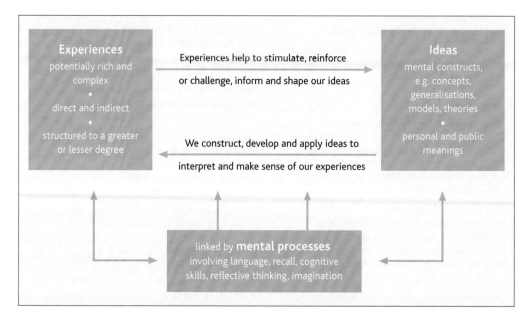

it and as they become more aware of its nuanced uses. This makes it difficult to assess conceptual understanding in simple ways.

Some geographical concepts are more difficult than others. Concrete geographical concepts tend to be easier to grasp than abstract concepts, but they vary in difficulty, tending to be more difficult if:

▲ the concept relates to something beyond the experience of students, e.g. for most UK students 'glacier' would be more difficult than 'beach'

▲ the concept relates to something that is very large, e.g. 'conurbation' is more difficult than 'town'

▲ students hear the word only in the geography classroom, e.g. precipitation

▲ the word used for a geographical concept has different meanings in other subjects and/or everyday life, e.g. energy.

Abstract concepts also vary in difficulty. They tend to be easier to understand if the concept can be clearly defined, e.g. 'honeypot', or if they can be related to students' everyday experiences, e.g. life expectancy. Abstract concepts tend to be more difficult if:

▲ the concept requires understanding of other concepts, e.g. biome.

▲ the concept has multiple contested meanings and is used differently in different contexts, e.g. sustainable development, globalisation.

▲ the concept is very abstract, e.g. social justice.

▲ the word for the concept is used in different ways at different levels of thinking, e.g. place, space, scale.

Are threshold concepts and associated ideas useful for school geography?

Threshold concepts

The idea of threshold concepts emerged during research into the quality of undergraduate courses and has been applied to a wide range of disciplines in higher education (Cousin, 2006). Meyer and Land (2003) argued that certain 'threshold' concepts were central to the mastery of a subject:

'A threshold concept can be considered as akin to a portal, opening up a new and previously inaccessible way of thinking about something. It represents a transformed way of understanding, or interpreting, or viewing something without which the learner cannot progress. As a consequence of comprehending a threshold concept there may thus be a transformed internal view of subject matter, subject landscape, or even worldview' (p. 412).

All learning of new concepts transforms existing ideas to some extent, but threshold concepts are big concepts which, because of the way they link with other concepts, can enable students to integrate their thinking across a subject area in a powerful way; they enable them to see the bigger picture.

Cousin, from her research (2010), quotes one student as saying 'There are some things you learn, you suddenly think, wow, suddenly everything seems different … you now see the world quite differently'.

Threshold concepts are not like building blocks which add to other concepts; instead they lead to a change in conceptual understanding. Before students understand threshold concepts, they tend to understand a subject in more fragmented ways which can create a barrier to their progress.

Evidence from a small-scale geography curriculum development project, carried out by Renshaw and Wood (2011), suggests that the idea of threshold concepts could be valuable for school geography (Figure 9.5).

Liminal spaces

Threshold concepts are difficult to grasp and the process of understanding them takes time. Crossing the threshold to understanding, therefore, is not like crossing a line, but more like entering a space

---

Threshold concepts in geography

The project

Renshaw and Wood (2011) carried out an exploratory small-scale curriculum development project focusing on two of the key concepts listed in the geography national curriculum: interdependence and physical processes (QCA, 2007). They provided the conceptual framework for a unit of work for 13–14 year olds investigating atmosphere, oceans, volcanoes and glaciers. Identifying 'interdependence' as a threshold concept, they speculated that 'if students are able to understand interdependence, seeing geography as an interconnected whole, their view of the subject may well be transformed' (p. 367).

Underpinning ideas

The project was underpinned by the view that 'knowledge is more deeply understood if seen as holistic and interdependent'. Renshaw and Wood wanted students to understand:

- ▲ how the elements of what they were studying were related to each other

- ▲ the relational nature of the concepts of interdependence and physical processes, i.e. how they were part of a web linking them with each other and other concepts.

Another important idea was that the understanding of difficult conceptual knowledge needed an extended period of exposure to the concepts, during which students are in transition between not understanding and understanding a concept. Such transitional spaces have been referred to as 'liminal spaces'. So it was important that students had time and space to grapple with both the content and the key concepts.

Curriculum content and approach

The content areas of the units of work (volcanoes, atmosphere, ice and oceans) was inspired by the BBC series *Earth: The power of the planet*. Students were provided with key questions to consider within each content area:

- ▲ What physical processes underpin each of these planetary forces?

- ▲ How are each of these processes linked to the global climate?

- ▲ How do these processes shape the planet's landscape?

- ▲ What impact have these forces had on the evolution of life on Earth?

- ▲ What contribution do these forces make to climate change and the future of Earth?

Two pedagogical approaches were used to provide the students with 'liminal spaces' in which they could develop their understanding:

- ▲ An enquiry approach, in which students were encouraged to ask questions at the start of each unit of work and to add to these during the work. Students were expected to revisit their questions and reflect on what they had found out. Within the broad framework of the questions listed above, they had space to think and question for themselves.

- ▲ Concept mapping, in which students identified links between the four planetary forces. At the start of each unit of work students identified links between the four planetary forces. They had opportunities while they were working on the units of work to add new links.

Research findings

The project was carried out with 13 different year 9 mixed ability classes between 2006 and 2009. Interviews were carried out with the class teacher and with two student focus groups for each class. Renshaw and Wood found that:

- ▲ The clear focus on interdependence as a threshold concept while planning and using the units of work contributed to students' growing understanding of the concept.

- ▲ The two pedagogical approaches used were popular with the students.

- ▲ Although it took time for students to develop their questioning skills, questioning helped their thinking and ability to understand 'interdependence'.

- ▲ The use of concept maps gave the students a way of organising ideas and content in a relational pattern so that they could begin to understand knowledge more holistically.

- ▲ The use of concept maps was thought to be particularly significant. The teacher thought they contributed to a 'fundamental change in how they're seeing the world'.

- ▲ There was some evidence that understanding a threshold concept such as interdependence could transform students' understanding of the subject.

Figure 9.5: An example of research into threshold concepts in geography.

in which the learner must struggle to understand. This space has been referred to as 'liminal space' (Meyer and Land, 2005). If learners are to grasp the meaning of the threshold concept then they need to be motivated to struggle with the meaning, to think their way through their misunderstandings and confusions and be prepared to think in more integrative ways. The aim is for students to develop a deep understanding of the concept and be able to apply it across a subject, rather than a surface understanding enabling them only to reproduce a definition and apply the concept in limited cases. Although the term 'liminal spaces' has been developed in relation to threshold concepts, it seems a useful idea to apply to all difficult abstract concepts in geography. If students are to develop deep understanding, then they need time and space to ask questions, discuss their ideas and to admit if they are confused.

It is worth considering which if any of geography's big ideas, listed in Figure 9.2, could be considered threshold concepts at school level. Do any of these concepts, when well understood, have the power to transform the way secondary school students think about the subject? Is it feasible for such transformation to take place within a unit of work? Perhaps, for some key concepts such as place and space, rather than expecting an 'aha' moment, it is better to think of students deepening their understanding throughout their geographical education.

What can be done within an enquiry approach to support conceptual development?

I would suggest the following 10 points when planning and using a unit of work.

1. Consider which, if any, of geography's key concepts should underpin the unit of work (and influence the key enquiry questions, sources used and activities).

2. Identify the new concepts that need to be developed to investigate the key question framing the unit and list them in plans for units of work and for individual lessons.

3. Consider which related everyday concepts students are likely to have. How can they be used to provide a link with new geographical concepts? How can any existing understanding and/or misconceptions be elicited and discussed?

4. Decide which concepts students are likely to find particularly difficult. Could students be helped to understand by connecting with their everyday lives or through the use of photographs, film, diagrams, maps, graphs, objects or anecdotes? It might be best to introduce difficult concepts through whole-class activity and discussion.

5. Ensure that there are opportunities for students to hear, say, read and write the words representing the concept. Learning geography, with its large conceptual vocabulary, resembles learning a foreign language. Students are more likely to develop an understanding of new concepts if they hear the words representing the concept and are encouraged to use this new geographical vocabulary themselves when contributing to whole-class and small-group discussion. Teachers can become more aware of the extent to which students understand a concept by listening carefully to how they use its vocabulary.

6. Learning new geographical concepts, like learning vocabulary in a foreign language, benefits from frequent reinforcement through reading, writing and through being used in subsequent lessons.

7. Consider how the choice of geographical examples used in an investigation can contribute to a deeper understanding of the concepts.

8. Consider including activities within the unit of work that promote the understanding of concepts (Figure 9.6).

9. Recognise the role of the teacher in supporting the acquisition of new concepts. If students are investigating questions relatively independently, provide the scaffolding through discussion with groups and individuals, probing their understanding, challenging their reasons and exploring students' understanding of the meaning of the concept. Make it acceptable for them to be hesitant, to be confused, to voice their confusions and try to identify their trouble spots.

10. Recognise that it is difficult to assess the extent to which a student has understood a concept. Can students explain it in their own words? Can they apply it to a new context? Questions such as these cannot be addressed by giving correct answers to simple questions or by indicating understanding by showing 'traffic lights'. Activities which are likely to be more revealing of the extent of a student's understanding are outlined in Figure 9.6.

Activities to support the development of conceptual understanding

Taboo

Taboo is a guessing game in which players take turns to describe the top word on a card without using any of the additional five words below. The other players have to listen and guess the word.

Rationale: to encourage students to think carefully about the meaning of a geographical concept and to explain it to others so that they can identify it from the description. The activity requires a good understanding of the concept so that the person describing it can do so without using the obvious words listed.

Procedure (small group or whole class activity): One person in the group or class is given a Taboo card and has to describe the concept listed at the top of the card without using any of the other words listed. The person who guesses the word correctly has the next turn.

Sources of suggestions for cards

Nichols, A. and Kinninmart, D. (eds) (2000) *More Thinking Through Geography.* Cambridge: Chris Kington Publishing, page 76. Set of 11 cards on the water cycle.

Staffordshire Learning Network website: *www.sln.org.uk/geography/georevision.htm*
Sets of cards on weather and climate (9 cards), coasts (18 cards), settlement (9 cards).

Thinking Through Geography website: *www.geoworld.co.uk/tabpupil.htm*
Set of 48 cards on tectonic processes.

Pictionary

Pictionary is a guessing game in which players have to guess a specific word from another player's drawing.

Rationale: to encourage students to think of the meaning of a concept and how it could be represented. It is challenging both to the person drawing and to the people guessing. Students' drawings can reveal both their understanding and their misunderstandings.

Procedure (small group or whole class activity): One person in the group is given a word representing a concept and has to represent the concept in a picture, using no words, on paper or on a whiteboard. The person who guesses the word correctly has the next turn.

The words chosen can be the concepts related to a unit of work or, for revision purposes, to concepts developed during a whole year.

Spider diagrams and mind maps

See Chapter 15.

Concept maps

See Chapter 16.

Representing a concept graphically

Students represent a concept graphically at the start of a unit of work to reveal prior knowledge and understanding of a concept. For example, students could be asked to represent the greenhouse effect in a picture or diagram and to label as much as they can. They could then annotate their sketch, labelling aspects of it they are unsure of and adding questions about things they still want to know.

Students represent a concept pictorially after studying geographical source material, e.g. a film, or a text. Chapter 19 provides an example of a DART activity in which a piece of text on the concept of eutrophication is reconstructed as a picture.

Producing a booklet or programme for younger children

Rationale: to clarify thinking about a concept and encourage students to explain a set of concepts clearly in their own words, possibly with illustrations.

Applying a framework of criteria to a particular case study

Digby (2007) used a framework of criteria, based on 'green rules' produced by Greenpeace, in a four lesson investigation of urban sustainability. His year 12 students used the criteria to investigate the extent to which the Sydney Olympic Games were 'green'.

Many examples of criteria to assess sustainable development can be found on the internet. Two examples in Figures 9.7 and 9.8 could be applied to rural and urban areas respectively.

Criteria frameworks could be used in various ways to increase students' understanding of the complexity of, and some possible contradictions in, sustainable development policies:

▲ Students apply the criteria to particular case studies, as in Digby's example, allocating scores to each criterion, to determine whether a project or development satisfied the criteria.

▲ Students categorise the criteria: economic, social, environmental and other. The meaning of each of the criteria could be probed and illustrated with examples and any conflicts discussed.

▲ Students examine the framework critically. They decide whether they agree with all of the criteria, whether there are any they would exclude and whether there are any they would add. To which criteria would they give priority? Are the criteria biased towards economic, social or environmental aims?

Using definitions

▲ Select different definitions of a complex concept, e.g. globalisation (Figure 9.9). Students map out different aspects of the concepts on a spider diagram. Discuss emphases and meanings.

▲ Use a few definitions of a concept. Students underline key words and annotate the definition with queries and with examples from prior knowledge and experience.

▲ Use one or two definitions of a concept and apply to a particular case study.

Figure 9.6: Activities which support the development of conceptual understanding.

The Peak District Sustainable Development Fund

'The Peak District Sustainable Development Fund supports projects that bring environmental, social, economic and cultural benefits to the National Park. We are particularly interested in projects that help to reduce the impact of climate change and its effects on the Peak District. All projects must involve some form of sustainable development and should demonstrate clear links with the Peak District National Park.'

Projects are assessed against the selection criteria below.

1. Meeting sustainable development objectives

▲ Does the project deliver long-term benefit for future generations?

▲ Is the project a model for sustainable living?

▲ Does the project increase awareness of sustainable development in the local and/or wider community?

2. Meeting social objectives

▲ Does the project impact upon and meet the social needs of members of the community?

▲ Does the project directly involve community groups?

▲ Does the project create new partnerships or networking structures?

▲ Does the project specifically involve young and/or older people?

▲ Does the project tackle social exclusion?

3. Meeting National Park and environmental objectives

▲ Does the project conserve and enhance the special qualities of the Park?

▲ Does the project promote opportunity for understanding and enjoyment of the Park?

▲ Does the project provide a model for countryside management?

▲ Does the project have an environmental impact upon the Park, its individuals or communities?

▲ Does the project encourage careful use of natural resources and/or use of renewable energy?

4. Meeting economic objectives

▲ Does the project have an economic impact upon individuals, groups or businesses in finding new ways to generate wealth?

▲ Does the project fully explore opportunities for leverage of funds in cash or in kind?

▲ Does the project demonstrate new urban and/or rural links?

5. Other scheme objectives

▲ Does the project have an innovative, imaginative approach to a problem?

▲ Will the project go ahead regardless of SDF funding?

▲ Will the project continue in some form after SDF funding ceases?

▲ Does the project have potential for replication inside or outside the Park?

The Greater London Plan

Objectives:

1: meet the challenge of growth
2: support a competitive economy
3: support the neighbourhoods
4: delight the senses
5: improve the environment
6: improve access/transport

No	Performance indicators
1	Maximise the proportion of development taking place on previously developed land
2	Optimise the density of residential development
3	Minimise the loss of open space
4	Increase the supply of new homes
5	Increase supply of affordable homes
6	Reduce health inequalities
7	Sustain economic activity
8	Ensure that there is sufficient development capacity in the office market
9	Ensure that there is sufficient employment land available
10	Increase employment in outer London
11	Increase employment opportunities for those suffering from disadvantage in the employment market
12	Improve the provision of social infrastructure and related services
13–16	Achieve a reduced reliance on the private car and a more sustainable modal split for journeys
17	Increase the number of jobs located in areas with high public transport accessibility level (PTAL) values
18	Protect biodiversity habitat
19	Increase municipal waste recycled or composted and elimination of waste to landfill by 2031
20	Reduce carbon dioxide emissions through new development
21	Increase energy generated from renewable sources
22	Increase urban greening
23	Improve London's Blue Ribbon Network (rivers, canals, docks, reservoirs and lakes)
24	Protect and improve London's heritage and public realm

Figure 9.8: The Greater London Plan: objectives and performance indicators. Source: Greater London Authority, 2011.

What activities can promote conceptual understanding?

The best way of promoting conceptual understanding is by paying particular attention to students' understanding of concepts during what I refer to in Chapter 11 as 'dialogues of learning', i.e. through whole-class discussion, dialogues with individuals and small groups and responses to written work.

Understanding of concepts develops gradually and what students say needs to be probed; they need to be able to apply a concept to a new situation or to their everyday lives.

The activities listed in Figure 9.6 could be incorporated into an enquiry-based unit of work to support conceptual development.

(a) Selected definitions of globalisation from Al-Rodhan (2006)

Source	Definition
David Harvey (1989) *The Condition of Postmodernity.* Oxford: Blackwell.	'the compression of time and space'
Anthony Giddens (1990) *The Consequences of Modernity.* Cambridge: Polity Press, p. 64.	'the intensification of worldwide social relations which link distant localities in such a way that local happenings are shaped by events occurring many miles away and vice versa'
Martin Khor (1995) cited in Jan Aarte Scholte 'The globalization of world politics', in Baylis, J. and Smith, S. (eds) (1999) *The Globalization of World Politics: An Introduction to international relations.* New York, NY: Oxford University Press, p. 15.	'Globalization is what we in the Third World have for several centuries called colonization'
Mark Ritchie (1996) 'Globalization vs. Globalism', *International Forum on Globalization*	'the process of corporations moving their money, factories and products around the planet at ever more rapid rates of speed in search of cheaper labor and raw materials and governments willing to ignore or abandon consumer, labor and environmental protection laws. As an ideology, it is largely unfettered by ethical or moral considerations.'
Thomas Friedman (1999) *The Lexus and the Olive Tree.* New York: Farrar, Straus and Giroux, pp. 7–8.	'the inexorable integration of markets, nation-states and technologies to a degree never witnessed before – in a way that is enabling individuals, corporations and nation-states to reach around the world farther, faster, deeper and cheaper than ever before, and in a way that is also producing a powerful backlash from those brutalized or left behind by this new system … Globalization means the spread of free-market capitalism to virtually every country in the world.'
David Held, Anthony McGrew, David Goldblatt and Jonathan Perraton (1999) *Global Transformations, Politics, Economics and Culture.* Stanford, CA: Stanford University Press, p. 2.	'the widening, deepening and speeding up of worldwide interconnectedness in all aspects of contemporary social life, from the cultural to the criminal, the financial to the spiritual'
Tomas Larsson (2001) *The Race to the Top: The real story of globalization. Washington,* DC: Cato Institute, p. 9.	'the process of world shrinkage, of distances getting shorter, things moving closer. It pertains to the increasing ease with which somebody on one side of the world can interact, to mutual benefit, with somebody on the other side of the world'
George Soros (2002) *George Soros on Globalization.* Cambridge, MA: PublicAffairs, p.13.	'development of global financial markets, growth of transnational corporations and their growing dominance over national economies'
International Monetary Fund (2002) *Globalization: Threat or opportunity?* Available online at *www.imf.org/external/np/exr/ ib/2000/041200to.htm* (last accessed 8 February 2013).	'Economic "globalization" is a historical process, the result of human innovation and technological progress. It refers to the increasing integration of economies around the world, particularly through trade and financial flows. The term sometimes also refers to the movement of people (labor) and knowledge (technology) across international borders. There are also broader cultural, political and environmental dimensions of globalization.'
OECD (2005) *OECD Handbook on Economic Globalisation Indicators.* Paris: OECD, p. 11.	'The term "globalisation" has been widely used to describe the increasing internationalisation of financial markets and of markets for goods and services. Globalisation refers above all to a dynamic and multidimensional process of economic integration whereby national resources become more and more internationally mobile while national economies become increasingly interdependent.'
E Marketing, 21 web resource: *www.manufacturing.net/articles/2010/06/ the-pros-and-cons-of-globalization*	'People around the globe are more connected to each other than ever before. Information and money flow more quickly than ever. Goods and services produced in one part of the world are increasingly available in all parts of the world. International travel is more frequent. International communication is commonplace. This phenomenon has been titled "globalisation".'

(b) Some alternative definitions of globalisation

Adil Najam, David Runnalls and Mark Halle (2007) *Environment and Globalization: five propositions*. Winnipeg: International Institute for Sustainable Development	'The processes that we now think of as globalization were central to the environmental cause well before the term "globalization" came into its current usage. Global environmental concerns were born out of the recognition that ecological processes do not always respect national boundaries and that environmental problems often have impacts beyond borders; sometimes globally. Connected to this was the notion that the ability of humans to act and think at a global scale also brings with it a new dimension of global responsibility not only to planetary resources but also to planetary fairness.'
Doreen Massey (2010) 'Is the world getting smaller or larger?'. Available online at *www.opendemocracy.net/globalization-vision_ reflections/world_small_4354.jsp* (last accessed 8 February 2013).	'It is not true that all places are reachable in the same time-span ("no-time") ... The centralisation of fast travel through hubs has rendered some places in-between all the harder to get at. 'In the thesis of the shrinking world, because "we all" have mobile phones, drink Starbucks coffee, these differences are underplayed. The George W Bush–Tony Blair global project fails to understand (or refuses to respect) the depth of variation (cultural, economic, political) between the multiple stories whose contemporaneous coexistence makes up our spatially differentiated "now". 'If the world seems to be getting smaller perhaps it is in part because we don't look, or listen, or (precisely) take enough time; or because we focus on the world coming to us at the expense of looking outwards. It is impossible to be aware of all those other stories going on "right now", as we struggle on with our lives. But that is not the point. Rather it is a question of the angle of vision, of a stance in relation to the world, an outward-lookingness of the imagination.'
Massey, D. (2006) 'Is the world really shrinking?' First Open University radio lecture, available online at *www.open.edu/openlearn/society/ politics-policy-people/geography/ou-radio-lecture-2006-the-world-really-shrinking* (last accessed 8 February 2013).	'So: the world is indeed more interconnected. We are, indeed, more interdependent, but the variety of this planet and its people has not been eradicated and that is both a source of richness and a challenge (and we should perhaps pay more respect to that). Economically, inequality is increasing.'
Harvey Perkins and David Thorns (2012) *Place, Identity and Everyday Life in a Globalizing World.* Basingstoke: Palgrave Macmillan, p. 25.	'The world is globalizing. People are connecting in an increasing number of ways. The working out of these developments over the past 50 years or so has raised questions about whether we are now living in a new epoch. But despite globalization there are still deep and enduring differences among the Earth's people, and considerable, and in many cases, growing inequalities in access to resources and services across the globe. The impact of change is thus uneven. It is also clear that in the face of globalization the ways everyday life is constituted are still shaped by local experience of place and by where people live locally, regionally and nationally and by the access they have to resources and opportunities in those settings. It is important therefore not to fall into the trap of seeing global change as creating a sense of universal cultural and economic homogeneity.'

Figure 9.9: Some of the many definitions of globalisation: (a) from Al-Rodhan, 2006; (b) alternative definitions.

Summary

If students are to benefit from geographical ways of seeing the world they need to develop understanding of a large range of concepts, both those related to the content of what they are investigating and geography's permeating big concepts. Developing conceptual understanding takes time: when planning enquiry-based work, teachers need to consider how students can relate their everyday concepts to new concepts and what kinds of activities could support conceptual development.

Suggestions for research

1. Explore how students' understanding of one of geography's key concepts is developed through the geography curriculum, analysing the ways in which different meanings are conveyed through the resources presented to students and through activities.

2. Investigate students' understanding of one of geography's big concepts (see Walshe, 2007, and Hopwood, 2007, who investigated students' understandings of sustainability, and Picton, 2010, who investigated students' understandings of globalisation).

References

Al-Rodhan, N. (2006) *Definitions of Globalization: A comprehensive overview and a proposed definition*. Geneva: Geneva Centre for Security Policy. Available online at *www.sustainablehistory.com/articles/definitions-of-globalization.pdf* (last accessed 22 April 2013).

Australian Curriculum, Assessment and Reporting Authority (ACARA) (2012) *Geography Curriculum (Draft)*. Available online at *www.acara.edu.au/verve/_resources/2._Draft–F-12–Australian_Curriculum_-_Geography.pdf* (last accessed 19 August 2013).

Bennetts, T. (2005) 'The links between understanding, progression and assessment in the secondary school curriculum', *Geography*, 90, 2, pp. 152–70.

Castree, N. (2005) *Nature*. London: Routledge.

Clifford, N., Holloway, S., Rice, S. and Valentine, G. (eds) (2009) *Key Concepts in Geography*. London: Sage.

Cloke, P., Crang, P. and Goodwin, M. (2005) *Introducing Human Geographies* (2nd edition). London: Hodder Arnold.

Counsell, C. (2011) 'Disciplinary knowledge for all: the secondary history curriculum and history teachers' achievement', *Curriculum Journal*, 22, 2, pp. 201–25.

Cousin, G. (2006) 'An introduction to threshold concepts', *Planet*, 17, pp. 4–5.

Cousin, G. (2010) 'Neither teacher-centred nor student-centred: threshold concepts and research partnerships', *Journal of Learning Development in Higher Education*, 2, pp. 1–9.

Digby, B. (2007) 'Teaching about the Olympics', *Teaching Geography*, 32, 3, pp. 73–9.

Geographical Association (2012) 'Thinking geographically'. Available online at *www.geography.org.uk/download/GA_GINCConsultation12ThinkingGeographically.pdf* (last accessed 18 January 2013).

Greater London Authority (2011) *The Greater London Plan: Spatial development strategy for Greater London*. London: Greater London Authority. Available online at *www.london.gov.uk/publication/londonplan* (last accessed 18 January 2013).

Hanson, S. (2004) 'Who are "we"? An important question for geography's future', *Annals of the Association of American Geographers*, 94, 4, pp. 715–22.

Hopwood, N. (2007) 'Environmental education: pupils' perspectives on classroom experience', *Environmental Education Research*, 13, 4, pp. 453–65.

Jackson, P. (2006) 'Thinking geographically', *Geography*, 91, 3, pp. 199–204.

Lambert, D. and Morgan, J. (2010) *Teaching Geography 11–18: A conceptual approach*. Maidenhead: Open University Press.

Leat, D. (1998) *Thinking Through Geography*. Cambridge: Chris Kington Publishing.

Marsden, B. (1995) *Geography 11–18: Rekindling good practice*. London: David Fulton.

Meyer, J.H.F. and Land, R. (2003) 'Threshold concepts and troublesome knowledge: linkages to ways of thinking and practising' in Rust, C. (ed) *Improving Student Learning – Ten years on*. Oxford: Oxford Centre for Staff and Learning Development (OCSLD), pp. 412–24.

Meyer, J. and Land, R. (2005) 'Threshold concepts and troublesome knowledge (2): epistemological considerations and a conceptual framework for teaching and learning', *Higher Education*, 49, 3, pp. 373–88.

Naish, M. (1982) 'Mental development and the learning of geography' in Graves, N. (ed) *New UNESCO Source Book for Geography Teaching*. Harlow: Longman.

Nichols, A. and Kinninment, D. (2000) *More Thinking Through Geography*. Cambridge: Chris Kington Publishing.

Peak District National Park Authority website: 'SDF criteria – how we assess applications'. Available online at *www.peakdistrict.gov.uk/living-and-working/your-community/sdf/how-to-apply* (last assessed 14 June 2013).

Picton, O. (2010) 'Shrinking world? Globalisation at key stage 3', *Teaching Geography*, 35, 1, pp. 10–14.

QCA (2007) *Geography: Programme of study for key stage 3 and attainment target*. London: QCA.

Rawling, E. (2008) *Planning your Key Stage 3 Geography Curriculum*. Sheffield: The Geographical Association.

Renshaw, S. and Wood, P. (2011) 'Holistic understanding in geography education (HUGE): an alternative approach to curriculum development and learning at key stage 3', *Curriculum Journal*, 22, 3, pp. 365–79.

Taylor, L. (2008) 'Key concepts and medium term planning', *Teaching Geography*, 31, 2, pp. 50–4.

Taylor, L. (2009) 'Think Piece: Concepts in geography'. Available online at *www.geography.org.uk/gtip/thinkpieces/concepts/#5821* (last accessed 18 January 2013).

Vygotsky, L. (1962) *Thought and Language*. Cambridge, MA: Massachusetts Institute of Technology Press.

Walshe, N. (2007) 'Year 8 students' conceptions of sustainability', *Teaching Geography*, 32, 3, pp. 139–43.

Teachers' talk in the enquiry classroom

'Many teachers do not plan and conduct classroom dialogue in ways that might help students to learn' (Black *et al.*, 2004, p. 11).

Introduction

Alexander (2000), drawing on his comparative research in primary schools in five countries, identified five categories of classroom talk: rote; recitation (question and answer); instruction/exposition; discussion; dialogue (Figure 10.1). He found that the first three categories, in which teacher talk is dominant, were most commonly used. This chapter examines the role of teachers' talk in an enquiry approach to learning geography and addresses the following questions:

▲ Why are talking and listening so important?

▲ How much geography is there in classroom talk?

▲ Is there a place for presentational talk by the teacher in an enquiry approach?

▲ What kind of questioning is typical in most classrooms?

▲ What kinds of questions might contribute to learning geography through enquiry?

▲ How can teachers improve their questioning skills?

Why are talking and listening so important?

I would identify two reasons why the spoken language is so important in learning geography through enquiry. First, it introduces students to the language of geography. Second, talk can be used to work on and develop students' understanding. The first reason underpins this chapter while the second reason underpins Chapter 11.

Geographers have developed particular ways of looking at the world and understanding it. They use geographical vocabulary to name features, processes and concepts. They have developed explanations of why places, patterns and environments are as they are. If geographical education is aimed at enabling students to see the world in a different way, they need to learn the language of geography. Although students encounter it through what they read, the spoken word is more accessible. Modern language teachers emphasise the importance of four processes in learning languages: listening, speaking, reading and writing. I think geography could give similar emphasis to all four processes. Students should get used to hearing how the vocabulary of geography is used and pronounced and how geographical ideas are expressed. They should be encouraged to use the language of geography when they speak in the classroom.

How much geography is there in classroom talk?

As a PGCE tutor and external examiner I have had the privilege of observing hundreds of geography

---

Repertoires of classroom talk

▲ Rote (teacher–class): the drilling of facts. Ideas and routines through constant repetition.

▲ Recitation (teacher–class or teacher–group): the accumulation of knowledge and understanding through questions designed to test or stimulate recall of what has been previously encountered or to cue students to work out the answer from clues provided in the question.

▲ Instruction/exposition (teacher–class, teacher–group or teacher–individual): telling the students what to do and/or imparting information, and/or explaining facts, principles or procedures.

▲ Discussion (teacher–class, teacher–group or student–student): the exchange of ideas with a view to sharing information and solving problems.

▲ Dialogue (teacher–class, teacher–group, teacher–individual or student–student): achieving common understanding through structured, cumulative questioning and discussion which guide and prompt, reduce choices, minimise risk and error and expedite 'handover' of concepts and principles.

Figure 10.1: Repertoires of classroom talk identified by Alexander (2000).

lessons. Since my earliest years of teaching I have been interested in the role of language in geographical education. So, when I observed lessons, I paid attention to what people were saying throughout the lesson, jotting down as much as I could of what was said, both in whole-class dialogues and in dialogues between the teacher and small groups. After the lesson, the student teacher and I studied my notes together, trying to analyse what was going on in the lesson. I found it useful to identify three categories of talk. The following examples are from my lesson observation notes:

▲ Managerial talk (behaviour), e.g. 'If you two carry on talking, I'll split you up'; 'Some of you are working well – I'm really pleased with you'

▲ Managerial talk (activities), e.g. 'You need to go round the spider diagram and write about each point'; 'You have three more minutes to get as much done as possible'

▲ Geographical talk: talking about the subject matter of what was being studied or investigated, e.g. 'We can see from the graphs how the employment structure has changed over time'; 'Do you think what the Yanomami are doing is sustainable?'

There were huge variations in the proportion of talk in each category. Sometimes 'managing behaviour' talk was dominant, sometimes talk to manage activities. In other lessons, but not so frequently, geographical talk was dominant. In some lessons there was astonishingly little geographical talk. This could have been because I was observing beginner teachers and they were concerned about managing behaviour and getting through their lesson plan, but it worried me. It seemed that the teacher was conveying implicitly that the purpose of the lesson was to get through the planned activities rather than to develop an understanding of geography.

It is worth developing an awareness of how much geographical talk there is. I would suggest the following professional development activity.

▲ If possible, record or film the lesson. Alternatively, get a colleague to write down as much as possible of what is said by the teacher.

▲ Use the three categories of talk (behaviour, activity, geography) to analyse the teacher's talk.

▲ Reflect on the extent to which the different categories of talk were necessary or desirable.

▲ What messages about the purposes of the lesson were conveyed by the talk?

▲ What messages about geography were conveyed by what was said by the teacher?

Is there a place for presentational talk by the teacher in an enquiry approach?

By presentational talk, which Alexander refers to as 'instructional/expositional' talk, I mean occasions when teachers talk and students listen. It is through this kind of talk that students hear the language of geography and become familiar with its vocabulary and way of developing arguments. It is through presentational talk that the teacher can show curiosity in the big question of the enquiry, convey an interest in what is being studied and generate enthusiasm among students. Presentational talk by the teacher can be used to:

▲ Give instructions about how to proceed with an enquiry or with an activity.

▲ Give background information about what is to be investigated. For example, in the public meeting role play lessons (Chapter 18) the chair of the meeting, in role, can provide essential contextual information about the issue.

▲ Explain a difficult concept or process. Some ideas and processes are difficult for students to understand simply from studying resources. A teacher presentation provides opportunities for students to ask questions and clarify their understanding before investigating an issue. For example, in an investigation of the impact of the monsoon climate on different parts of the Indian subcontinent, the teacher could explain why there are monsoons, using maps, diagrams and photographs. Students could then study climate graphs of different parts of India to investigate its differential impact.

▲ Share a personal experience or an anecdote. Many geography teachers have travelled widely and have first-hand experiences of themes and places being studied. Some have studied issues in the field at undergraduate or postgraduate level. For example, I have worked with PGCE students who have variously spent time working in Japan, Kenya, Ghana, Peru and Australia; who have studied deforestation in Nepal or glacier retreat in Switzerland; who have experienced earthquakes and seen volcanic eruptions. These experiences, often backed up by photographs, can be used as a resource. A teacher's presentation based on first-hand experience can be much more vivid and detailed than accounts in geography textbooks and often provokes genuine questions. It can help students realise that their own personal experiences of the world can be relevant to what they are learning in the classroom.

▲ Read a piece of text. Before students study a piece of text it is sometimes helpful for the teacher to read it out loud. This enables students to hear the pronunciation of geographical vocabulary and helps them read difficult passages. This is recommended for directed activities related to text (Chapter 19).

▲ Read a text which students study only through listening. Some texts can be presented orally by the teacher for students. This could include: reports; weather forecasts; extracts from fiction and non-fiction; poems; songs. They might be asked simply to listen and remember, to jot down key points, or to translate what they hear into a diagram. Two of David Leat's thinking skills strategies, 'Mind movies' and 'Story telling', require students to listen to teachers reading a passage and are designed to access students' prior knowledge, practise skills of memorising and develop key concepts (Leat, 1998).

Presentational talk by the teacher can be valuable. It is therefore worth considering whether there is a role for presentational talk in a particular unit of work and, if so, incorporating it into curriculum plans.

What kind of questioning is typical in most classrooms?

A lot of importance has been attached to teachers' questions in the classroom. Researchers and INSET providers have investigated:

▲ the types of questions asked

▲ what might constitute good practice in using questions in the classroom

▲ how teachers might develop questioning skills.

Presentational talk typically follows a question and answer routine, which is sometimes referred to as 'recitation' and sometimes as 'IRF' (initiation, response, feedback). The pattern of IRF is as follows:

▲ Initiation: the teacher asks a question.

▲ Response: a student answers the question.

▲ Feedback: the teacher comments on the reply.

IRF is found in different subjects in classrooms all over the world (Alexander, 2000). IRF depends on both teachers and students accepting certain conversational rules or ground rules, which Mercer and Dawes (2008) identified as:

▲ Only a teacher can nominate who should speak.

▲ Only a teacher can ask a question without seeking permission.

- Only a teacher can evaluate a comment made by a participant.

- Students should try to provide answers to teachers' questions which are as relevant and brief as possible.

- Students should not speak freely when a teacher asks a question but raise their hands and wait to be nominated.

Ground rules are not usually made explicit, but are established gradually through practice, e.g. by the teacher asking a particular student, or prefacing the question with 'put your hands up' or by saying 'no calling out'.

IRF is used so widely all over the world that teachers must find it valuable. It can:

- Help classroom management by maintaining students' attention.

- Give students an opportunity to contribute to the lesson.

- Be used to reinforce key facts and information.

- Be used to check on and assess students' knowledge and understanding.

- Be developed into sequences of questions devised to help students understand complex ideas.

- Be developed into genuine discussion.

IRF, however, does have limitations:

- Most questions asked by teachers are closed, low-level questions, which have one correct answer and require recall of information.

- Brief correct responses do not necessarily indicate understanding.

- Student participation is limited; they are not usually expected to provide lengthy answers, voice uncertainties, express their own ideas, ask questions or work on their own understanding of geography.

- There is insufficient time in any one lesson for all students to be involved, unless other strategies are used (see below).

- Feedback from teachers is often brief and evaluative, e.g. 'good'. Such feedback does not help to develop students' understanding.

- Direct questions are not thought to be the best way to get people to talk; IRF is not the best way of initiating classroom discussion.

- There is no evidence that students learn much from IRF, or that it stimulates their thinking.

In spite of these limitations, I have included IRF in this book, partly because it has some value, and partly because it is ingrained in classroom practice, schools often encourage it and it will continue to take place. It is therefore worth considering how to make IRF as effective as possible.

What kinds of questions might contribute to learning geography through enquiry?

Understanding classroom dialogues

Classroom talk is complicated and it is not possible to know or evaluate exactly what is going on by paying attention only to the talk taking place in one particular lesson (Mercer and Littleton, 2007). Teachers and classes build up shared understandings; they know what has been talked about in previous lessons and sometimes what is going to happen in the following lessons. So what is meant by particular questions and what is understood by students might not be evident to an observer. Also, teachers' questions are used for different purposes and the purpose might depend on intonation or when they are saying it rather than the wording. For example, a question at the start of a unit of work might be to elicit prior knowledge whereas the same question at the end of a unit of work might be to check what has been learnt. So great care needs to be taken when interpreting observations or transcripts of classroom dialogues.

Closed and open questions

Most questions asked in the classroom are closed: there is one acceptable answer in the teacher's mind. It is often stated that open questions, in contrast, are those for which there is more than one answer, but this needs probing a bit. Some questions for which there are several answers are not really open in that the teacher has a list of correct answers in mind, e.g. giving names of countries in the EU. Questions starting with why, how, explain etc. can be closed if they demand simple recall of something that has been taught or read. In my opinion, open questions are those in which the purpose is to get inside the students' minds, to find out what and how they are thinking.

Although closed questions are limited, it is not a case of 'closed questions bad, open questions good'; it is possible to justify the use of closed questions. They can be used for a rapid recap and reinforcement of facts and vocabulary introduced in previous lessons or to check a skill in using a resource, e.g. reading a figure from a graph or identifying a symbol on a map. So, in an enquiry approach, it is not a case of avoiding closed questions, but of thinking of when it is appropriate to use them. Open questions invite more varied and usually more extended responses and can enable teachers to get into students' minds, to know how they are thinking. Asking more open questions gives students more chance to explain their ideas, voice their opinions and be more involved.

Lower order and higher order questions

The majority of questions asked in the classroom are lower order questions, demanding little thinking by students; they require simple recall of what has been learned, often in one-word responses which rarely indicate whether students have made sense of what they are learning. Higher order questions demand responses that require students to think and to reason: they reveal what students understand.

Bloom's taxonomy (1956) is widely used to categorise teachers' questions as lower order and higher order questions. The taxonomy had its origin in examiners' meetings in which it was found that there were different understandings of terms and what was assessed. Bloom wanted to produce a standard, precise list of objectives in order to help those dealing with curriculum and assessment in education 'to discuss the problems with greater precision' and reach common understandings (*ibid.*, p. 1). In spite of criticisms of the taxonomy and it being neglected in the UK for decades, it was revived enthusiastically in a modified form through the National Strategy and applied to teachers' questions.

Although people refer to Bloom's taxonomy, many of the versions in use differ from Bloom's original conception. Bloom divided his taxonomy into three domains: the cognitive domain, related to intellectual abilities; the affective domain, related to feelings and values; and the psychomotor domain,

which was never completed, related to ability to manipulate things physically. Most versions used in relation to questions use only the cognitive domain. His taxonomy was a list of educational objectives, a classification of educational goals, together with guidance about how they might be tested. Bloom's taxonomy provided a framework of objectives describing what students should learn to do; it was not designed as a framework for analysing questions.

Bloom divided each of his categories (evaluation, synthesis, analysis, application, comprehension, knowledge) into sub-categories – see Figure 10.2. Frameworks for analysing questions do not usually include sub-categories. His lowest level of cognitive objective, knowledge, was about remembering by recall or recognition. In this category Bloom included: knowledge of specifics (recall of facts, terminology); knowledge of ways and means of dealing with specifics (classifications, criteria, trends and sequences and methodology); and knowledge of universals and abstractions in a field (principles, generalisation and theories). These types of knowledge are more varied and complex than those included in frameworks used to analyse questions.

Two different versions of Bloom's taxonomy tend to be used to categorise classroom questions (Figure 10.2): Bloom's original hierarchy of cognitive objectives and a revised version by Anderson, one of Bloom's students (Anderson and Krathwohl, 2001). In the revised version nouns have been changed into verbs, some terminology has changed (knowledge to remembering; comprehension to understanding; and synthesis to creating), the order of the two highest categories has been reversed and what is included in each category has been changed (Figure 10.3).

Figure 10.2: Framework of levels based on Bloom's taxonomy of cognitive objectives.

Bloom's categories	Bloom's definitions	Bloom's sub-categories	Possible examples of questions related to Bloom's categories
Evaluation	Judgements about the value of materials and methods for given purposes	Internal criteria External criteria	Is the data presented in the survey valid and reliable? Does the report on the earthquake deal with all relevant aspects?
Synthesis	Putting parts together to form a new whole	Production of a unique communication Production of a plan Ability to form hypotheses	What would you include in a 3-minute TV report on a recent volcanic eruption?
Analysis	Breaking down into constituent elements	Of elements Of relationships Of organisational principles	Identify the social, economic and environmental impacts and possible legacy of the 2012 London Olympics and Paralympics.
Application	The use of ideas in particular and concrete situations	(no sub-division)	How has globalisation influenced this town/area? How could this school be made more sustainable?
Comprehension	Ability to grasp meaning of material	Translation Interpretation Extrapolation	What does the graph show? Describe the photograph. Identify the coastal features shown on an Ordnance Survey map.
Knowledge	Recall of specifics and universals Remembering previously learned material	Terminology Specific facts	What is GDP? Which is the largest ocean?
		Trends Classifications Methodologies Evaluative criteria Methods of 'inquiry'	What different types of soils are there? How is precipitation measured?
		Principles and generalisations Theories and structures	What is the theory of plate tectonics?

While it is useful to distinguish between low level questions that demand little of students and higher level ones that demand more thinking, the limitations of Bloom's taxonomy, in any of its versions, for analysing questions should be recognised.

▲ The taxonomy does not include the affective domain so excludes questions that are useful for investigating issues or geography's ethical dimension, including values or for making judgements about evidence.

▲ The distinction between knowledge and the 'higher' intellectual processes is 'unsound' (Pring, 1971). To know something, other than in the most simplistic rote-learning sense, implies some degree of understanding and application

to the real world. There is little educational value in knowing a fact or a definition unless it has meaning, can be related to other information or applied to a situation.

▲ The separation of intellectual processes into a hierarchy is not supported by research. Understanding, analysis and application are related intellectual processes. Pring (1971) describes the distinctions as 'not logically acceptable' and as 'a misrepresentation of what is going on' (p. 91).

▲ Although the taxonomy is represented as a hierarchy there could be different levels of difficulty in each of the categories, meaning that a question categorised as lower level could in

Cognitive Level	Bloom (1956)	Anderson and Krathwohl (2001)
Highest	Evaluation	Creating
	Synthesis	Evaluating
	Analysis	Analysing
	Application	Applying
	Comprehension	Understanding
Lowest	Knowledge	Remembering

Figure 10.3:
Comparison of original and revised versions of Bloom's taxonomy. Sources: Bloom, 1956; Anderson and Krathwohl, 2001; Krathwohl, 2002.

Anderson and Krathwohl (2001) published a revised version of Bloom's taxonomy in which they listed the revised categories and subdivisions as follows:

1.0   Remember: retrieving relevant knowledge from long-term memory
1.1   Recognising
1.2   Recalling

2.0   Understand: determining the meaning of instructional messages, including oral, written and graphic communication
2.1   Interpreting
2.2   Exemplifying
2.3   Classifying
2.4   Summarising
2.5   Inferring
2.6   Comparing
2.7   Explaining

3.0   Apply: carrying out or using a procedure in a given situation
3.1   Executing
3.2   Implementing

4.0   Analyse: breaking material to its constituent parts and detecting how the parts relate to one another and to an overall structure or purpose
4.1   Differentiating
4.2   Organising
4.3   Attributing

5.0   Evaluate: making judgements based on criteria and standards
5.1   Checking
5.2   Critiquing

6.0   Create: putting elements together to form a novel, coherent whole or make an original product
6.1   Generating
6.2   Planning

fact be more demanding than one categorised as higher level. For example, remembering a theory (in the low-level knowledge category) would be demanding unless students just repeated it parrot fashion. Understanding and interpreting a table of complex statistics could be more demanding than applying an idea to the school grounds or analysing factors affecting something.

▲ The taxonomy is a generic one and does not take account of the structure of disciplinary knowledge. It does not specifically encourage questions that probe different aspects of geography.

▲ Although the original taxonomy included procedural knowledge (knowledge of how to do things) this is listed under knowledge, i.e. the ability to recall it, rather than to apply it.

Because of these limitations, it would be better to use professional judgement to distinguish between low level undemanding questions and high level demanding questions and about the level of difficulty involved in answering specific questions. This depends as much on the complexity of the subject matter as on the particular verbs used to introduce a question.

More appropriate for learning geography through enquiry would be a specifically geographical framework which analyses teachers' questions. Figure 10.4 shows the categories of questions used in the development compass rose (Birmingham DEC, 1995) and in the route for enquiry (Rawling, 2008). Using these categories would reveal the amount of attention given to different aspects of geography. Figure 10.5 shows an alternative framework, with illustrative examples, designed to promote a critical enquiry approach to geography.

Figure 10.4: Alternative frameworks for analysing teachers' questions. Sources: Birmingham DEC, 1995; Rawling, 2008.

Questions based on the development compass rose

Category of question	How defined by Birmingham DEC
Natural	These are questions about the environment: energy, air, water, soil, living things and their relationships to each other. These questions are also about the built as well as the 'natural' environment.
Social	These are questions about people, their relationships, their traditions, culture and they way they live. They include questions about how, for example, gender, race, disability, class and age affect social relationships.
Economic	These are questions about money, trading, aid, ownership, buying and selling.
Who decides	These are questions about power, who makes choices and decides what is to happen, who benefits and loses as a result of these decisions and at what cost.

Questions based on the route for enquiry (Rawling, 2008)

Sequence of questions
What?
When and where?
How and why?
What might happen?   What impact?   What decision?
What do I think?   Why?   What will I do next?

The advantage of using frameworks is that they can reveal patterns of questioning behaviour. They should be used to guide and illuminate practice rather than as strait-jackets. The most important thing is to reflect on the type of questions asked and consider the extent to which they are supporting the learning of geography.

The kinds of questions teachers ask convey messages to students about what geography is about and the purpose of learning it. If, for example, the majority of questions demand the recall of factual information, this suggests that geography is about learning facts. Questions that demand the understanding of data presented on graphs, photographs, etc., suggest that learning geography is about developing skills to interpret data. Questions that require students to analyse an issue, to think about relationships, processes or factors, etc., suggest that geography is about developing reasoning. Questions such as 'what ought?' 'what might?' and 'what do you think about ...?' suggest that geography includes ethical dimensions. Questions that probe sources and the validity of data convey a critical attitude towards evidence.

Experienced teachers ask questions routinely without necessarily having to pre-plan them. However, because there is a tendency for questions to be closed and low level, it is worthwhile to plan in advance some questions which help students focus on the key question being investigated, on the evidence being used, on the key concepts and the types of reasoning that are required.

How can teachers improve their questioning skills?

Teachers' questions can be improved by paying attention to the classroom processes involved in question and answer sessions and the skills involved in managing these processes. Research by Black and Wiliam (1998) and Black *et al.* (2004) suggests that questioning can be improved by:

▲ Distributing questions so that different students answer. Only a minority of students volunteer to answer questions and only a minority answer questions in any one lesson. Questions can be directed at particular students, and over a series of lessons all students could have the opportunity to answer questions.

▲ Pausing after asking a question. After asking a question, many teachers wait less than one second and then, if there is no response, either answer the question themselves or ask another question (Black *et al.*, 2004). It was suggested that wait time should be extended to several seconds, although teachers find this difficult at first.

▲ Giving students time to think before they answer questions in front of the whole class. Black and Wiliam suggest that students should be given time to respond by:

'asking them to discuss their thinking in pairs or in small groups, so that a respondent is speaking on behalf of others; giving pupils a choice between different possible answers and asking them to vote on the options; asking all of them to write down an answer and then reading out a selected few: and so on. What is essential is that any dialogue should evoke thoughtful reflection in which all pupils can be encouraged to take part' (Black and Wiliam, 1998, p. 8).

Type of question	applied to coastal erosion in Humberside	applied to theme of carbon emissions
Focusing on factual information – from memory, from sources. Significance of factual information	In which part of England is the coast eroding quickly? Why is this important to some people?	How much have carbon emissions increased in the last xxx years? Which countries emit most? Why does it matter?
Focusing on understanding of concepts	What do you understand by coastal erosion/longshore drift?	What do you understand by 'carbon emissions'? What are the sources of carbon emissions?
Focusing on geographical sources as evidence	What evidence is there for coastal erosion in Holderness? What evidence is there about the rate of change?	What evidence is there for an increase in carbon emissions? Who publishes this evidence? To what extent can predictions be made from this evidence?
Focusing on reasoning about processes	What factors affect coastal erosion? Why does the Holderness coast erode so quickly? To what extent can erosion be prevented?	Why has there been an increase in carbon emissions in the last 150 years? How could they be reduced?
Focusing on different viewpoints	Why do people living in different parts of the coastline have different viewpoints about building coastal defences?	Why do countries have different views about the extent to which they should reduce carbon emissions?
Probing assumptions	What assumptions are behind different views? What ways do different groups see the world? e.g. related to market forces, role of government, role of communities	What assumptions are behind different views? What ways do different groups see the world? e.g. related to market forces, role of government, role of communities
Asking for judgements or conclusions	Should we allow nature to take its course and let the coast erode naturally?	Should the UK attempt to reduce carbon emissions? Why/Why not?
Asking for opinions on ethical matters	Is it important to protect areas of special scientific interest along the coast?	Should all countries be expected to reduce carbon emissions equally? Should the rich countries of the world give financial help to the poorer countries of the world to enable them to reduce carbon emissions?

Figure 10.5: A framework of categories of questions devised to encourage a critical enquiry approach to learning geography.

▲ Listening and responding carefully. Responding to students' responses can include:

– Evaluating a response. This might involve a quick reply such as 'good', 'excellent'. It is important that students are aware if a response is incorrect or inappropriate. This can be done for closed questions by giving the correct answer, by probing inappropriate responses to open questions or by asking for other suggestions.

– Giving prompts. The prompts are best if they guide thinking rather than give clues to correct answers, such as the initial letter of a word or place.

– Probing responses. This is time consuming but valuable. Socratic questions (see Chapter 11) are useful for probing responses.

– Commenting on a student's response – adding to it or making a geographical comment.

Although it is taken for granted that it is desirable for as many students as possible to be involved in answering questions, Alexander (2000) noted a different practice in some classrooms in Russia. The teacher invited one or two students to the front of the class and they answered a sequence of questions. Alexander commented: 'the child who comes to the front and works through a problem, aloud and at length, is less an individual being tested and compared with others than their representative. For the moment, that child is the class and all are participating' (p. 454). He thought that children learnt from listening to 'the sustained discourse' and saw that mistakes were not negatively assessed but part of the process of learning. What I find interesting about cross-cultural research is the way it challenges accepted practices and advice. Could this practice promote learning in a different classroom culture?

Summary

An enquiry approach to learning geography does not mean that there is no role for teacher talk. Presentational talk by the teacher can introduce students to geographical vocabulary and ways of thinking; it can be used to support students' reading and, when based on experiences related to what is being studied, it can be a vivid, interesting resource. Typical patterns of question and answer have some value, but they cannot be considered as 'discussion'. It is worth reflecting on when it is appropriate to ask open and closed questions. Frameworks which categorise question types can help teachers vary the kinds of questions they ask and the demands made on students' thinking. Frameworks based on Bloom's taxonomy are widely used, but frameworks designed for geography and for enquiry would encourage more purposeful questioning. Research has suggested various ways in which teachers might improve their questioning skills.

Suggestion for research

Investigate the nature of teacher talk in a series of lessons and examine its contribution to students' learning. The investigation could use video and tape recordings of lessons to collect evidence and include an analysis of the types of talk, analysis of a teacher's questions, and analysis of the way a teacher responds to student responses.

References

Alexander, R. (2000) *Culture and Pedagogy: International comparisons in primary education.* Oxford: Blackwell.

Anderson, L. and Krathwohl, D. (eds) (2001) *A Taxonomy for Learning, Teaching and Assessing: A revision of Bloom's taxonomy of educational objectives.* New York: Addison Wesley Longman.

Birmingham DEC (1995) *The Development Compass Rose.* Available online at *www.tidec.org/sites/default/files/uploads/2c.50%20Compass%20rose_1.pdf* (last accessed 13 March 2013).

Black, P. and Wiliam, D. (1998) *Inside the Black Box: Raising standards through classroom assessment.* London: King's College.

Black, P., Harrison, C., Lee, C., Marshall, B. and Wiliam, D. (2004) 'Working inside the black box: assessment for learning in the classroom', *Phi Delta Kappan,* 86, 1, pp. 9–12. Available online at *http://education.vermont.gov/new/pdfdoc/pgm_curriculum/science/resources/cd_materials/local_assessment/Formative%20Assessment/WorkingInsidetheBlackBox.pdf* (last accessed 13 March 2013).

Bloom, B. (ed) (1956) *Taxonomy of Educational Objectives, Handbook 1: Cognitive domain.* New York: McKay.

Krathwohl, D. (2002) 'A revision of Bloom's taxonomy: an overview', *Theory into Practice,* 41, 4, pp. 212–18.

Leat, D. (1998) *Thinking through Geography.* Cambridge: Chris Kington Publishing.

Mercer, N. and Dawes, L. (2008) 'The value of exploratory talk' in Mercer, N. and Hodgkinson, S. (eds) *Exploring Talk in School.* London: Sage.

Mercer, N. and Littleton, K. (2007) *Dialogue and the Development of Children's Thinking: A socio-cultural approach.* London: Routledge.

Pring, R. (1971) 'Bloom's taxonomy: a philosophical critique', *Cambridge Journal of Education,* 1, 2, pp. 83–91.

Rawling, E. (2008) *Planning your Key Stage 3 Geography Curriculum.* Sheffield: The Geographical Association.

CHAPTER 11

Discussion, dialogic teaching and Socratic questions

'Dialogic teaching reflects a view that knowledge and understanding come from testing evidence, analysing ideas and exploring values, rather than unquestioningly accepting somebody else's ideas' (Alexander, 2011, p. 32).

Introduction

The word 'discussion' is used fairly loosely both in everyday life and by educators. I have heard it used to refer to any kind of interactive talk, including conversations and classroom question and answer sequences. In this book I am using 'discussion' to mean periods of purposeful classroom talk focused on geography when students are expected to talk for at least 50% of the time. This chapter addresses the following questions:

▲ Why is discussion important?

▲ What are the characteristics of dialogic teaching?

▲ How can dialogic talk be encouraged in whole-class situations?

▲ How can talk in small groups contribute to geographical enquiry?

▲ What are Socratic questions and how can they be used?

Why is discussion important?

There is a large body of research, including that carried out by Barnes, Mercer, Alexander and Wells, indicating that students learn more effectively when they have been actively involved in discussion.

Barnes and Todd (1995), from their research into students' discussion in small groups, found that their talk was an important way of them 'working on understanding'. They found that 'One of the most important ways of working on understanding is through talk, either in formal education or as part of the learning in everyday life. New ways of talking about things lead to new ways of seeing things' (p. 12). Barnes emphasises the value of what he termed 'exploratory talk':

'Exploratory talk is hesitant and incomplete because it enables the speaker to try out ideas, to hear how they sound, to see what others make of them, to arrange information and ideas into different patterns. The difference between the two functions of talk is that in presentational talk the speaker's attention is primarily focused on adjusting the language, content and matter to the needs of an audience and in exploratory talk the speaker is more concerned with sorting out his or her own thoughts' (Barnes, 2008, p. 5).

Mercer and Littleton's research on classroom talk (2007) has focused on ways in which teachers and students can, through discussion, work on knowledge and understanding together. Influenced by Vygotsky's (1962) work, Mercer emphasises the importance of dialogue in what he has referred to as 'the joint creation of knowledge' (2000, p. 9) in any society. Mercer set up a research project, 'Thinking Together', which encouraged a dialogue-based approach to students' thinking and studied the effect of guided support on students' talk in small groups. The project carried out research in a large number of classrooms, mainly in England and Mexico, which found that students involved in the project were more engaged with tasks in small group work, that the quality of talk changed significantly and that educational attainment improved (Thinking Together project, 2012). The project team developed practical activities for developing the talk of students aged 11–14 in geography (Dawes *et al.*, 2005).

Alexander (2000) found that of the five categories of classroom talk he had identified (see Figure 10.1, p. 95), discussion and dialogue, although they had the greatest cognitive potential, were the least used. He used the term 'dialogic teaching' to embrace both discussion and dialogue and to include various kinds of teacher–student and student–student interactions in both whole-class and small group teaching. He explained its value:

'Dialogic teaching harnesses the power of talk to stimulate and extend students' thinking and advance their learning and understanding. It helps the teacher more precisely to diagnose students' needs,

frame their learning task and assess their progress. It empowers the student for lifelong learning and active citizenship. But classroom dialogue is not just any talk. It is as distinct from the question-answer and listen-tell routines of traditional or even so-called "interactive" teaching as it is from the casual conversation of information discussion, aiming to be more consistently searching and empowering than any of these' (Alexander, 2011).

In addition to justifying dialogic teaching in terms of what it can achieve in school, Alexander also justifies it in terms of society: 'Democracies need citizens who can argue, reason, challenge, question, present cases and evaluate them' and that 'democracies decline when citizens listen rather than talk and when they comply rather than debate' (2011, p. 54). Alexander's concept of dialogic teaching has been taken up by many local authorities in the UK and there has been growing international interest.

Wells and Ball (2008), who have carried out research into primary pupils' talk, emphasise the relationship between 'inquiry', with its emphasis on questioning and evidence, and a 'dialogic stance':

'Adopting inquiry as a pedagogical approach means more than adopting piecemeal strategies such as increasing "wait time" after a question or including more "hands-on" activities in the daily classroom repertoire. Adopting inquiry as a pedagogical approach means adopting a dialogic stance toward experience and information, that is to say a willingness on the part of all participants, teacher as well as students, to wonder, to ask questions and to answer those questions through the collection of relevant evidence by various means, both empirical and library-based, and to present the findings to one's peers for critical review and improvement' (p. 183).

The value that is placed on discussion by the above researchers is theoretically grounded in the work of Vygotsky, Bakhtin and Bruner. Vygotsky (1962) valued the role of talk between learners and more knowledgeable people in advancing learners' understanding in the 'zone of proximal development'. Bakhtin argued that dialogue pervades all written and spoken language. He pointed out that 'we do not take words from a dictionary but from the mouths of other speakers and so they carry with them the voice of those who have used them before' (Wegerif, 2008, p. 349). Words therefore carry meanings from how they have been used previously and the values and assumptions of those using them. Bakhtin argued that it is through dialogue that we get to know the different meanings other people attach to words

and develop our understanding. He thought that the exchange, acquisition and refinement of meanings were what education was all about (Alexander, 2011).

In summary, evidence from research has shown that dialogic teaching can contribute to learning geography through enquiry by helping students to:

▲ participate more in discussion, to get more involved in what they are investigating

▲ ask questions of the teacher and of each other

▲ generate their own questions

▲ relate their existing knowledge and experience to new ideas

▲ participate in the construction of their knowledge and contribute to their understanding of the nature of geographical knowledge

▲ work on their understanding

▲ hear and consider a range of ideas and opinions

▲ clarify their own ideas and opinions by having opportunities to share them

▲ think at higher levels

▲ take part in problem-solving and decision making.

What are the characteristics of dialogic teaching?

Alexander uses the term 'dialogic teaching' to mean an approach to classroom practice that is characterised by five criteria or principles. Dialogic teaching is:

▲ collective, in that teachers and students address learning tasks together, whether as a group or as a class

▲ reciprocal, in that teachers and students listen to each other, share ideas and consider alternative viewpoints

▲ supportive, in that students articulate their ideas freely, without the fear of embarrassment over 'wrong' answers, and help each other to reach common understandings

▲ cumulative, in that teachers and students build on each other's ideas and chain them into coherent lines of thinking and enquiry

▲ purposeful, in that teachers plan and steer classroom talk with specific educational goals in view (Alexander, 2011).

Cotton (2006), in her research into the discussion of controversial issues in geography, recorded and transcribed some classroom discussions, one of

An example of dialogic talk

1 Teacher: OK, do you think ... it is the sole responsibility of these different states? What about NGOs, what about non-government organizations?

2 Dan: I think they should have a major say in it as well.

3 Teacher: Why?

4 Paul: Non-government, non-elected in other words?

5 Dan: Yeah, because they do sometimes have good qualities to point out.

6 Paul: They're unelected though ...

7 Dan: [Interrupting] Yeah, but often they're ...

8 Teacher: Paul, Paul, make your point.

9 Paul: People like Greenpeace aren't representation of a whole thing, they're not elected, they're just a business ...

10 Jake: No, they don't have the facilities and the resources to, erm, have so much, er ... research stations as the government.

11 Lara: But they don't have darkened motives.

12 Jake: How do you know?

13 Paul: Not darkened motives! Of course, they do.

14 Vanessa: [Jokingly] They're not evil, Paul.

15 Teacher: Vanessa, what were you saying? Why do you think they're needed?

16 Vanessa: [Laughs] I was just saying... Well, they give some protection to the ... country.

17 Teacher: Is that necessary here?

18 Vanessa: Well, yes ...

19 Dan: Yes.

20 Vanessa: It'd be plundered otherwise.

21 Teacher: Would it? According to the Treaty, they're not going to plunder it.

22 Vanessa: Yeah well!

23 Dan: No, that's only because Greenpeace have a say in the Treaty because they are sort of ...

24 Paul: What? They have nothing to do with the Treaty.

25 Dan: Yes, they do, because they go into the meetings, they suggest ...

26 Paul: Oh yeah, alright then. But they're just a limited company in Britain, no more than that. They're not elected, they're not ...

27 Teacher: So ...

28 Vanessa: It doesn't mean they're stupid and ignorant, Paul.

29 Paul: Well, it means that they shouldn't have the right to rule the world if they're non-elected.

30 Vanessa: We're not giving them the right to rule the world.

31 Dan: Paul, we're not giving you the right to rule the world!

32 Paul: What?

33 Jake: What? ... Irrelevant, Dan [laughs] ...

34 Teacher: How many of you do feel that it's a good thing that Greenpeace are kind of on the edge of all of this? Put your hands up [Dan, Jake, Lara, Vanessa, Jenni agree].

35 Jake: It's a good thing to have all these green things. They raise questions and make the public aware and make sure that the, er, some of these things do ... But to give them as much power to have a huge right of say into something like this is ridiculous. It shouldn't be done!

36 Teacher: Right, so you...?

37 Jake: You should have them lobbying on the outside instead.

38 Teacher: OK, so that's what you think their role is? And, Paul, what do you think of that? Cause you were kind of 'no' [laughs].

39 Paul: Well, they shouldn't have any power, obviously, but they can express their feelings ...

40 Vanessa: The point is ... OK, right. You've got a continent that is totally natural, yeah. It hasn't got any inhabitants ...

41 Jake: Yeah, why should a body though, unelected ...

42 Teacher: No, let her finish, Jake ... Jake, let her finish!

43 Vanessa: Yeah, right. So, it's totally uninhabited yeah, and you want to come in and exploit it and take all the minerals out [Jake: yeah] and they want to conserve it [Jake: yeah] ... which is fair enough because ... But, but then they don't have to have any sort of political training [unclear]. Yeah, but they don't ... nothing needs to be politically run in Antarctica. They don't need to govern ... No, but they don't you see, they don't need to say, OK, right then, we'll give money, they have no idea how to do that. That's a totally irrelevant issue.

44 Jake: Exactly, and why should we give a job such as running a continent into the hands of amateurs? [Confused uproar apparently from rest of class.]

45 Vanessa: Yes, no but ...

46 Jake: They haven't got the resources to, erm ... run a continent!

47 Vanessa: Yeah, but it's a totally different ...

48 Teacher: Jake, are we saying run it, or are we saying be part of the process?

49 Jake: To run a continent, to have power, to have power over a continent is ... to run a continent. It's exactly the same thing.

50 Vanessa: Yes, but it's a continent with no people on it ...

51 Jake: Well, there could be people. That's the whole point. It's land.

52 Paul: You're making a decision to preserve it without consulting ...

Figure 11.1: An example of dialogic talk focused on the development of Antarctica. Gaps indicate some dialogue omitted, and comments have been renumbered from original. Source: Cotton, 2006.

which provides a good example of dialogic teaching (Figure 11.1). The discussion was focused on the role of non-governmental organisations (NGOs) in the development of Antarctica. The dialogue is collective, in that the teacher and students are working together to discuss how Antarctica should be managed. It is reciprocal and cumulative, in that the students listen to each other and comment on each other's ideas, gradually developing their opinions (comments 16–30 and 40–47). The teacher has evidently created an atmosphere in the class which is supportive. Students are able to air their views and disagree with each other and help each other understand their arguments. The teacher keeps the discussion purposeful by enabling everyone to express a viewpoint with a show of hands (comment 34) and by checking the meaning of what students are saying (comments 38 and 48).

This dialogue is strikingly different from typical question/answer routines and provides a good example of exploratory talk. The teacher talks much less than the students and does not intervene after each student's contribution. She does not evaluate their contributions. The students direct their talk not just to the teacher but to other students; they ask each other questions and comment on each other's ideas. The teacher allows the discussion to flow but her infrequent contributions are significant in enabling this kind of talk. She initiates the discussion by asking an open question about the students' opinions. She probes some of their responses and checks their meaning, e.g. 'Why do you think they are needed?' (comment 15), 'So…' (27), '… are we saying run it, or are we just saying be part of the process?' (48). She gives information where she thinks it will help, 'According to the Treaty, they're not going to plunder it' (21). She makes sure that people can have their say and make their point, e.g. 'No, let her finish, Jake' (42).

I feel best with others when they …

I feel uncomfortable with others when they …

It is easy to share my feelings with others when they …

It is hard to share my feelings with others when they …

In our class I hope that …

In our class I am most concerned about …

What I want to get out of these lessons is …

I feel warmest towards others when they …

What I can give to this group is …

I would like to discuss …

Figure 11.2: Sentence starters for students to complete before a PHSE discussion-based course.

How can dialogic talk be encouraged in whole class situations?

A shift in classroom culture

The kind of talk illustrated in Figure 11.1 is not easy to achieve. It requires us to rethink classroom talk and to adopt a different stance towards students' contributions. Although Alexander (2011) insists that all five principles of dialogic pedagogy are essential, he suggests that:

'If we want to make the transformation of classroom talk achievable for other than the most talented teachers, we might concentrate first on getting the ethos, dynamics and affective climate right; that is by making the talk collective, reciprocal and supportive. In those classrooms where these conditions and qualities are established, we can then attend more closely to the other two principles' (p. 112).

A shift to dialogic pedagogy requires a shift in classroom culture, which is difficult to achieve if traditional patterns of classroom talk are prevalent in a school across all subjects. Research has shown, however, that a dialogic approach to talk can be successful if ground rules are made explicit, certain strategies are adopted and structured activities are used.

Ground rules

The ground rules for genuine discussion are very different from the implicit ground rules of traditional classroom talk, which were listed in Chapter 10.

Ground rules need to be made explicit and agreed with students. By far the best way of producing a list of ground rules is to use students' ideas to develop them. Personal, social and health education (PSHE) lessons at King Edward VII School, Sheffield, are taught entirely through discussion and ground rules are negotiated with each class. At the start of the course, year 7 students complete a sheet of sentence starters setting out their feelings about classroom discussion (Figure 11.2). The teacher uses their completed sentences to compile a list of ground rules for that particular class. In the next lesson students discuss the meaning of each rule and if the teacher feels that something essential has been missed out, suggests it for consideration. Students' responses, plus any amendments or additions, become the agreed ground rules for that particular class and are referred to throughout the year. Figure 11.3 shows the ground rules produced by one year 7 class. At the beginning of years 8 and 9, when the students are taught in the same groups, the ground rules

We do want people to:

Include others

Listen

Be warm

Help others

Show respect

Be trustworthy

Be considerate

Get along

Co-operate

Become confident

Encourage

Show interest

Show understanding

Share views/feelings

Argue well

Be open

Have fun

Get to know others

We don't want people to:

Make fun of others

Bully

Giggle

Feel embarrassed

Pick on others

Exclude people

Feel ignored

Be secretive

Tease

Be mean

Feel shy

Be put under the spotlight

Whisper

Be racist

Use put-downs

Talk behind people's backs

Mess about

Stop others learning

Figure 11.3: Some ground rules devised by a year 7 PSHE class.

are looked at and renegotiated. In year 10, when PSHE lessons are in newly formed groups, students complete sentence starters to establish new ground rules.

Because the year 7 students have negotiated their own ground rules they take into account their particular concerns; the students also understand them better than abstract, general rules imposed on them. If we are to use the potential of classroom discussion in learning geography through enquiry then it is worth using the procedure used in the PSHE example. A different list of sentence starters, suggested in Figure 11.4, would be more relevant to investigating geography. These could be used at the start of each academic year and the responses used to produce and negotiate ground rules for discussion in geography.

Strategies to encourage whole class discussion

Discussion is more likely to take place if some of the following conditions apply:

▲ Ground rules have been made explicit and students are reminded of them if necessary.

▲ The issue being discussed is controversial and has been introduced through the use of a stimulus or a contentious statement.

▲ Students have already studied evidence on the issue or have some data to which they can refer during their discussion.

▲ Students have information about different views on the issue.

I feel best with others in a discussion when they ...

I feel uncomfortable with others in a discussion when they ...

It is easy to ask questions about things if ...

It is difficult to ask questions about things if ...

It is easy to say I do not know something if ...

It is hard to say I do not know something if ...

It is easy to say I do not understand something if ...

It is hard to say I do not understand something if ...

It is easy to share my ideas and opinions with others when they ...

It is hard to share my ideas and opinions with others when they ...

It is easy to comment on the ideas of other people if ...

It is hard to comment on the ideas of other people if ...

In our class I am most concerned about ...

I feel uncomfortable if after I say something the teacher ...

Figure 11.4: Sentence starters to generate ground rules for discussion in geography.

▲ Students have the opportunity to discuss the issue in pairs or small groups before whole-class discussion takes place.

▲ The teacher allows discussion to flow without commenting on or evaluating every contribution.

▲ The teacher manages the discussion, enabling students to complete what they have to say, stopping people from interrupting and inviting others to join in.

▲ The teacher intervenes when appropriate to correct inaccuracies or supply additional information.

▲ The teacher occasionally asks for a show of hands about who is for and against a point of view and invites people to explain why they voted as they did.

▲ The teacher probes responses using Socratic questions (see below).

▲ The discussion is part of a structured activity with specific procedures and ground rules of its own, e.g. a public meeting role play.

▲ The discussion is preceded by an activity about which students want to talk.

▲ Classroom seating arrangements are such that all students can see each other easily, either in a horseshoe/conference arrangement or in groups sitting at tables.

Discussion-based activities

The most successful lessons I have observed in which there have been whole-class discussions have been public meeting role plays (see Chapter 18). These give opportunities for different kinds of classroom talk:

▲ Exploratory talk in small groups when students prepare their presentations.

▲ Presentational talk when groups make their formal presentations to the whole class.

▲ Dialogic talk when the groups question each other in a purposeful way.

▲ Dialogic talk during the debriefing.

When students have been engaged in challenging activities, they often have a lot to talk about and the value of the activities is enhanced by debriefing. If exploratory talk is to be encouraged, then debriefing needs to be more than a brief plenary activity to finish a lesson. Instead, students should be given time for discussion, to 'work on their understanding' and feel free to ask questions and to voice uncertainties. Time needs to be allowed for this kind of debriefing which could follow the following activities:

▲ intelligent guesswork (Chapter 13)

▲ Five Key Points (Chapter 14)

▲ concept maps (Chapter 16)

▲ layers of inference (Chapter 17)

▲ public meeting role play (Chapter 18)

▲ the use of a game or simulation, e.g. the trading game

▲ activities in which students rank the importance of particular viewpoints or a choice of projects.

The most impressive debriefing I have seen of a public meeting role play lasted the whole of the following lesson.

How can talk in small groups contribute to geographical enquiry?

Exploratory talk, in which students have opportunities to share their knowledge, understanding and opinions tentatively, is more likely to take place in small groups than in the public arena of whole-class discussion.

Managing small groups

Research does not suggest one correct way of managing small group work in terms of size of groups, composition of groups or time allocated. Groups of two, three, four and five students have been used successfully. Barnes and Todd (1995) recommend a group size of three or four but note advantages of both smaller and larger group sizes. The smaller the group the greater is the potential for involvement of each individual to be involved. The larger the group the greater the potential for diversity of views and pooling of ideas. If group sizes are larger than four, it is advisable to allocate particular roles to students within the group, e.g. chair, secretary, and to structure the activity to ensure that each person takes part in discussion.

Students find it more comfortable to work in friendship groups, but such groups 'can seek consensus at the expense of a rigorous examination of the topic in hand' (Barnes and Todd, 1995, p. 93). Working with different people can enable students to encounter more new ideas and opinions and encourage them to explain themselves more clearly. Teachers can have particular reasons for selecting students for groups, related to differentiated activities, the need for different gender or cultural perspectives, etc. Ultimately it comes down to the professional judgement of the teacher, who knows the class and individuals in it well. Group work can vary from short two-minute discussions in pairs to collaborative work spanning several lessons.

Ground rules for small group work

Mercer and Dawes (2008) suggest the following ground rules, which could be discussed or negotiated, for small groups:

▲ Partners engage critically but constructively with each other's ideas.

▲ Everyone participates.

▲ Tentative ideas are treated with respect.

▲ Ideas offered for joint consideration may be challenged.

▲ Challenges are justified and alternative ideas or understandings are offered.

▲ Opinions are sought and considered before decisions are jointly made.

▲ Knowledge is made publicly accountable (and so reasoning is visible in the talk).

Activities suitable for small group work

Small group work is more likely to be successful if there is a specific but open task for which students have some relevant data or a specific end product to plan for. Small group activities which have been used successfully in geography include:

▲ devising questions or subsidiary questions to frame an enquiry

▲ devising questions for a visiting speaker

▲ a DARTs activity, usually carried out in pairs (see Chapter 19)

▲ producing concept maps in groups of two, three or four (see Chapter 16)

▲ putting a list in rank order according to preference, e.g. list of possible locations, priorities for funding

▲ planning a presentation to a whole class, e.g. in a role play or formal debate

▲ devising a plan, e.g. for a piece of land

▲ making a model, e.g. of a river basin

▲ planning a display

▲ planning a dramatic representation of something geographical

▲ discussing a decision to be made

▲ searching for and selecting relevant data to download from the internet.

The teacher's role in small group work

The teacher has an important role to play in supporting small group work. In addition to planning the activity and providing guidelines, the teacher's observations and interventions can make a difference to what students learn from the activity. The teacher can support small group work by:

▲ ensuring that all students understand the purpose of the group work – what they are investigating

▲ managing the group by watching them to ensure that students understand what they have to do and that the ground rules are being followed. If necessary, the teacher could intervene to bring a student into the discussion or prevent one student from dominating

▲ eavesdropping on the group, listening carefully and taking mental or actual notes of points that would be useful to follow up after the group work

▲ showing an interest in what students are saying

▲ encouraging students to expand on what they are saying and to voice opinions

▲ using evaluative comments discriminately and rarely, avoiding habitual 'fantastic', 'brilliant', etc. and relating evaluating comments to the geographical content of what is said

▲ joining in the discussion building on previous point – modelling the way dialogic talk is cumulative

▲ encouraging students to ask Socratic questions (see below)

▲ asking Socratic questions that probe students' understanding or reasoning

▲ providing information if requested by students or to correct misunderstandings.

What are Socratic questions and how can they be used?

One way of promoting dialogic talk is through use of Socratic questions. They are named after the Greek philosopher, Socrates, who lived around 477–399 BC, who taught by asking questions. Socrates thought that through questioning he could get his students to examine ideas logically and to develop reliable knowledge.

Paul (1993) used Socrates' ideas to develop his 'wheel of reasoning' in which he classified different types of critical thinking. I have adapted Paul's ideas and other frameworks of Socratic questions to produce a framework of questions suitable for geographical enquiry (Figure 11.5). This framework can be used to help both teachers and students to:

▲ check understanding

▲ probe assumptions implicit in evidence

▲ probe reasons and evidence

▲ become aware of different viewpoints

▲ consider implications

▲ pay attention to the big question framing the enquiry.

Socratic questions can be introduced to students by a teacher modelling their use in whole-class discussion. If Socratic questions are being used for the first time, it might be simplest to use just one or two of the categories of questions. For example, the teacher could make explicit use of questions probing reasons and evidence when discussing a film the students have just observed, to get both teachers and students familiar with how these types of questions are used. Students could be encouraged to use Socratic questions in both whole-class and small group discussions.

The following ground rules have been designed specifically for Socratic questions:

▲ Students are encouraged to ask each other questions and to reply to each other.

▲ Students should ask questions if they are not clear about the meaning of the data.

▲ Students should ask questions if they are not clear about what others are saying.

▲ Students should refer to geographical information when answering questions, linking their replies to the evidence.

▲ Students and teachers should treat all contributions as needing further clarification or development.

▲ Students and teachers should follow each contribution to discussion with further questions if possible.

Questions that seek clarification: trying to understand what others are saying	Questions about viewpoints and perspectives
What do you mean by …? What is the main point you are making …? Is your main point …? Could you put it another way? Could you give me an example of …? How does it relate to what we have been talking about? Could you explain that a bit more?	Whose points of view are represented? What different ways are there of looking at it? Who benefits from this? Who loses? Why is it better than …? What are the strengths and weaknesses of …? Is there another point of view we should consider? What is the counter-argument?
Questions that probe assumptions	**Questions that probe implications and consequences**
You seem to be assuming that … Is that always the case? Does your reasoning depend on the idea that …? Are you taking for granted …? What else could we assume? Why might someone make that assumption?	When you say …, are you implying …? But, if that happened, what else would happen as a result? Why? What effect would that have? Would that necessarily happen or only probably/possibly happen? What would be the consequences of that? What are the implications of that?
Questions that probe reasons and evidence	**Questions about the question**
How can we find out if it is true/accurate? Why do you think that is true? What evidence are you basing that on? Do you have any evidence for …? What are your reasons for saying …? Are these reasons enough? Why do you say that? Is there any reason to doubt the evidence? Why is that happening? Are these reasons a good enough explanation? Can you explain your reasoning? Could there be another explanation?	Why is this issue important? How can we find out? Are there other questions we need to ask? Can we break the question down a bit? How far have we got? Are we any nearer to answering the question?

Figure 11.5: Categories of Socratic questions.

Summary

The substantial amount of research into the use of exploratory and dialogic talk in the classroom has shown its educational value. The emphasis of the research has been on using language to increase understanding. Geography education has a lot to learn from this ongoing research. The value of the activities included in this book would be enhanced by being followed by discussion and by the use of Socratic questions to probe meanings. Exploratory talk in small groups can help students work on their understanding.

Suggestion for research

Develop Alexander's ideas about dialogic teaching in your classroom. Record dialogues of whole-class and/or small group talk. Analyse transcripts using Alexander's criteria. Reflect on the conditions which encourage dialogic teaching and on the extent to which it promotes geographical understanding.

References

Alexander, R. (2000) *Culture and Pedagogy: International comparisons in primary education*. Oxford: Blackwell.

Alexander, R. (2011) *Towards Dialogic Teaching: Rethinking classroom talk* (4th edition). York: Dialogos.

Barnes, D. (2008) 'Exploratory talk for learning' in Mercer, N. and Hodgkinson, S. (eds) *Exploring Talk in Schools*. London: Sage.

Barnes, D. and Todd, F. (1995) *Communication and Learning Revisited: Making meaning through talk*. Portsmouth, NH: Heinemann.

Cotton, D. (2006) 'Teaching controversial environmental issues: neutrality and balance in the reality of the classroom', *Educational Research*, 48, 2, pp. 223–41.

Dawes, L., English, J., Holmwood, R., Giles, G. and Mercer, N. (2005) *Thinking Together in Geography*. Stevenage: Badger Publishing.

Mercer, N. (2000) *Words and Minds: How we use language to think together*. London: Routledge.

Mercer, N. and Dawes, L. (2008) 'The value of exploratory talk' in Mercer, N. and Hodgkinson, S. (eds) *Exploring Talk in Schools*. London: Sage.

Mercer, N. and Littleton, K. (2007) *Dialogue and the Development of Children's Thinking*. London: Routledge.

Paul, R. (1993) *Critical Thinking: How to prepare students for a rapidly changing world. An anthology on critical thinking and educational reform*. Santa Rosa, CA: Foundation for Critical Thinking.

Thinking Together (2012) Available online at *http://thinkingtogether.educ.cam.ac.uk* (last accessed 21 January 2013).

Vygotsky, L. (1962) *Thought and Language*. Cambridge, MA: Massachusetts Institute of Technology.

Wegerif, R. (2008) 'Dialogic or dialectic? The significance of ontological assumptions in research on educational dialogue', *British Educational Research Journal*, 34, 3, pp. 347–61.

Wells, G. and Ball, T. (2008) 'Exploratory talk and dialogic inquiry' in Mercer, N. and Hodgkinson, S. (eds) *Exploring Talk in Schools*. London: Sage.

12

Controversial issues in geography

'One of the reasons to have geography on the curriculum is to guard against indoctrination and propaganda' (Lambert, interviewed on BBC Today Programme, 2002).

Introduction

Almost everything that anyone says or writes about the teaching of controversial issues in geography is in itself controversial; different people would respond in different ways to the questions that this chapter sets out to examine:

▲ What is a controversial issue?

▲ What are wicked problems and super-wicked problems?

▲ Why should controversial issues be investigated in school geography?

▲ Which controversial issues should be included in the geography curriculum?

▲ What is the role of the teacher when controversial issues are being investigated?

▲ How could a critical approach to controversial issues be encouraged?

▲ What classroom activities can support students' investigation of controversial issues?

What is a controversial issue?

A controversial issue is a matter about which individuals and groups disagree. This sounds simple enough, but there are different kinds of controversial issues and different reasons for disagreement that need to be taken into account when investigating them.

Some issues are controversial because there is insufficient evidence to support one particular theory or explanation

For example, the theory of plate tectonics was not finally accepted until the 1960s; before that there had been fierce disputes about whether parts of the Earth's crust could move around.

Disputes about conflicting theories are common in science but the expectation is that eventually, through the accumulation of evidence, they can be resolved. Although scientific knowledge is always provisional in that it can be revised in light of new evidence and although, like all knowledge, it is socially constructed, this does not make it controversial. Sometimes, however, even when there is overwhelming scientific evidence for a theory, e.g. the theory of evolution, some people do not accept it and for them the issue remains controversial. Many issues which have been resolved through scientific research have implications for society, so even when scientific aspects are considered resolved, other aspects remain controversial for one or more of the reasons listed below.

Some issues are controversial because of differences of interpretation

For example, there are different interpretations of the impact of the British Empire on Britain's former colonies; some accounts emphasise the positive impacts while others the negative. These interpretations are influenced by which aspects of Empire are looked at, which evidence is given most attention and which voices are listened to. In this case, although the views use evidence, the differences of opinion are related to different ways of looking at colonialism, different mind-sets. Although this might seem more relevant to interpretations of history, it is also relevant to geography as different ways of thinking about, for example, development, globalisation or sustainability, influence the questions asked, the evidence used and the interpretation of that evidence.

Some issues are controversial because there are different opinions about what should be done

Opinions can vary for one or more of the following reasons:

▲ There is a conflict of interests between different groups of people, organisations or nations affected by a decision; some would gain and others lose. For example, the possible expansion of Heathrow Airport brings advantages to some and disadvantages to others. Some of those who might lose from the development oppose it. This is an example of NIMBYism (not in my back yard) i.e. the protection of self interest.

▲ There is a conflict of values between the different groups involved. Any planning and policy decisions that have an impact on the environment are likely to be controversial. Some groups would give priority to protecting the environment, other groups to social considerations such as employment and others to economic interests. For example, creating game reserves in Kenya might help endangered species to survive, but could be at the expense of the livelihoods of displaced people.

▲ There is a conflict of ideologies, i.e. ways of seeing the world and thinking about it. For example, some would consider Western capitalism as a pre-condition for dealing with current issues related to the global economy while others would see it as incapable of doing so. People have profound disagreements about the role that market forces, or government, should be allowed to have in patterns of production and consumption.

▲ There is uncertainty about the implications of decisions. Any decisions affecting the future can have unanticipated outcomes or elements of risk. Opinions vary about what risks are acceptable.

Some issues are considered controversial for ethical reasons

Ethics deal with moral questions about what is considered right/wrong or good/bad. Some decisions and policies, related to human rights or social justice for example, are considered morally wrong in an absolute sense; e.g. I thought that the apartheid system in South Africa was morally wrong. Also some actions and policies might be considered wrong for religious reasons, e.g. population control. Other issues have ethical dimensions because they can be judged as good or bad according to their potential impacts. Figure 12.1 provides some examples of moral dilemmas related to geographical issues.

Only the first kind of controversial issue, related to scientific research, is likely to be resolved simply by collecting data and using evidence. For controversial issues which have different interpretations, conflicts of interest, values or world views, or in which there are ethical issues, it is not enough to examine evidence. It is also important to examine the

Moral dilemmas

The following moral dilemmas could be investigated in geography. They are related to actions which have good outcomes for some people and bad outcomes for others. The decisions people and governments make about such issues have implications for people in different parts of the world and influence places and how they relate to each other.

▲ Should we buy a Valentine Day's rose from Kenya? (Ellis, 2009)

▲ Should we go on a long-haul 'responsible tourism' holiday?

▲ Should we buy clothes that are made by child labour? (Pumpkin Interactive, 2011)

▲ Should we become vegetarian?

▲ Should we try to buy only British produce and products?

▲ Should we give money to buy a goat to help combat poverty? (Jackson, 2006)

▲ Should we boycott products from a country whose policies we disapprove of?

▲ Should we build new housing developments on the Green Belt?

▲ Should Britain grow as much of its own food as possible?

Published examples

McPartland (2006) has created a narrative related to the issue of the use of pesticides in Benin. The dilemma he presents is 'Should Nestor, a graduate student of chemistry in the UK, leave the course and accept a job back home working in Benin for a pesticide firm?' McPartland analyses arguments for and against (pp. 175–6).

Bustin (2007) created a narrative with five characters about water supply in a village in Sudan, and devised a ranking process through which students investigated the moral issues in the story. First, students ranked the characters in order of who they think are morally the best and worst, drawing on their pre-existing views of right and wrong. Then they ranked the characters according to their motives: which character had the noblest intentions? Then they looked at the consequences of each character's actions and ranked them accordingly. Finally, students compared these three ways of moral reasoning, identifying the advantages and disadvantages of each.

Figure 12.1:
Controversial issues with an ethical dimension.

values and ideologies that underpin the different viewpoints and to consider who has the power to influence decisions.

What are wicked problems and super-wicked problems?

Rittel and Webber (1973) describe some kinds of planning problems as 'wicked' problems. They thought that policy makers had been misled into thinking that planning problems could be solved in the way that scientists solve problems. They argue that:

'The kinds of problems that planners deal with, societal problems, are inherently different from the problems that scientists and perhaps some classes of engineers deal with. Planning problems are inherently wicked' (p. 160).

They use the term 'wicked' to mean something like vicious (like a vicious circle) in contrast to what they term the 'benign' problems of scientists which can be resolved through experiment, evidence and reasoning. They identify ten distinguishing properties of wicked problems (Figure 12.2).

The term 'wicked problem' is now commonly used by policy makers to describe issues with these properties.

Many controversial issues studied in geography are 'wicked'; they cannot be resolved simply on the basis of evidence. We need to recognise that for many controversial issues:

▲ there are different ways and scales of conceptualising them

▲ they are connected with a network of other issues

▲ their solutions have wide-ranging implications.

Levin *et al.* (2009) identify a new class of 'superwicked' problems. These have all the features of wicked problems but with four additional features:

▲ time is running out

▲ the central authority needed to address them is weak or non-existent

▲ those who cause the problem also seek to create a solution

Wicked problems

1. **It is not possible to define the problem clearly**

   'The information needed to understand the problem depends on one's idea of solving it. ... In order to anticipate all questions, knowledge of all conceivable solutions is required.'

   Example: poverty.

2. **The search for solutions never stops**

   '... because there is not an end to the causal chains that link interacting open systems, the would-be planner can always try to be better. Some additional investment of effort might increase the chances of finding a better solution.'

3. **Solutions are not true or false, but good or bad**

   'Normally many parties are equally equipped, interested and/or entitled to judge the solutions. Their judgements are likely to differ widely to accord with their group or personal interests, their special value sets and their ideological predilections.'

4. **There is no immediate and no ultimate way of evaluating a solution**

   'Any solution, after being implemented, will generate waves of consequences over an extended period of time ... the consequences of the solution may yield undesirable repercussions which outweigh the intended advantages.'

5. **There is no opportunity to learn by trial and error; every attempt counts**

   'Every implemented solution is consequential. It leaves "traces" that cannot be undone ... Many people's lives will have been irreversibly influenced.'

   Example: building a new motorway.

6. **There are many possible potential solutions**

   'There are no criteria which enable one to prove that all solutions to a wicked problem have been identified and considered ... a host of potential solutions arises; and another host is never thought up. It is a matter of judgement which of these solutions should be pursued and implemented.'

   Example: combating street crime.

7. **Every wicked problem is essentially unique**

   'Despite long lists of similarities between a current problem and a previous one, there always might be an additional distinguishing property that is of overriding importance'.

8. **Every wicked problem can be considered to be a symptom of another problem**

   'Crime in the streets can be considered as the symptom of general moral decay, or permissiveness, or deficient opportunity or wealth, or poverty ...'

9. **A wicked problem can be explained in numerous ways**

   'The choice of explanation is arbitrary ... People choose those explanations which are most plausible to them ... The analyst's world view is the strongest determining factor in explaining a discrepancy and therefore in resolving a wicked problem.'

   Example: street crime.

10. **The planner has no right to be wrong**

    'In the scientific world it is accepted that hypotheses can be proved wrong. In the world of planning ... the aim is not to find the truth but to improve some characteristics of the world where people live. Planners are liable for the consequences of the actions they generate; the effects can matter a great deal to those people that are touched by those actions.'

Figure 12.2: Ten properties of 'wicked' problems. Source: Rittel and Webber, 1973.

▲ responses are pushed into the future when immediate action is required to set up long-term policy solutions.

They cite dealing with climate change as a superwicked problem.

Why should controversial issues be investigated in school geography?

There are several justifications for including controversial issues in the geography curriculum, together with the values and ethical issues associated with them.

The present geography of the world has been shaped by decisions made in the past

Almost everything studied in geography, the physical landscape as well as the more obvious patterns resulting from human use of land and resources, has been influenced by past decisions, most of which would have been controversial. The study of current controversial issues can increase students' awareness of the complexity of processes and factors that have influenced the places and themes they are studying.

Many current issues have geographical dimensions

The media make us aware that people have different views about current issues, many of which have geographical dimensions. Issues that divide people and which get into the news can vary from local issues, such as changes to bus routes, to global issues, such as the ethics of carbon trading. Online comments on newspaper articles, blogs, radio phone-in programmes and social networking sites such as Facebook and Twitter have enabled a greater number of people to voice their opinions publicly. Young people have easy access to different views on current issues. Hopwood (2007) writes that geography can help students navigate 'complex and sometimes unsettling issues'.

Geography is a political subject

Keith Joseph, Secretary of State for Education and Science (1981–86), recognised that 'geography is in many ways a political subject; and it is of course a value-laden subject' (Joseph, 1985, p. 292). He wrote:

'When patterns which are observed arise as a result of human decisions and behaviour and when the observations themselves, as well as the evaluation of the evidence, may be coloured by personal attitudes and values, then choices between alternative explanations may not be capable of being reached by scientific method alone' (ibid., p. 292).

Joseph thought that 'factual knowledge on its own is not enough' and wanted students to be 'sensitive to the nature and complexity' of the issues and problems they studied:

'To my mind, teachers do no service to their pupils if they give them the impression that such problems are easily defined, that the processes involved are well understood so that their occurrence can be straightforwardly explained and that there are always practicable solutions available. Issues such as the ones I have mentioned [changes taking place in a city, regional differences in employment, pollution] are matters of legitimate dispute precisely because there are often strong disagreements about diagnoses, goals and strategies' (ibid., p. 294).

Values and ideologies are inherent in geographical knowledge

Sherman et al. (2005) emphasise that geography is a 'contested discipline':

'There is more than one way of knowing about the world and not necessarily any single correct way … it would be surprising if the assumptions we made about what counts as facts, how causes operate, whether our own values should enter our explanations and other such issues were the same for all conceivable phenomena. What's more, even accounts of the same processes, say domestic labour by migrant workers, could look very different depending on whether one's understanding was influenced by feminism or by mathematical modelling'.

Proctor (1998) in writing about the ethical dimension of geography, commented on the increasing attention paid to the 'values inherent in the practice of geography and of the substantive issue of the values inherent in the subject matter of geography' (p. 8). He adds that values are as much part of geography as facts.

Slater (2001) argued similarly that:

'Geography in education, like all subjects, is not neutral. Its substance, as one source of its value-ladenness, does not stand apart from our constructions and interpretations of spatial and environmental relations. So geography is shot through with a values bias, linked among other things to people's experience, perception and conception of their environment, how they evaluate it and seek to live in it' (p. 43).

Sources of geographical information are never neutral, but are shaped by the kinds of geography that produced them. It is important to recognise the ideologies and values that underpin geographical knowledge and our choices of what and how to teach (Slater, 1996).

The study of controversial issues can equip students to guard against indoctrination

Geography can increase students' awareness of underpinning values and can enable them to examine viewpoints critically. Fien and Slater (1981) identify four possible approaches to values education that could be used in geography, each of which has different educational purposes (Figure 12.3).

Values analysis, values clarification and action learning were incorporated into the Schools Council 16–19 Geography Project's 'route for enquiry' (Figure 12.4) designed to support the investigation of questions, issues and problems (Naish et al., 1987). Instead of values being treated as something separate, to be investigated after the facts of an issue are established, the route for enquiry encouraged the use of 'more objective' data and 'subjective' data throughout the investigation of an issue. The framework included 'values clarification', encouraging students to consider what they thought about the issue. Finally, students were asked to consider whether they would take action on the issue or not.

The route for enquiry encouraged rigorous examination of geographical sources and made students aware of different viewpoints and possible actions. The route for enquiry does not, at any stage, advocate particular viewpoints.

Students are interested in current issues and want to study them in school

Research carried out by Ipsos MORI (2009) on behalf of the Geographical Association found, from interviews with 11–14 year olds, that the great majority (93%) thought it was important to learn about issues affecting different parts of the world and about how the world could change. Most (63%) thought that there was not enough time spent learning about the wider world in school. They studied issues in geography more than in other subjects and it was in geography that they expected to study issues related to the economy and jobs, the environment, poverty and hunger.

These findings confirm previous research carried out in the UK and Australia. Young people are interested in issues that will affect their future, want to be better informed about issues, want to study local and international issues in school and want to have opportunities to discuss them and voice their opinions. They have expressed particular interest in issues to do with injustice, inequality and the environment (Hicks, 2007).

Students can learn a wide range of skills through the study of controversial issues

Stradling (1984) distinguishes between two approaches to the teaching of controversial issues. Some emphasise intrinsic reasons for studying them: students should know about topical issues which are relevant to their lives. The emphasis is on knowledge and understanding of the issue. Others emphasise skills that students learn through the process of studying issues: academic skills of collecting and evaluating evidence and social skills

Approach	Purpose
Values analysis	Helps students identify different viewpoints on an issue and assess the evidence on which they are based
Moral reasoning	Helps students discuss reasons for adopting a particular viewpoint
Values clarification	Helps students become aware of their own values in relation to issues they discuss
Action learning	Focuses on students having a reasoned base for actions they might take in relation to specific social or environmental issues

Figure 12.3:
Approaches to values education. Source: Fien and Slater, 1981.

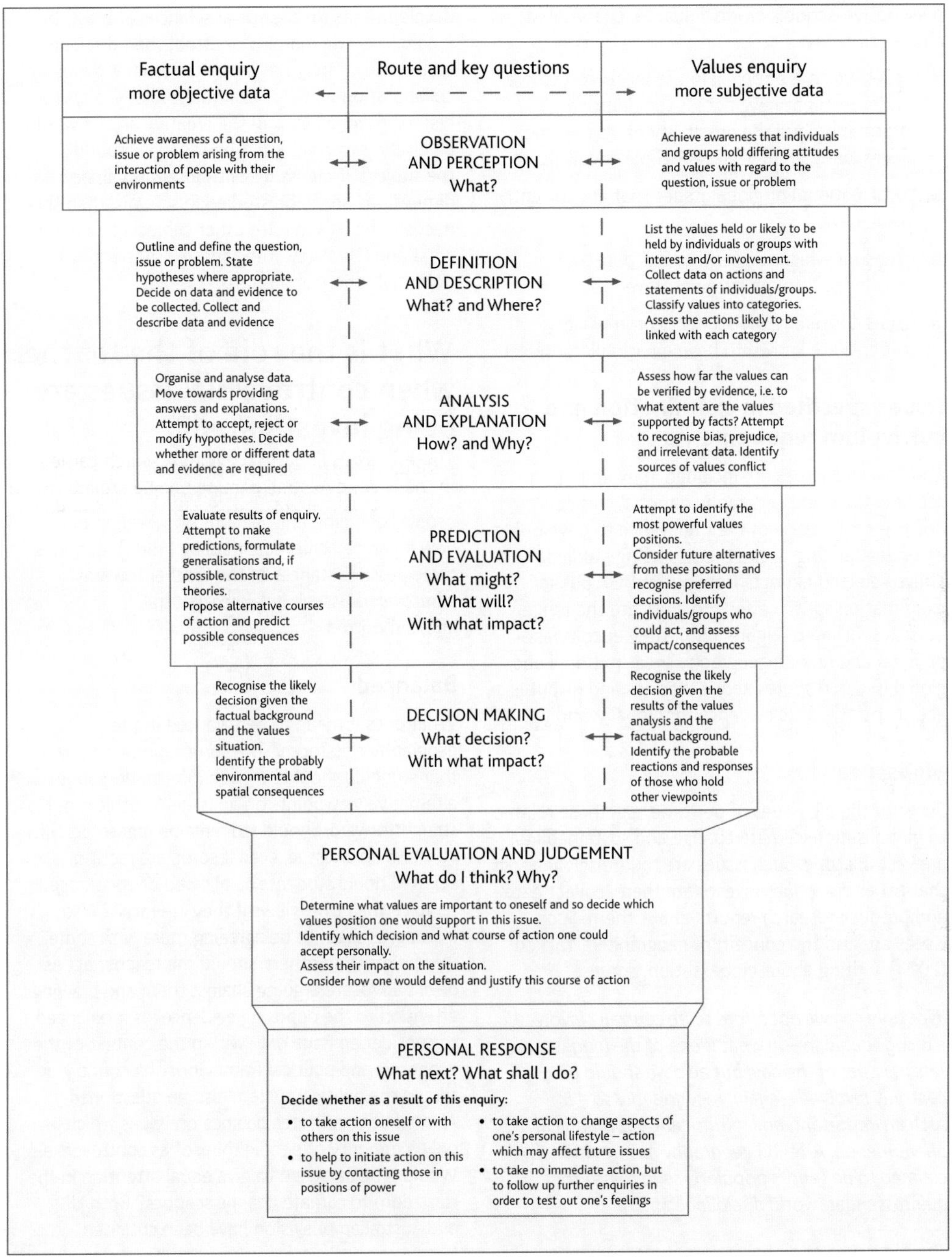
Factual enquiry
more objective data
Route and key questions
Values enquiry
more subjective data
Achieve awareness of a question, issue or problem arising from the interaction of people with their environments
OBSERVATION AND PERCEPTION
What?
Achieve awareness that individuals and groups hold differing attitudes and values with regard to the question, issue or problem
Outline and define the question, issue or problem. State hypotheses where appropriate. Decide on data and evidence to be collected. Collect and describe data and evidence
DEFINITION AND DESCRIPTION
What? and Where?
List the values held or likely to be held by individuals or groups with interest and/or involvement. Collect data on actions and statements of individuals/groups. Classify values into categories. Assess the actions likely to be linked with each category
Organise and analyse data. Move towards providing answers and explanations. Attempt to accept, reject or modify hypotheses. Decide whether more or different data and evidence are required
ANALYSIS AND EXPLANATION
How? and Why?
Assess how far the values can be verified by evidence, i.e. to what extent are the values supported by facts? Attempt to recognise bias, prejudice, and irrelevant data. Identify sources of values conflict
Evaluate results of enquiry. Attempt to make predictions, formulate generalisations and, if possible, construct theories. Propose alternative courses of action and predict possible consequences
PREDICTION AND EVALUATION
What might?
What will?
With what impact?
Attempt to identify the most powerful values positions. Consider future alternatives from these positions and recognise preferred decisions. Identify individuals/groups who could act, and assess impact/consequences
Recognise the likely decision given the factual background and the values situation. Identify the probably environmental and spatial consequences
DECISION MAKING
What decision?
With what impact?
Recognise the likely decision given the results of the values analysis and the factual background. Identify the probable reactions and responses of those who hold other viewpoints
PERSONAL EVALUATION AND JUDGEMENT
What do I think? Why?
Determine what values are important to oneself and so decide which values position one would support in this issue. Identify which decision and what course of action one could accept personally. Assess their impact on the situation. Consider how one would defend and justify this course of action
PERSONAL RESPONSE
What next? What shall I do?
Decide whether as a result of this enquiry:
• to take action oneself or with others on this issue
• to help to initiate action on this issue by contacting those in positions of power
• to take action to change aspects of one's personal lifestyle – action which may affect future issues
• to take no immediate action, but to follow up further enquiries in order to test out one's feelings

Figure 12.4: Route for enquiry. Source: Naish *et al.*, 1987.

of communicating with others and cooperating in projects. I would suggest that these approaches are not mutually exclusive. It would seem limiting to teach any geographical issue without developing skills. It would seem equally limiting to develop skills without applying them to something that was worth knowing about and understanding.

Which controversial issues should be included in the geography curriculum?

Issues chosen because of their particular relevance

When national curricula are not completely

prescriptive, schools or individual teachers could choose to study:

▲ Issues which are topical in the local area, where students might have access to additional information and the possibility of visiting the places, or listening to local people, involved.

▲ Local, national or global issues that are currently in the news.

▲ Issues for which the teacher has particular knowledge through study or travel.

▲ Issues chosen by the students or in which students are known to have a particular interest.

Issues specified in examination and curriculum requirements

Controversial issues are included in examination specifications and geography national curriculum documents because of their relevance to developing an understanding of the themes being studied. I have selected extracts from current UK public examination specifications to illustrate the range of issues included (Figure 12.5). They encompass physical and human geography, local, national and global issues, disputes about theories and disputes about the scientific evidence for global warming.

Big issues

Some of the big issues of our time, e.g. those related to globalisation, climate change and sustainability, are vast in scope. Such issues are multidisciplinary in that other disciplines investigate them, collect data and produce research reports about them. Such issues are also the concern of geographers. Dicken (2004), writing about globalisation, argues:

'Not only can we not afford to be centrally involved – recognisably so – in what is one of the biggest sets of issues of the day, but also we should be centrally involved – again, recognisably so – in such an important, and intrinsically geographical phenomenon. After all geography has traditionally claimed to be (and is popularly seen to be) the quintessential "world discipline"' (p. 6).

The big issues of globalisation, climate change and sustainability should be studied in school geography for two reasons. First, they have geographical dimensions and geography contributes to our understanding of them. Second, such big issues cannot be ignored in schools and they are more likely to be studied in geography than other subjects. As geographers we pride ourselves on geography being an integrative subject; we should not be afraid of working its margins. Jackson (1996) argues that 'many of the most exciting recent

developments (in the social sciences at least) have emerged at the margins of established disciplines' (p. 82). Geography has benefited from working in collaboration with, for example, biology, physics, history, psychology and the creative arts. It would be limiting to erect strict boundaries around the subject. If big issues with interdisciplinary dimensions are to be studied in schools, then there needs to be liaison with other subjects to find out what and how they study these issues and the potential for collaboration.

What is the role of the teacher when controversial issues are being investigated?

Although all teachers want to be 'fair' and avoid indoctrination when teaching controversial issues, people have different opinions on whether and how it can be achieved. Stradling (1984) identifies three possible stances of the teacher towards controversial issues: balanced, neutral and committed.

Balanced

What does it mean to be balanced in the geography classroom? The common sense view is that students should be given information about alternative viewpoints on an issue. But this is not straightforward. Should students be presented with all views on an issue, even if some are racist or sexist? Should students be allowed or encouraged to voice their own views if they are racist? Also, if students seem to be agreeing more with some viewpoints than others, should the teacher act as devil's advocate arguing against them and drawing attention to the opposing evidence? Is it balanced to consider an issue only within the context of the economic and political framework of a country or should the political system also be questioned? Also, what constitutes balance on issues which only a minority of people think of as controversial? Would it be balanced to give equal attention in the classroom to climate change sceptics? Both UK and Australian television have been criticised for giving equal time on news and discussion programmes to majority scientific views and to climate change sceptics.

Cotton's research (2006) has shown that it is never easy to be balanced. She studied a geography teacher discussing the role of NGOs in Antarctica (Figure 11.1 shows part of the transcript). Although the teacher aimed to be balanced, she tended to probe students' presentation of different viewpoints differently.

Neutral stance

Two projects in particular have advocated that the teacher should adopt a neutral stance: the Humanities Curriculum Project and Philosophy for Children (Figure 12.6).

There has been some criticism of procedural neutrality. People have argued that:

▲ It is unsuitable for some issues, e.g. racism.

▲ It is impossible because teachers' views would influence their choice of resources and how they managed discussion.

▲ It is unnecessary in secondary schools as students are unlikely to be influenced by teachers' views.

▲ Teachers feel that they have relinquished their authority.

There is some evidence from classroom practice and from research that procedural neutrality encourages discussion.

Committed stance

There are two ways of adopting a committed stance: through letting students know the teacher's viewpoint and through advocating certain values.

Letting students know the teacher's viewpoint

An alternative to neutrality is for teachers to disclose their own views, but there are disagreements about when this should be done and why. Some argue that a teacher should tell students at the outset of the study of a controversial issue so that they can take it into account. Whether this stance is adopted might depend on the age of the students and the extent to which it is thought they can take a teacher's views into account in thinking for themselves about issues. Others argue for procedural neutrality to encourage free discussion but think that teachers should disclose opinions at the end of an investigation as students are entitled to know what teachers think.

Geography examination	Extract from specifications
GCSE AQA A	Government strategies to cope with an ageing population and the incentives suggested for encouraging an increase in a country's birth rate
GCSE AQA B	There are frequently conflicting demands on coastal areas and this creates a need for management strategies
GCSE Edexcel A	Case study: a dispute between countries, or areas within a country, over water transfer
GCSE Edexcel B	Investigate the growing local pressures on a named and located marine eco-system. Examine the conflicting views about how the chosen eco-system should be managed
GCSE OCR A	Topical analysis of one recent energy supply issue
GCSE OCR B	A case study of a specific development where conflicts exist between economic development and environmental damage
GCSE WJEC A	Should we change our approach to river and floodplain management in the future?
GCSE WJEC B	Who is involved in planning decisions in residential places? How and why do conflicts occur?
GCE AQA	Managing hot desert environments and their margins – to consider and evaluate the strategies adopted with regard to land use and agriculture
GCE Edexcel	The conflicting views and role of the key players in managing climate change – including governments, business, NGOs, individuals and groups. The complexities of a global agreement
GCE OCR	What are the social and economic issues associated with rural change?
GCE WJEC	What types of strategies exist for reducing the development gap and how effective are these strategies?

Figure 12.5: Examples of controversial issues in UK geography examination specifications.

Procedural neutrality

The **Humanities Curriculum Project** (HCP), directed by Lawrence Stenhouse, was a research and curriculum development project, set up in 1967. Its aim was 'to develop an understanding of social situations and human acts and of the controversial value issues which they raise' (Stenhouse, 1971, p. 155). There were three distinctive features of its approach to studying controversial issues:

▲ students investigated issues through discussion rather than through 'instruction'

▲ evidence was provided in the form of resources which included photographs, pictures, extracts from newspapers and books, statistical tables, advertisements, maps, cartoons and audio tapes. As Ruddock (1986) commented, this guarded against 'the mere pooling of ignorance' (p. 9).

▲ the teacher aspired to be 'neutral'. The teacher who chaired the discussion adopted a role of what Stenhouse termed 'procedural neutrality'. He did not want teachers to use their own bias and authoritative position to influence students' views or to inhibit discussion. The role of the teacher was to develop students' understanding of the issue through promoting high quality, rational discussion, to enable them to use evidence as appropriate and express different views.

Philosophy for Children (P4C) originated in a project by Matthew Lipman in 1972 and its approach has been widely used. P4C aims to enable children to become more intellectually curious and critical and to help adults and children to think together. Lipman *et al.* (1980) thought that certain conditions needed to be met when using the P4C approach: 'the readiness to reason; mutual respect (of children towards one another, and of children and teachers towards one another) and an absence of indoctrination' (p. 45).

In a typical P4C lesson, students are provided with a stimulus from which they generate questions for discussion, one of which is chosen. The students discuss the question in what has been referred to as a 'community of enquiry' (Lipman *et al.*, 1980, p. 45). The teacher does not offer opinions, but both teacher and students use Socratic questions to probe what is said. The P4C approach has been adapted for use in environmental education to investigate specific issues that affect Morecambe Bay (Rowley and Lewis, 2003), focusing particularly on the development of thinking skills and conceptual understanding.

Advocating certain values

Schlottman (2012) defines an advocate as 'someone who openly supports, recommends, or furthers a particular cause, policy or idea' (p. 77). Should schools generally, and geography teachers in particular, be advocates of anything? There is no simple answer; there is a spectrum varying from permissible advocacy at one end to indoctrination at the other. What might be deemed permissible could vary according to national and school contexts.

At the permissible end of the spectrum, it can be argued that advocacy of certain behaviours, types of knowledge and ways of working are acceptable. Schools advocate what is acceptable behaviour within the classroom and school although these norms vary from school to school. Schools have anti-bullying and anti-racist policies which discourage certain behaviours. Generally, schools do not expect students to debate or challenge them. Where knowledge is considered settled, e.g. the theory of plate tectonics or the theory of evolution, it is permissible to promote this

theory. I would include the scientific consensus on anthropomorphic climate change at this end of the spectrum for the same reason; I consider it permissible to emphasise the supporting scientific evidence. Advocacy of particular religious beliefs is acceptable at schools with religious affiliations but would be considered indoctrination at secular schools. It also seems permissible and desirable to promote certain educational values, e.g. encouraging curiosity, intellectual honesty and critical thinking.

At the centre of the advocacy spectrum are a range of concerns related to the environment and human rights, raised from 1987 onwards in international reports (see Figure 12.7) for which there could be disagreement on what is permissible advocacy. These reports identify concerns related to the future of the planet and refer to: 'profound change'; 'a defining moment in history'; 'a critical moment in the Earth's history' and 'central challenges', and suggest that education can contribute to meeting these challenges by:

1987: The report of the World Commission on Environment and Development, Our Common Future (the Brundtland Report)

'Over the course of this century, the relationship between the human world and the planet that sustains it has undergone a profound change. When the century began, neither human numbers nor technology had the power to radically alter planetary systems. As the century closes, not only do vastly increased human numbers and their activities have that power, but major, unintended changes are occurring in the atmosphere, in soils, in waters, among plants and animals, and in the relationships among all of these. The rate of change is outstripping the ability of scientific disciplines and our current capabilities to assess and advise. It is frustrating the attempts of political and economic institutions, which evolved in a different, more fragmented world, to adapt and cope. It deeply worries many people who are seeking ways to place those concerns on the political agendas' (Paragraph 1.02, p. 26).

Available online at *www.un-documents.net/ our-common-future.pdf*

2000: The Earth Charter

'We stand at a critical moment in Earth's history, a time when humanity must choose its future. As the world becomes increasingly interdependent and fragile, the future at once holds great peril and great promise. To move forward we must recognize that in the midst of a magnificent diversity of cultures and life forms we are one human family and one Earth community with a common destiny. We must join together to bring forth a sustainable global society founded on respect for nature, universal human rights, economic justice, and a culture of peace. Towards this end, it is imperative that we, the peoples of Earth, declare our responsibility to one another, to the greater community of life, and to future generations' (preamble)

Available online at *www.unesco.org/education/tlsf/mods/ theme_a/img/02_earthcharter.pdf*

1992: Agenda 21: the United Nations Programme of Action from Rio

'Humanity stands at a defining moment in history. We are confronted with a perpetuation of disparities between and within nations, a worsening of poverty, hunger, ill health and illiteracy, and the continuing deterioration of the ecosystems on which we depend for our well-being. However, integration of environment and development concerns and greater attention to them will lead to the fulfilment of basic needs, improved living standards for all, better protected and managed ecosystems and a safer, more prosperous future. No nation can achieve this on its own; but together we can – in a global partnership for sustainable development' (preamble).

Available online at *http://habitat.igc.org/agenda21/a21-01.htm*

2000: United Nations Millennium Declaration

'We believe that the central challenge we face today is to ensure that globalization becomes a positive force for all the world's people. For while globalization offers great opportunities, at present its benefits are very unevenly shared, while its costs are unevenly distributed. We recognize that developing countries and countries with economies in transition face special difficulties in responding to this central challenge. Thus, only through broad and sustained efforts to create a shared future, based upon our common humanity in all its diversity, can globalization be made fully inclusive and equitable. These efforts must include policies and measures, at the global level, which correspond to the needs of developing countries and economies in transition and are formulated and implemented with their effective participation'

Available online at *www.un.org/millennium/declaration/ ares552e.pdf*

Figure 12.7: International concerns about challenges for the planet.

Which of the following do you think is permissible or impermissible advocacy in geography?	Permissible	Not sure	Impermissible
Keeping students informed about environmental issues			
Encouraging a caring, responsible attitude towards the environment			
Letting students know how they could take action on environmental issues			
Getting students involved in monitoring the environment			
Getting students involved in 'improving' the environment			
Getting students to put ideas, e.g. related to waste and energy, into practice within the school			
Encouraging students to put ideas, e.g. related to waste and energy, into practice outside the school			
Convincing students that there are serious environmental concerns			

Figure 12.8: What should geography teachers advocate?

▲ presenting 'the best available scientific information including the natural, behavioural and social sciences and taking into account aesthetic and ethical dimensions' (Agenda 21)

▲ developing knowledge, values and skills to participate in decisions (UN Decade of Sustainability)

▲ fostering a sense of responsibility (Brundtland Report)

▲ changing people's attitudes so that they have the capacity to assess and address concerns (Agenda 21)

▲ students learning to monitor, protect and improve the environment (Brundtland Report)

▲ empowering students so that they can contribute actively to sustainable development (Earth Charter)

▲ putting ideas related to, for example, waste and energy, into practice (Eco-Schools Initiative)

▲ encouraging students to get involved in, for example, saving energy, taking charge of waste audits (UK Sustainable Schools).

What should be the role of school geography in relation to these documents? Are we justified in advocating what these documents and policies suggest? What is permissible and what might be considered indoctrination? Figure 12.8 provides a list of possible actions. Does what is permissible depend on particular local and global contexts? For example:

▲ If a school is involved in the International Eco-Schools Initiative should the geography teacher support what the school is doing to change students' behaviour within the school or encourage students to question or even challenge it?

▲ If there is broad international agreement that certain actions and behaviours are necessary because of the plight of the planet, does this justify advocacy?

▲ How serious would international concerns about the planet have to be before it would be permissible to try to change students' behaviour?

At the far impermissible end of the spectrum is indoctrination. Geography teachers generally would find it impermissible to promote particular viewpoints on contested issues, e.g. nuclear energy, migration policies, congestion charges, GM crops; they would want students to study a range of viewpoints. There can, however, be unintentional, implicit advocacy at this end of the spectrum if:

▲ uncritical acceptance of one particular viewpoint is encouraged

▲ one point of view is emphasised in the resources presented

▲ all the resources and activities are underpinned by a particular ideology or way of looking at the world

▲ the activities and discussion encourage students to adopt one viewpoint

- emotive images are presented to students without opening them up to critical scrutiny

- it is suggested that facts are neutral.

In order to guard against indoctrination, it is important for teachers to reflect on how the controversial issues are investigated and whether there is any unintentional, implicit advocacy for particular viewpoints.

How could a critical approach to controversial issues be encouraged?

There are two ways in which 'critical' is used in relation to classroom practice: encouraging critical thinking and adopting critical pedagogy. Although these approaches have things in common, it is worth distinguishing between what they are trying to achieve.

Critical thinking is an approach to education underpinned by commitment to rigour and rational reasoning. Critical thinking aims for students to:

- learn how to assess evidence

- identify assertions which are not based on evidence

- identify evidence which is based on false authority

- recognise faulty arguments

- probe the assumptions behind what is claimed to be true

- explore ambiguous concepts

- develop a way of looking at the world and a disposition towards learning which is driven by seeking reasons and evidence.

An emphasis on critical thinking would encourage students to expose sloppy thinking, to improve their reasoning and to be more rigorous in investigating evidence related to controversial issues.

Critical pedagogy is an approach to education underpinned by commitment to equality and social justice. It draws on the work of Freire and many other radical thinkers and movements. It is concerned with probing beneath the surface, taking into account how political, economic and cultural contexts and systems of belief influence knowledge and impact on people.

Critical pedagogy aims for students to:

- recognise the political nature of issues

- find out who are the interested parties in a dispute and the reasons for their interest

- ask questions that challenge the status quo

- consider questions which probe ethical issues: What ought to happen? What would be a just solution? Who would benefit and who would lose from a particular decision?

- ask fundamental questions about data and evidence: What is the source of this evidence? Why are these claims being made now? Who has funded the research? Who is promoting the findings?

- expose the hidden meanings of data, to be aware of what is not being said and why

- examine power relationships involved in an issue: What opportunities do different parties in a dispute have to make their views felt and influence the outcome?

- consider the underlying political and economic structures which influence an issue

- understand different perspectives on issues, e.g. gendered perspectives

- develop awareness of actions that might be taken.

Instead of advocating a particular policy, e.g. the Earth Charter, critical pedagogy aims for students to be able to look at such documents critically. It wants students to be:

'capable of critically assessing arguments and policy prescriptions from across the political spectrum, and acting on those they personally and collectively find to be most rationally and ethically defensible. These might include the ideas of market fundamentalists, national protectionists, regulatory liberals, cosmopolitan liberals and anti-capitalists' (Huckle, 2010, p. 140).

Critical pedagogy encourages debate, dialogue and critical literacy. The differences between critical literacy and other forms of reading are summarised by Open Spaces for Dialogue and Enquiry (OSDE) (2009).

What classroom activities can support students' investigation of controversial issues?

Several activities and frameworks in this book are particularly useful for investigating controversial issues:

- Public meeting role play (Chapter 18)

- Structured academic controversy (Chapter 8 and Figure 8.7)

- Teachers' questions (Figure 10.5)

▲ Student record of using a geographical source (Figure 6.6)

▲ Considering criteria for assessing sustainability in development projects (Figures 9.7 and 9.8)

The following activities could be focused on a controversial issue:

▲ Mind maps and spider diagrams (Chapter 15)

▲ DARTs (Chapter 19)

▲ Questionnaire surveys (Chapter 20)

▲ Web enquiries (Chapter 21)

Figure 12.9 suggests some additional activities.

Summary

The study of many themes and places in geography involves consideration of issues that are for various reasons controversial. They cannot be resolved simply by using evidence. Underpinning controversial issues are conflicts of ideologies and values. Many current issues have geographical dimensions and school geography has a role in helping students understand them.

Suggestions for research

1. Read Cotton's article and develop her work from data collected in your own classroom.

2. Investigate how a geography textbook represents a controversial issue, examining the text, supporting information and suggestions for student activities. To what extent does it enable students to study the issue critically? Is there any evidence of unintentional promotion of particular viewpoints?

Investigating controversial issues

Investigating an issue through different perspectives

Focusing the investigation on perspectives related to, for example, age, gender, ethnicity, class, disability. Examples of issues in which these perspectives could be different and relevant are:

▲ use of space, e.g. in school, urban areas, shopping centres, parks, national parks

▲ feelings of safety

▲ public transport

▲ location of retail outlets

▲ priorities in tourist developments.

Decision-making activity

Using a variety of source materials, students decide and justify a decision about, for example:

▲ a choice of site for a development

▲ a choice of policy e.g. a coastal management policy, or to promote 'sustainable development'

▲ priorities for development

▲ conflicts over use of a resource.

Many varied examples of decision-making activities together with useful source materials, can be found in past public examination papers available from examination boards.

Diamond ranking

A set of nine cards on each of which is written, for example:

▲ a priority for a future development

▲ a viewpoint on an issue

▲ a factor that might be taken into account in making a decision about an issue

▲ a person or organisation that would be influenced by a decision.

Preferably working in pairs or small groups to encourage discussion, students arrange the cards in a diamond pattern with the most important/significant at the top and the least important/significant at the bottom.

Using frameworks

A framework with the following headings could be used to analyse an article, a film, a set of resources or information found on the internet:

▲ Who is involved in the issue?

▲ Why are they interested in the issues?

▲ What assumptions are they making about the issue?

▲ What power do they have to influence decisions?

▲ What could they gain from the decision?

▲ What could they lose from the decision?

Is the issue a 'wicked' or a super-wicked problem?

An issue could be analysed using the properties of 'wicked' problems (Figure 12.2). The properties that apply to the issue could be represented on a spider diagram which could be annotated with evidence and ideas related to the issue.

The issue of global warming could be analysed using the four additional properties of 'super-wicked' problems.

Figure 12.9: Activities to support the investigation of controversial issues.

References

Bustin, R. (2007) 'Whose right? Moral issues in geography', *Teaching Geography*, 32, 1, pp. 41–4.

Cotton, D. (2006) 'Teaching controversial environmental issues: neutrality and balance in the reality of the classroom', *Educational Research*, 48, 2, pp. 223–41.

Dicken, P. (2004) 'Geographers and "globalisation": (yet) another missed boat?', *Transactions of the Institute of British Geographers*, 29, 1, pp. 5–26.

Ellis, L. (2009) *A Thorny Issue: Should I buy a Valentine's rose?* Sheffield: The Geographical Association.

Fien, J. and Slater, F. (1981) 'Four strategies for values education in geography', *Geographical Education*, 4, 1, pp. 39–52.

Hicks, D. (2007) 'Lessons for the future: a geographical contribution', *Geography*, 92, 3, pp. 179–88.

Hopwood, N. (2007) 'Values and controversial issues', GTIP Think Piece. Available online at *www.geography.org.uk/gtip/thinkpieces/valuesandcontroversialissues* (last accessed 21 January 2013).

Huckle, J. (2010) 'ESD and the current crisis of capitalism: teaching beyond green new deals', *Journal of Education for Sustainable Development*, 4, 1, pp. 135–42.

Ipsos MORI (2009) *World Issues Survey. Outline findings and PowerPoint presentation*. Available online at *www.geography.org.uk/resources/adifferentview/worldissuessurvey/#top* (last accessed 21 January 2013).

Jackson, P. (1996) 'Only connect: approaches to human geography' in Rawling, E. and Daugherty, R. (eds) *Geography into the Twenty-First Century*. Chichester: John Wiley and Sons.

Jackson, P. (2006) 'Thinking geographically', *Geography*, 91, 3, pp. 199–204.

Joseph, K. (1985) 'Geography in the school curriculum', *Geography*, 70, 4, pp. 290–7.

Lambert, D. (2002) BBC Today Programme: Interview of David Lambert and Alex Standish: 'Does the teaching of geography matter any more?'. Transcript available online at *http://openlearn.open.ac.uk/file.php/2471/!via/oucontent/course/188/geog_sk6_09s_transcript_4.pdf* (last accessed 21 January 2013).

Levin, K., Cashore, B., Bernstein, S. and Auld, G. (2009) 'Playing it forward: path dependency, progressive incrementalism and the "super wicked" problem of global climate change', IOP Conference Series: *Earth and Environmental Science*, 50. Available online at *http://iopscience.iop.org/1755-1315/6/50/502002* (last accessed 21 January 2013).

Lipman, M., Sharp, A. and Oskanyan, F. (1980) *Philosophy in the Classroom*. Philadelphia, PA: Temple University Press.

McPartland, M. (2006) 'Strategies for approaching values education' in Balderstone, D. (ed) *Secondary Geography Handbook*. Sheffield: The Geographical Association, pp. 170–9.

Naish, M., Rawling, E. and Hart, C. (1987) *Geography 16–19: The contribution of a curriculum project to 16–19 education*. London: Longman.

OSDE (2009) 'Critical Literacy'. Available online at *www.osdemethodology.org.uk/criticalliteracy.html* (last accessed 21 January 2013).

Proctor, J. (1998) 'Ethics in geography: giving moral form to the geographical imagination', *Area*, 30, 1, pp. 8–18.

Pumpkin Interactive (2011) *Issues in Globalisation: How Fair is Fashion?* (DVD). Bristol: Pumpkin Interactive.

Rittel, W. and Webber, M. (1973) 'Dilemmas in a general theory of planning', *Policy Sciences*, 4, 2, pp. 155–69.

Rowley, C. and Lewis, L. (2003) *Thinking on the Edge: Thinking activities to develop citizenship and environmental awareness around Morecambe Bay*. Bowness-on-Windermere: Badger Press Ltd.

Ruddock, J. (1986) 'A strategy for handling controversial issues in the classroom' in Wellington, J. (ed) *Controversial Issues in the Curriculum*. Oxford: Blackwell.

Schlottman, C. (2012) *Conceptual Challenges for Environmental Education*. New York: Peter Lang.

Sherman, D., Rogers, A. and Castree, N. (2005) 'Introduction: questioning geography' in Castree, N., Rogers, A. and Sherman, D. (eds) (2005) *Questioning Geography: Fundamental debates*. Oxford: Blackwell.

Slater, F. (1996) 'Values: towards mapping their locations in a geography education' in Kent, A., Lambert, D., Naish, M. and Slater, F. (eds) *Geography in Education: Viewpoints on teaching and learning*. Cambridge: Cambridge University Press.

Slater, F. (2001) 'Values and values education in the geography curriculum in relation to concepts of citizenship' in Lambert, D. and Machon, P. (eds) *Citizenship through Secondary Education*. London: Falmer.

Stenhouse, L. (1971) 'The Humanities Curriculum Project: the rationale', *Theory into Practice*, 10, 3, pp. 154–62.

Stradling, R. (1984) 'The teaching of controversial issues: an evaluation', *Educational Review*, 36, 2, pp. 121–9.

CHAPTER 13

Intelligent guesswork

'For if we do nothing else we should somehow give to children a respect for their own powers of thinking, for their power to generate good questions, to come up with interesting informed guesses' (Bruner, 1966, p. 96).

'Intelligent guesswork' is the term I have given to a strategy that involves students making informed guesses about something, e.g. guessing where a photograph was taken, guessing what a place to be seen on film is going to be like, guessing a set of statistics. This chapter addresses the following questions:

- ▲ What kinds of geographical source material can be used for intelligent guesswork?

- ▲ What are the purposes of using intelligent guesswork?

- ▲ What needs to be considered when planning to use intelligent guesswork?

- ▲ What is the general procedure for using intelligent guesswork?

The chapter then presents two examples with comments on their use:

- ▲ Guessing life expectancy at birth

- ▲ What might Patriot Hills in Antarctica be like?

What kinds of geographical source material can be used for intelligent guesswork?

Intelligent guesswork can be used with different forms of stimulus, e.g. photographs, film, statistics, maps. Several guessing activities referred to in earlier chapters are ways of using intelligent guesswork:

- ▲ speculating on how something was formed (see examples in Chapter 4)

- ▲ guessing facts and figures (see examples in Chapter 4)

- ▲ where in the world? (Figure 7.2)

- ▲ Amazon or not? and variations on this idea (Figure 7.2).

What are the purposes of using intelligent guesswork?

The strategy of intelligent guesswork is rooted in a constructivist theory of learning which emphasises the importance of taking existing knowledge into account when introducing new knowledge. Intelligent guesswork is an effective way of eliciting students' prior knowledge and understanding. Unless they just guess randomly, students have to draw on what they already know to make their guesses. Their 'knowledge' might also include misconceptions and stereotypical images which can be revealed and corrected or discussed during the debriefing.

Another reason to use intelligent guesswork is to spark curiosity. Jerome Bruner used a similar strategy, which he termed 'Informed guessing', in 'Man: A course of study', the humanities course he developed in the 1960s. He wanted students to hypothesise, to make conjectures, to guess, as part of the process of making them more curious and inquisitive (Bruner, 1966). In my experience, intelligent guesswork always creates a need to know.

What needs to be considered when planning to use intelligent guesswork?

- ▲ How does the activity relate to the key question being investigated? Does it contribute to what is being learnt?

- ▲ Is it reasonable to assume that students will have sufficient prior knowledge or reasoning power to make informed guesses of what is being asked? For example, it would be unlikely that students in England could guess the population density of the different states of India unless they were given other information to support their guesses; but they might be able to guess life expectancy of different countries in the world, or what a place in Antarctica is like.

- ▲ What kind of data could to be presented to students to enable them to make their guesses? (e.g. photograph, film, lists of places, a map).

- Would the activity benefit from a structured worksheet on which students write their guesses and which could then be used as a basis for discussion?

- Is this just a brief strategy, requiring a simple guess and brief follow up discussion, or is it worth spending most of the lesson on the activity plus debrief?

- How should the activity be debriefed?

- How can the activity be linked to activities that are to follow?

What is the general procedure for using intelligent guesswork?

- Ensure that students are aware of the focus of the enquiry.

- Make it clear that it is not a test and that you are really interested in their guesses.

- Ask students to speculate individually or in small groups – allow sufficient time for them to come up with ideas.

- Gather information and ideas from the class – probe, in a curious rather than threatening way, the reasoning and thinking behind each contribution. If misunderstandings occur, note these down so that they can be addressed later.

- Ask whether students want to know the answer. The reply is invariably yes.

- Provide the answer(s).

- Debrief the activity. What was guessed correctly? Why was this? What was guessed incorrectly? Why might this have been? In what ways has the activity changed the previously held knowledge?

Example: Guessing life expectancy at birth

This activity could be used as part of a unit of work on development, on global inequalities or on world health issues. It could be focused on other indices of development. I have used the activity frequently, varying the procedure outlined below according to the purpose of using it, the time available and the group.

The first thing I do is to find up-to-date statistics. At the time of writing, good online sources of statistics on life expectancy at birth are:

- the World Health Organisation, which gives estimates for 2009

- the Central Intelligence Agency (CIA), which gives estimates for 2012

- the World Bank, which gives an estimate for each country for 2007–11

- the United Nations, which provides estimates for years up to 2011

- Gapminder, which provides estimates for years up to 2011.

These are all based on official statistics and explain the source of the figures. The figures vary between these sites because of the different dates of the data used and the way estimates are calculated. I would not advise using websites which do not update data regularly or which do not explain how the figures were derived, even if the websites have been designed for geography teachers.

I then choose a list of between 16 and 20 countries, aiming to include countries in different parts of the world and a fairly representative range of life expectancy figures. I also take into account countries that students are likely to know something about or are likely to be using in the curriculum. For example, in England I usually included Brazil, Italy, Japan and Kenya because they were at the time likely to have been studied in school. I also include some of the countries in which some students' parents or grandparents have been born, e.g. Poland, Jamaica, Pakistan, India, Bangladesh and Somalia. When I worked with Singaporean teachers, I included Singapore and also Cambodia. For the countries with low life expectancy, I always include South Africa, one other African country and one country with a lower life expectancy than Bangladesh. I always include Bangladesh, because of the way the responses can be used to expose stereotyping. At the higher end, I always include USA, Japan, Italy and Australia because they generate interesting reasoning.

In the classroom/workshop, I introduce the participants to the activity, explaining how it relates to what we are investigating and give them a worksheet (Figure 13.1) to use. I also check that they understand the meaning of 'life expectancy at birth' or give them one of the following definitions:

- *'The average number of years that a newborn could expect to live, if he or she were to pass through life exposed to the sex- and age-specific death rates prevailing at the time of his or her birth, for a specific year, in a given country, territory, or geographic area'* (WHO website).

- *'The average number of years a newborn child would live if current mortality patterns were to stay the same'* (Gapminder website).

It is worth emphasising that the figures are averages and what this means; some people will live longer

Figure 13.1: Intelligent guesswork: average life expectancy at birth.

Country	Rank	Estimate (my guess)	Statistics (to be completed from data)
Australia			
Bangladesh			
Bolivia			
Brazil			
Cambodia			
China			
Egypt			
Germany			
India			
Italy			
Jamaica			
Japan			
Kenya			
Lesotho*			
Malawi*			
Malaysia			
Mexico			
Pakistan			
Poland			
Russia			
Saudi Arabia			
Singapore			
Somalia*			
South Africa			
United Kingdom			
USA			

NB Include only one of the countries marked *

and some will not live so long; also that the figures for males and females are different and life expectancy figures are usually given as an average of both. With a class it might be worth explaining this by using a few figures as an example. There are often misunderstandings, e.g. that if the life expectancy is 50 there will not be any old people in a country. Discussing the meaning of the figures could be left until after the guessing.

Sometimes I ask students to work individually and silently for a few minutes, starting by identifying the three countries they think are highest and the three they think are lowest. I then ask them to work in pairs or small groups and try to reach a consensus about the three top and three bottom countries. If there is time, the groups can try to complete the whole table. It can be useful to eavesdrop on what the groups are saying, to pick up points for later discussion and to see which countries each group has identified. I have allowed between 5 and 10 minutes for this part of the activity.

I collect all their guesses for the top three and bottom three countries and list them on a white board or flip-chart, without comment at this stage. Usually, nominations for the top three include about five different countries; depending on the list provided, they might include: Japan, Italy, UK, USA, Australia and Singapore. Similarly, there are usually about five nominations for the bottom three, which might include: Lesotho, Cambodia, Bangladesh, Bolivia and Kenya. I then collect the highest and lowest estimates for each of these countries.

I then probe their choices, going through each one in turn and annotating the list with reasons. I start with asking: Why did you choose country X? Or what were your reasons for choosing country Y?

If they give one-word answers then I probe these, using Socratic questions. One-word answers I have

received are: for Bangladesh – floods; for Italy – olive oil; for Lesotho – conflict; for Australia – relaxed lifestyle or space; for Japan – diet; for the UK – NHS (a common response in Singapore).

The kinds of questions I use to elicit their thinking have included:

▲ How can floods/olive oil affect life expectancy?

▲ What is the connection between a relaxed lifestyle and life expectancy?

▲ Has Japan/Singapore got a relaxed lifestyle?

▲ What evidence do you have to support that?

▲ How could we find out if that reason was valid?

▲ What is your evidence for conflict in Lesotho (this is inaccurate and reflects stereotypical views of Africa)

▲ What are you assuming about Lesotho?

▲ Do different factors affect different places?

▲ What are you saying are the most important factors?

▲ Do the countries you have nominated in the top three list have anything in common?

Can flooding, diet or lifestyle affect life expectancy?
Photos: Will Ellis and Ernst Moeksis (Creative Commons licence).

▲ Do the countries you have nominated in the bottom three list have anything in common?

▲ How does wealth/poverty affect life expectancy?

At some stage during the discussion I find out their estimated figures; these can be used to reinforce the fact that life expectancy figures are average figures. For example, some put exceptionally high figures for Japan, based on newspaper reports of people living to be over 100.

After eliciting reasons and probing them, I try to use what they have said to generalise about the factors they seem to think affect life expectancy. By this time they are sometimes getting impatient and want to know the figures. (I sometimes comment that they did not come into the room wanting to know the life expectancy of people in Lesotho. The activity always creates a need to know.)

I then display the most up-to-date figures I can find. Figure 13.2 shows statistics available at the end of 2012 and is included to illustrate the range of life expectancies. The first thing participants want to do is to comment to each other in groups. After this, I ask them to write the correct figures in the last column of their estimates table (Figure 13.1).

I then debrief the activity by asking:

▲ How accurate were your guesses: in identifying countries? in identifying figures?

▲ Which countries and which figures were most accurate in your guesses? Why do you think this was?

▲ Which countries/figures were most surprising? Why do you think this was?

▲ Which of your explanations of the figures seem most likely? How would you find out?

This activity can be followed up in various ways:

▲ Students could investigate the world pattern of life expectancy, using atlases or online maps (World Bank, WHO and Gapminder websites) and produce their own annotated maps to identify key features, show the pattern or produce a list of generalisations.

▲ Students could investigate factors affecting life expectancy in particular countries.

▲ Students could investigate how life expectancy at birth relates to other indices of social and economic development.

I have found that this activity produces very valuable dialogic discussion and it is worth allowing time for the activity, the initial discussion and the debriefing.

Country	Life expectancy at birth
Australia	82
Bangladesh	65
Bolivia	68
Brazil	73
Cambodia	61
China	74
Egypt	71
Germany	80
India	65
Italy	82
Jamaica	71
Japan	83
Kenya	60
Lesotho*	48
Malawi*	47
Malaysia	73
Mexico	76
Pakistan	63
Poland	76
Russia	68
Saudi Arabia	72
Singapore	82
Somalia*	51
South Africa	54
United Kingdom	80
USA	79

Figure 13.2: Average life expectancy at birth.
Source: World Health Organisation, 2012.

Example: What might Patriot Hills in Antarctica be like?

This activity could be used as an introduction to an investigation of aspects of Antarctica, e.g. issues related to its use by different nations and for different purposes. It is designed to elicit what students already know about Antarctica and to introduce them to some background geographical information about the continent. It has been very successful when I have used it with PGCE students, and when they have used it in schools.

The context for the activity was deciding how useful the final episode of the BBC series *Pole to Pole* (1992) would be to introduce students to an investigation of an issue related to Antarctica. I use the following procedure.

1. I explain to students that they are going to make an imaginary journey from Chile to Patriot Hills in Antarctica.

2. I show a ten-minute extract from the programme, starting when the passengers are getting on the plane in Chile and stopping it just before the plane lands at Patriot Hills. (It is important to preview the film to know exactly when to stop: the whole point of the activity is lost if the plane has actually landed. A good point to stop might be after Michael Palin has been shown the map of Antarctica on the plane.)

3. After stopping the film, I invite students to speculate on what Patriot Hills might be like. Sometimes I have asked them to jot down ideas individually before sharing in pairs or small groups. Sometimes I have suggested categories, such as weather, landscape and what will be at Patriot Hills.

4. I collect in their ideas and write them down without comment, usually in these categories: landscape; weather; Patriot Hills itself; buildings; with speculative prompts – I wonder what the weather will be like when they land? How cold do you think it will be? I collect as many different responses as possible. For temperature, responses often vary from -5°C to -40°C. Responses for what will be at Patriot Hills are usually the most varied. Some students think it will all be very high tech with a good airport and sophisticated buildings designed to withstand the cold. Some think there will be shops and even a McDonald's. Some think there will be a few huts. We discuss why they think this and what are the most likely things.

5. I ask if they want to see what Patriot Hills is like and they invariably say 'yes'. Again, the activity has created a need to know. I show the next ten-minute extract and ask them to concentrate both on what they see and what they hear.

Photo: NASA Goddard Photo and Video (Creative Commons Licence).

6. I debrief the activity by going though the categories of landscape, weather, buildings and people and ask what surprised students and why. I ask 'How much can you tell about Antarctica from this extract?' 'In what ways might it be misleading?' 'What else do you need to find out?'

As a follow-up activity, students could list everything they have learnt about Antarctica so far from the two 10-minute extracts and use this to write a report. Alternatively students could complete a KWL grid (Chapter 5) or a 'layers of inference' diagram (Figure 17.1) about Patriot Hills.

PGCE students who have used this activity in schools often continue to show the whole episode, so that students get a bigger picture of Antarctica and because the activity has really sparked students' curiosity. It does meet the other purpose of using intelligent guesswork i.e. eliciting prior knowledge including misunderstandings which can be discussed before continuing with some sort of investigation of Antarctica.

Suggestion for research

Investigate students' prior knowledge and understanding of a theme or place by using the intelligent guesswork strategy.

References

BBC (1992) *Pole to Pole* (DVD). London: BBC Publications.

Bruner, J. (1966) *Toward a Theory of Instruction*. Cambridge, MA: Harvard University Press.

Central Intelligence Agency (CIA) website: Statistics for life expectancy at birth from *The World Factbook*. Available online at *https://www.cia.gov/library/publications/the-world-factbook/rankorder/2102rank.html* (last accessed 14 February 2013).

Gapminder website: Life expectancy at birth. Available online at *www.gapminder.org/?s=life+expectancy* (last accessed 15 December 2012). Data is presented in three forms:

▲ Spreadsheet: Statistics listed alphabetically by country, 1800 to 2011.

▲ Graph: Life expectancy plotted against GDP (or other chosen indicator) sliding graphics, 1800–2011.

▲ World map of life expectancy at birth sliding graphics, 1700–2011.

United Nations Department of Economic and Social Affairs website: Life expectancy at birth – both sexes (also separate statistics for male and female) spreadsheets, listed by area, region and country. Available online at *http://esa.un.org/wpp/Excel-Data/mortality.htm* (last accessed 15 December 2012)

World Bank website: Statistics for life expectancy at birth. Available online at *http://data.worldbank.org/indicator/SP.DYN.LE00.IN* (last accessed 15 November 2012).

World Health Organisation (2012) Life expectancy data table. Available online at *http://apps.who.int/gho/data/?vid=710* (last accessed 14 February 2013).

World Health Organisation website: Map of life expectancy at birth. Available online at *http://gamapserver.who.int/mapLibrary/Files/Maps/Global_LifeExpectancy_2009_bothsexes.png* (last accessed 15 December 2012).

Five Key Points

CHAPTER 14

'The desire to find order in the world is a fundamental human need' (Bonnett, 2008, p. 9).

'If you do not know why you are looking at data, if you are looking just to find a story with little idea of what may matter, you are very likely to make a mistake ... You should know why you are interested in what you are looking at before you try and determine what is happening' (Dorling, 2005, p. 249).

'Five Key Points' is the name I have given to a strategy in which students examine geographical source material and identify key points in the form of statements. The number of points could vary according to the source. This chapter addresses the following questions:

▲ What kinds of geographical source materials can be used for Five Key Points?

▲ What are the purposes of using Five Key Points?

▲ What needs to be considered when planning to use Five Key Points?

▲ What is the general procedure for using Five Key Points?

The chapter then presents two examples with comments on their use:

▲ Tourist arrivals in ASEAN countries

▲ Interpreting climate graphs

What kinds of geographical source materials can be used for Five Key Points?

The ideal source material presents secondary data which has not been 'processed' too much by a textbook or website author, so the key points have not already been identified. A wide range of geographical sources could be used including:

▲ A photograph or set of photographs

▲ A film

▲ A table of statistics

▲ A graph

▲ A topographical map

▲ An atlas map – e.g. a political map, a physical map or a distribution map

▲ A Worldmapper map (Figure 14.1)

▲ A Gapminder graph (Figure 14.2).

What are the purposes of using Five Key Points?

The main purpose of Five Key Points is to enable students to examine and interpret sources for themselves. The aim is that, through using the activity and discussing it, students would develop their skills in using sources, increase their knowledge and understanding of geography and gain confidence in using source materials independently.

What needs to be considered when planning to use Five Key Points?

▲ How does the activity relate to the key question being investigated? Does it contribute to what is being learnt?

▲ Do the students have sufficient skills to have an initial attempt? Do they need scaffolding of some sort before they use the strategy for the first time?

▲ Do the data lend themselves to this activity? Are there at least five key points?

▲ What are the key points? It is worth identifying some key points before the activity is used.

▲ How many key points should students be expected to identify? (It doesn't have to be five.) Students need to be clear that the point of the activity is to help them analyse and interpret data. They should not get the impression that there are only five points or that everyone should agree on them.

▲ How long should students have to identify key points?

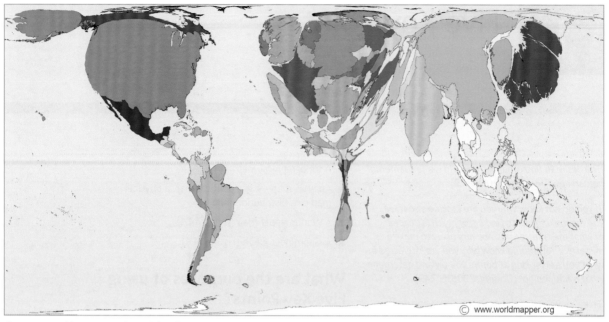

Figure 14.1: Worldmapper Map of Wealth (2002). The territory size shows the proportion of worldwide wealth found there when GDP is adjusted for local purchasing power. Source: © SASI Group (University of Sheffield) and Mark Newman (University of Michigan).

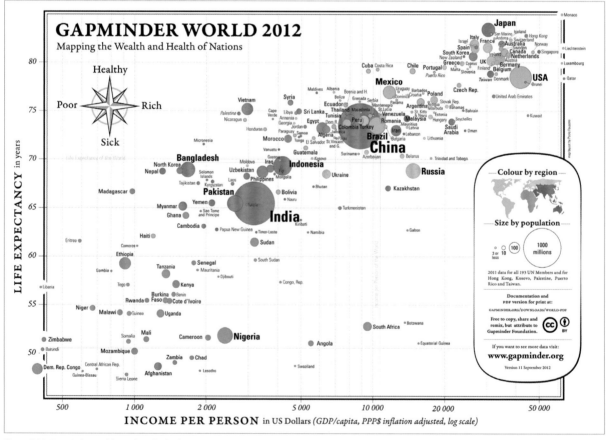

Figure 14.2: Gapminder World Map (2012). The chart compares all UN members and other countries and territories with more than 1 million people by income and health. Source: © Gapminder (www.gapminder.org)

- ▲ Should this be done individually or in pairs or groups?
- ▲ How is the activity going to be debriefed?
- ▲ How can the activity be linked to what students are going to do next?

What is the general procedure for using Five Key Points?

- ▲ Ensure that students are aware of the overall focus of the enquiry.
- ▲ Ask students to look carefully at the source material. If necessary, explain the meaning of any terms in the resources or draw attention to units of measurement used or scale of map, etc.
- ▲ Ask students individually or in pairs to write down five (or an appropriate number between 3 and 10) key statements, giving an example of each statement. A smaller number is preferable as it focuses attention and additional points can be added in discussion.
- ▲ Ask students to share their ideas with another person or in a small group and try to reach a consensus. Students could then write their key points on flip-chart paper.
- ▲ Get feedback from one group (or one statement from each group until there are no more key points) and display their points on the whiteboard or flip-chart paper. Then ask other groups if they have anything to add.
- ▲ Discuss the list of statements as a class. Which are the most important points? Why? Is the example illustrating this statement a good one? Which are less important points and why? If any important points have not been identified by students, they should be added to the list.
- ▲ Debriefing could include a discussion on the types of generalisations that can be made from different geographical source materials and how they need to be qualified.
- ▲ Students could be asked to make a record of the key points agreed by the class.

Although I have used this strategy with students in schools and with PGCE students, the example below is based on my most recent use of the strategy which was with teachers.

Example: Tourist arrivals in ASEAN countries

I used the statistics in Figure 14.3, related to tourist arrivals in the 10 Association of South East Asian Nations (ASEAN) countries, in workshops with teachers in Singapore. It was in the context of the revised Singapore O-level geography syllabus which advocates an enquiry approach. One of the six areas of content to be investigated is global tourism. This part of the syllabus includes an investigation of different types of tourism, trends in global tourism, long-haul and short-haul destinations, fluctuations from place to place and from year to year. The syllabus includes the skill of extracting information from tables and graphs. The purpose of using Five Key Points was to not to provide a definitive resource for the syllabus, but to explore the value of using this strategy, this kind of data and issues that might arise in the classroom.

I related what we were doing to the key question from the syllabus 'Why has tourism become a global phenomenon?' and its subsidiary questions related to trends and fluctuations. Before distributing the sheets containing the table of statistics I showed a map and list of ASEAN countries and asked each group to speculate on which country had the highest number of tourist arrivals and which had the least. I was using 'intelligent guesswork' as a three-minute stimulus activity. I wanted to ensure that they all knew the complete list of ASEAN countries and to provoke curiosity. I did not intend to discuss their choices of key points in detail, although this could be done with secondary school students if appropriate.

I then gave out the table of statistics, drawing their attention to the fact that the figures were in thousands. The intelligent guesswork had sparked their curiosity in that all groups immediately checked whether their initial ideas were correct and made comments to each other; they were interested to see the figures.

Next I asked them individually to identify what they thought were the five most important points they could make about tourist arrivals from these statistics. They annotated their tables of statistics and circled figures that could be used to exemplify the key points. I then asked them, in their groups, to share their decisions and reasoning. Each group listed their points on flip-chart papers. I asked one group to present their flip-chart list and the other groups if they had further key points to add. In all the workshops I ran, more than five key points were identified by the group as whole. The kinds of points they made were about significant individual figures and about trends.

Points made about significant individual figures:

- ▲ Overall maximum and minimum figures
- ▲ The country with the maximum number of tourist arrivals

ASEAN country	2007			2008			2009		
	Intra-ASEAN	Extra-ASEAN	Total	Intra-ASEAN	Extra-ASEAN	Total	Intra-ASEAN	Extra-ASEAN	Total
Brunei Darussalam	85	94	179	98	128	226	78	80	158
Cambodia	410	1605	2015	553	1573	2126	693	1469	2162
Indonesia	1523	3982	5506	2775	3654	6429	2102	4222	6324
Laos	1273	351	1624	1286	719	2005	1611	397	2008
Malaysia	15 620	4616	20 236	16 637	5416	22 053	18 386	5260	23 646
Myanmar	53	679	732	463	198	661	524	239	763
The Philippines	236	2856	3092	254	2885	3139	256	2762	3017
Singapore	3725	6563	10 288	3571	6545	10 117	3651	6030	9681
Thailand	3755	10 709	14 464	4125	10 472	14 598	4075	10 075	14 150
Vietnam	661	3488	4150	516	3738	4254	319	3453	3772
Total	27 341	34 943	62 285	30 276	35 329	65 606	31 694	33 987	65 680

▲ The country with the minimum number of tourist arrivals

▲ The country with the maximum number of tourists from within the ASEAN area

▲ The country with the minimum number of tourists from within the ASEAN area

▲ The country with the maximum number of tourists from outside the ASEAN area

▲ The country with the minimum number of tourists from outside the ASEAN area

Points made about trends: changes between 2007 and 2011:

▲ General changes

▲ General changes in arrivals within ASEAN countries

▲ General changes in arrivals from outside ASEAN countries

▲ Countries in which the trend was different from the general trend

▲ Years in which there were changes in the trend in specific countries

▲ Countries with the greatest increase (total or proportion)

▲ Countries with the smallest increase

I then debriefed the activity, asking questions such as: which are the most important of the points they identified? What kinds of things did they look for (maximum, minimum, trends, anomalies)? Did any figures surprise them? What might explain their statements?

We then stood back from the activity and I debriefed them as teachers. What was the value of getting students to do this? What problems might they have in using this kind of data? The teachers thought it was valuable in focusing attention on data and in considering the types of points that could be made from statistics. They thought the table too daunting for some students and suggested smaller tables of statistics when using this strategy for the first time.

Students could follow up this activity by:

▲ annotating a map of the area with the five key points and supporting statistics

▲ investigating tourism in one of these countries, chosen either by the teacher and supported with resources, or researched by students, with the teacher providing web links

▲ using other information on the ASEAN website to find out more about origins of tourists.

Example: Interpreting climate graphs

Climate graphs are valuable sources of geographical information and it is important that students can interpret them. Using the Five Key Points strategy with climate graphs, followed by discussion, could enable them to interpret them independently rather than relying on lists of questions telling them exactly what to do.

This strategy should be used when students need to interpret climate graphs for the theme they are investigating. For example they might be

ASEAN country	2010			2011		
	Intra-ASEAN	Extra-ASEAN	Total	Intra-ASEAN	Extra-ASEAN	Total
Brunei Darussalam	110	104	214	124	118	242
Cambodia	853	1655	2508	1101	1781	2882
Indonesia	2339	4664	7003	3259	4391	7650
Laos	1991	522	2513	2191	532	2724
Malaysia	18 937	5640	24 577	18 885	5829	24 714
Myanmar	512	279	791	100	716	816
The Philippines	298	3222	3520	332	3586	3918
Singapore	4780	6859	11 639	5372	7799	13 171
Thailand	4534	11 402	15 936	5530	13 568	19 098
Vietnam	466	4584	5050	838	5176	6014
Total	34 820	38 933	73 753	37733	43 496	81 229

Figure 14.3: Tourist arrivals in ASEAN countries as of 30 June 2012. Figures in thousands of arrivals. Source: ASEAN website. Note: details may not add up to totals due to rounding errors.

investigating, in relation to a particular part of the world:

▲ the influence of climate on vegetation

▲ the potential of an area for tourism

▲ the impact of the monsoon on India.

Students should understand why they need to examine and interpret climate graphs. They might need explanation of units of measurement or of the way average figures are calculated. They need to be aware of the differences between average temperature figures (as a monthly average of daily figures, then these figures averaged over a period of years) and average rainfall figures (which are total figures in a month, then the monthly totals averaged over a period of years). Some climate graphs require an understanding of negative numbers.

Procedure

Students work in pairs to identify five key points. Key points are shared between pairs: they agree on their five points and exemplify them with details from the graph. The key points are shared as a class.

Students then discuss the kinds of points that can be made from a study of climate graphs, with evidence for each statement being requested and checked. The following list suggests some of the points that might be made.

▲ Maximum temperature figure

▲ Minimum temperature figure

▲ Seasonal variations in temperature

▲ Range of temperature

▲ Distribution of rainfall throughout the year

▲ Total rainfall figure

▲ How the pattern of rainfall relates to the pattern of temperature

▲ What the figures suggest about the location of the place.

Using Five Key Points with climate graphs followed by discussion could enable students to:

▲ understand how the figures are calculated and therefore what they mean

▲ relate the figures to their own experiences of temperature and precipitation patterns

▲ understand the difference between weather and climate

▲ develop the skills of reading climate graphs so that they can read them independently

▲ develop knowledge about the climate of particular locations.

There are many sources of climate graphs, e.g. atlases and websites. It is worth looking for climate graphs that use conventions common in geography and in atlases: e.g. putting the scales for temperature and precipitation on different sides of the graph; using scales in degrees Celsius for temperature and millimetres for precipitation; showing average monthly temperatures on a single line graph or, if average maximum and average minimum monthly temperatures would be useful, then on two line graphs; showing average monthly precipitation totals on a bar graph.

Suggestion for research

Investigate the use of Five Key Points with different kinds of source materials. Analyse data from students' work, from debriefing discussions and from questionnaires or interviews. Evaluate the contribution Five Key Points makes to students' learning.

References

ASEAN website: *www.aseansec.org.* Statistics for 2007–10 taken from *www.aseansec.org/Stat/Table28.pdf* (last accessed 27 September 2012), updated with 2011 statistics from *www.asean.org/images/pdf/resources/statistics/table%2028%20n.pdf* (last accessed 3 December 2012).

Bonnett, A. (2008) *What is Geography?* London: Sage.

Dorling, D. (2005) 'Counting and measuring' in Castree, N., Rogers, A. and Sherman, D. (eds) *Questioning Geography.* Oxford: Blackwell.

Mind maps

CHAPTER 15

'*I always had trouble seeing the big picture and this has given me a skill to help bring it together.* (First year undergraduate, quoted in Lloyd *et al.*, 2010, p. 185).

Mind maps were developed by Tony Buzan to help his students with note-taking. He first published his ideas in 1974 in his book, *Use Your Head*. He continued developing ideas about how to use mind maps in educational and business contexts and in 1995 the first edition of his *Mind Map Book* was published. Several other books followed, including *Mind Maps for Kids* (Buzan, 2003). There is also a dedicated website through which it is possible to buy mind mapping software.

This chapter addresses the following questions:

▲ What are the differences between spider diagrams, mind maps and concept maps?

▲ What are the characteristics of mind maps?

▲ How can mind maps and spider diagrams be used?

▲ What needs to be considered when planning to use mind maps?

▲ What is the general procedure for using mind maps?

▲ What are the advantages and disadvantages of using mind maps?

The chapter then presents five examples of mind maps with comments on their use:

▲ Doing something about global warming

▲ Rivers, floods and management

▲ Water

▲ The future of Singapore

▲ Sea level rise.

What are the differences between spider diagrams, mind maps and concept maps?

The terms spider diagram, mind map and concept map are often used, in books and journals about geographical education, interchangeably, as if they all mean the same thing. So although the ideas of 'mind maps' and 'concept maps' were developed with very specific meanings, these have been subject to slippage because of the way the terms are used. It is, however, useful to distinguish between these three types of graphic organisers as they can achieve different purposes in geographical education (Davies, 2011). Figure 15.1 outlines their characteristics.

Mind maps serve the same purposes as spider diagrams but are more elaborate because of their use of colour and illustrations. Although I think spider diagrams are extremely useful as graphic organisers, I am not devoting a chapter to them, partly because they are already familiar to readers and partly because they were not initially developed with any specific rules. I would, however, encourage the use of spider diagrams as they are simple for students to use when sorting out ideas. However, I think it is confusing to refer to them as mind maps or concept maps, which were developed with specific characteristics, outlined in this chapter and the next.

What are the characteristics of mind maps?

A mind map is a sophisticated spider diagram with a hierarchical structure that uses colour and illustrations to categorise information and ideas. Buzan set out strict rules about how they should be drawn:

▲ They are focused on a theme, the name of which is centrally placed.

▲ Main branches radiate out from the centre, each branch representing a different aspect of the main

	Spider diagrams	Mind maps	Concept maps
What they look like			
Origin	In general use for decades	Tony Buzan, 1974	Novak, 1972
What they do	Categorise information and ideas into categories and sub-categories	Categorise information into categories and sub-categories	Identify relationships between concepts
Distinguishing features	No specific rules – developed as wanted Can be developed with sub-categories and links as considered useful No need to use colours to categorise	Emphasis on classification Labels categories and sub-categories Uses colour to classify categories Uses illustrations	Emphasis on labelling nature of links between concepts Nodes of diagram are concepts In original form, concepts arranged hierarchically

Figure 15.1: What are the differences between spider diagrams, mind maps and concept maps?

theme. Each branch is drawn in a different colour and labelled. Main branches are drawn thickly.

▲ Sub-branches are drawn growing out of the main branches to represent sub-topics. These, and the sub-branches growing out from them, are drawn in the same colour as the main branch from which they grow and are each labelled with a single word.

How can mind maps and spider diagrams be used?

Mind maps and less formally structured spider diagrams can be used for various aspects of geographical enquiry:

▲ to connect with prior knowledge and experience by asking students to draw mind maps of their current knowledge on the topic/issue being studied. This brainstorming can be carried out as a whole-class, a group or an individual activity

▲ to provide a scaffold or 'advanced organiser' for the enquiry, by presenting a skeleton mind map to students at the start of an enquiry with some branches and sub-branches named

▲ to provide an overview of a topic on a completed mind map from which questions can be generated

▲ for students to make notes, and as an analytical tool to sort out information and ideas presented in geographical sources, e.g. articles, film (Lloyd et al., 2010)

▲ for students to reconstruct information they have analysed in a DART (see Chapter 19)

▲ for students to make presentations to the rest of the class

▲ for students to review what has been investigated in a unit of work

▲ to help students plan what they are going to include in an essay or a report

▲ to assess students' knowledge: diagnostically at the start of a unit of work; formatively, part way through a unit of work or summatively, at the end of a unit of work

▲ to assess students in a formal examination (Lloyd et al., 2010)

▲ as a homework activity

▲ by students for revision purposes to check their own understanding and to provide a record that might be more easily memorable than notes

▲ by the teacher as a tool to help plan a unit of work, to identify the key topics/factors that will be introduced. The branches can relate either to different aspects of planning for enquiry, e.g. key questions; key concepts; creating a need to know; data to be used; activities for making sense of data; debriefing activities; opportunities for assessment; or to the content of the lesson, identifying its different geographical components.

What needs to be considered when planning to use mind maps?

▲ Does the topic or issue being investigated lend itself to being mapped on a mind map or spider diagram? Can the information or ideas be divided into categories and sub-categories?

▲ What is the purpose of using the mind map? Is it to spark curiosity, to elicit prior knowledge, to help students analyse geographical source material, or for assessment?

▲ If the mind map is to be applied to geographical resources, what categories and sub-categories are likely to be found?

▲ Should the activity be carried out individually, in pairs or in small groups (three or four maximum)?

▲ To what extent should students be free to develop their own mind map or would the activity benefit from teacher guidance, e.g. categories for the main branches?

▲ What support might students need, e.g. modelling the process, showing a finished mind map, providing skeleton mind maps or helping individuals and groups through discussion?

▲ How should the activity be debriefed?

What is the general procedure for using mind maps?

Ensure that students are aware of the focus of the enquiry and the purpose of constructing the mind map. If students are unfamiliar with mind maps it is worth modelling the process by demonstrating and talking through their construction. Students could be shown a completed mind map so that they know what they look like. Give clear instructions:

▲ Turn the paper or flip-chart paper sideways (landscape).

▲ Write the main topic in the centre of the page, so that there is room to extend the diagram in all directions.

▲ For each main topic or idea draw a branch from the centre with a curved line, using a different colour for each branch. Label the branch. Mind maps work best if there are between three and six main branches.

▲ Then add small sub-branches, branching out from the thick main branches, using the same colour as the main branch from which they come. Label each sub-branch. You could add sub-sub-branches. The width of the sub-branches

and sub-sub-branches should reduce in the same way as the branches and sub-branches of a tree get narrower the further they are from the trunk.

▲ Add illustrations where possible.

This procedure could be varied. If students find it difficult to categorise data, they could be given a list of the broad categories to include, or the broad categories for the main branches could be agreed through a whole-class discussion related to geographical data. At the end of an enquiry or this particular activity, one or two groups could present their mind maps to the class. This could be followed by class discussion, inviting different suggestions, probing students' reasoning, inviting students to express uncertainties, correcting misunderstandings.

Although Buzan developed strict procedures for the construction of mind maps, it is possible to draw versions of mind maps, e.g. extended spider diagrams, which do not use colour but which are still extremely useful.

What are the advantages and disadvantages of using mind maps?

Advantages

▲ They can provide an overview of a theme, at either the start or the end of an investigation.

▲ They can be used to sort out and categorise information or ideas.

▲ They encourage analytical thinking about a topic or issue.

▲ They can be more easily memorable than notes.

Disadvantages

▲ Mind maps are limited by their nature: they are designed to map out categories and sub-categories of information and ideas, not to explain the links between them.

▲ They can become over-complex and this would make them difficult to remember.

Example: Doing something about global warming

Focus of enquiry: Can we do anything about global warming?

Figure 15.2 maps out some ideas for 'solving global warming'. This could be used with students in different ways:

- To show students what a mind map looks like and how main branches, sub-branches, colour and illustrations have been used.
- To investigate, using other sources, the extent to which the things listed contribute to carbon emissions and their relative contributions.
- To discuss the relative importance of the proposed solutions.
- To probe the assumptions implicit in the mind map, e.g. that individuals rather than government or international action can 'solve global warming'.

Other mind maps on the same website (*http://learningfundamentals.com.au/resources*) include: energy saving tips for your school and impacts of global warming (related to degrees of warming). Instead of using these actual mind maps with students, they might generate ideas of what kinds of mind maps students could be asked to create themselves.

Example: Rivers, floods and management

Mind maps can be used to map out the content of a theme to be studied, providing students with an overview, an advanced organiser and a check list of what needs to be investigated. It

can also be used as a revision list. Figure 15.3 is an example of a mind map of the theme 'Rivers, floods and management' in the AQA geography AS/AS examination specification. It shows how mind maps do not necessarily have to adhere to Buzan's rules. This map has ten main branches, which is unusually large, does not use colour or illustrations. But it could be used as a model to demonstrate to students what a mind map looks like and to discuss the extent to which they find it useful to map out a theme in this way.

Example: Water

The mind map in Figure 15.4 was produced by a secondary school student in Singapore. Students investigating sources of water were given the categories of the main branches – sources, importance, uses and renewable – and were asked to develop the mind map from information from a textbook.

Example: The future of Singapore

The mind map in Figure 15.5 was produced by a secondary school student in Singapore during a social studies course focusing on Singapore's

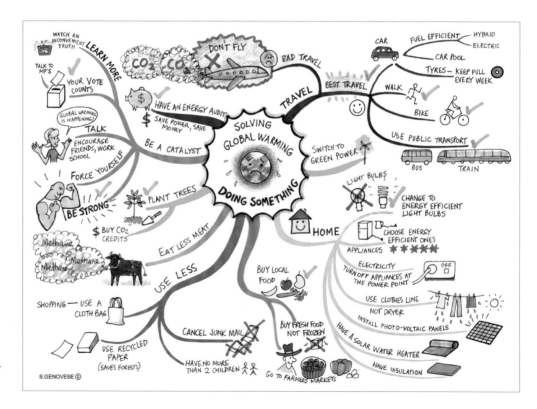

Figure 15.2: Mind map showing ways in which individuals could 'solve' global warming. Source: *www.learningfundamentals.com.au*

Causes of flooding
- Human causes
- Physical causes
- Frequency
- Magnitude
- Risk assessment
- MEDC case study
- LEDC case study

Impact of flooding
- MEDC case study
- LEDC case study

Rejuvenation
- Incised meanders
- River terraces
- Knick points
- Waterfalls

Landforms
- Erosional
  - Gorge
  - Waterfalls
  - Potholes
  - Rapids
  - Meanders
  - Oxbow lakes
- Depositional
  - Floodplains
  - Deltas
  - Braiding
  - Levees

Rivers, floods and management

Flood management
- Hard
  - Dams
  - Raising levees
  - Meander cut-through
  - Diversionary spillways
- Soft
  - Afforestation
  - Land use management
  - Forecasts and warning
  - River restoration
  - Wetland and river bank conservation

Hydrological cycle
- Closed system
- Water balance

Drainage basin
- Storm hydrograph
- Long profile
  - Upper course
  - Middle course
  - Lower course

Changing channel characteristics
- Roughness
- Cross-sectional area
- Wetted perimeter
- Hydraulic radius
- Velocity — Efficiency
- Discharge

Valley profiles
- Graded profile
- Cross-sectional profile
- Long profile
- Potential and kinetic energy

Processes
- Erosion
  - Hydraulic action
  - Corrasion
  - Corrosion
  - Attrition
- Transportation
  - Solution
  - Suspension
  - Bedload
    - Saltation
    - Traction
- Deposition
- Hjulström curve
- Types of load

Figure 15.3: Mind map showing what is included in the theme of rivers, floods and management in AQA AS/A2 geography specification, 2008.

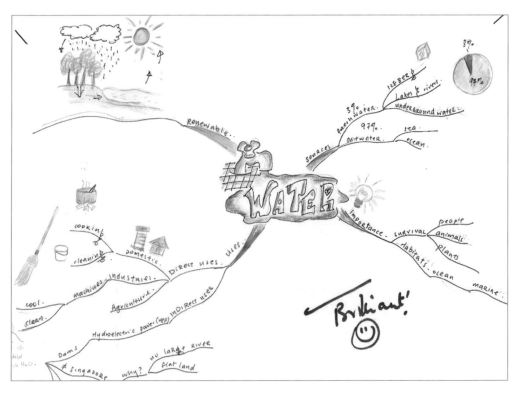

Figure 15.4: Sources, importance and uses of water.

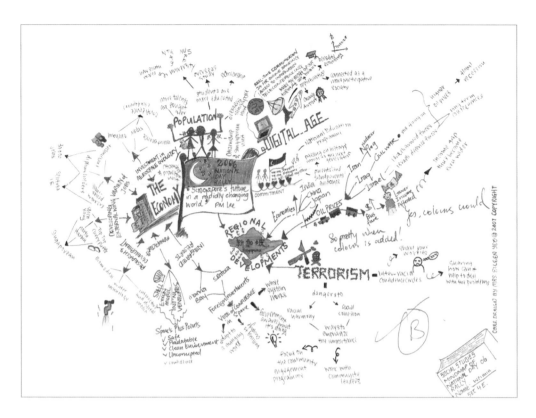

Figure 15.5: Mind map speculating on Singapore's future in a rapidly changing world.

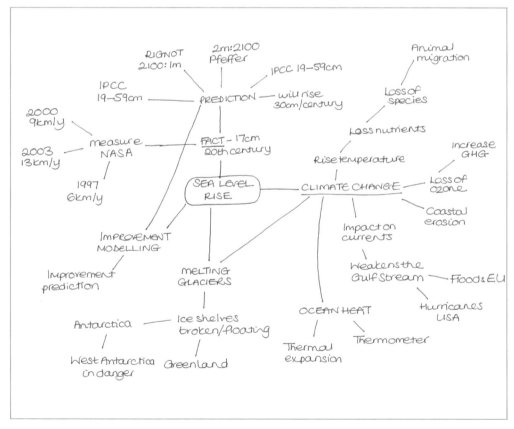

Figure 15.6: 'Mind map' on sea level rise.

future in a rapidly changing world. Categories were provided for the main branches of the mind map: population, the economy, the digital age and terrorism.

Example: Sea level rise

The spider diagram in Figure 15.6 was produced by a first-year undergraduate at Southern Cross University, Australia, during a course on global environmental issues. Students were asked to use mind maps to analyse journal articles relevant to the unit of study.

Suggestions for research

1. Investigate the different ways in which mind maps can be used in geography and evaluate the extent to which they can support learning.

2 Collect data in the form of students' completed mind maps and in questionnaires or interviews.

References

Buzan, T. (2003) *Mind Maps for Kids: An introduction*. London: Thorsons.

Buzan, T. (1995) *The Mind Map Book*. London: BBC Books.

Buzan, T. (1974) *Use Your Head*. London: BBC Books.

Davies, M. (2011) 'Concept mapping, mind mapping, argument mapping: what are the differences and do they matter?', *Higher Education,* 62, 3, pp. 279–301.

Lloyd, D., Boyd, B. and den Exter, K. (2010) 'Mind mapping as an interactive tool for engaging complex geographical issues', *New Zealand Geographer,* 66, 3, pp. 181–8.

Websites with information about mind mapping:

iMindMap, Mind Mapping software: *www.thinkbuzan.com/uk; www.thinkbuzan.com/uk/articles*

Mind map of rivers, floods and management, AQA AS/A2 geography, 2008: *http://zigzageducation.co.uk/synopses/2854.asp*

CHAPTER 16

Concept maps

'*Concept maps are graphical tools for organizing and representing knowledge. They include concepts, usually enclosed in circles or boxes of some type, and relationships between concepts indicated by a connecting line linking two concepts*' (Novak and Cañas, 2008).

The idea of concept maps was developed initially at Cornell University, USA, in 1972 by Joseph Novak and his research group. They were influenced by Ausubel's theory of meaningful learning (1963) which according to Ausubel (2010) depends on an active process of 'relating new potentially meaningful material to relevant ideas in the learner's cognitive structure' (p. 4). Novak continued to develop his ideas on concept maps (Novak, 2010; Novak and Cañas, 2008) and encouraged their widespread use.

This chapter addresses the following questions:

▲ What are the characteristics of concept maps?

▲ How can concept maps be used?

▲ What needs to be considered when planning to use concept maps?

▲ What is the general procedure for using concept maps?

▲ What are the advantages and disadvantages of using concept maps?

The chapter then presents an example of using concept maps with reflections on its use.

What are the characteristics of concept maps?

A concept map consists of two parts:

▲ Concept labels, which form the nodes of the diagram. Usually the concept labels are circled or enclosed in boxes.

▲ Links between the concepts, which are shown as lines, with words or phrases written on the line to indicate the nature of the relationship. Sometimes arrows are marked on the line to indicate the direction of the relationship.

Concept maps can be very simple, based on a few concepts, or can be more elaborate with as many as 25 concepts and many links and cross links. The word or phrases linking two concepts form a proposition, which could be expanded and expressed as a sentence stating how the concepts are related. Depending on the purpose for which concept maps are used, what is written on the links could either be speculative or it could be based on evidence.

Novak's concept maps have a hierarchical structure with the broadest, more general concepts at the top of the map and sub-concepts placed below. When used like this, concept maps have a classificatory function as well as being used to explore relationships. Concept maps can be educationally valuable even if the concepts are not arranged hierarchically.

How can concept maps be used?

Concept maps are relevant to all aspects of geographical enquiry. They can be used:

▲ to spark curiosity by encouraging students to use their existing knowledge to speculate on links between concepts, e.g. links between different indices of development. In this example, the speculative links could be checked at a later stage of the enquiry by using a database to look at the extent of correlation between the different indices

▲ to provide a scaffold or 'advanced organiser' (Ausubel, 1960) for the enquiry, by presenting what Novak (2010) calls 'expert skeleton concept maps' to students at the start of an enquiry

▲ to represent information presented in geographical sources, e.g. in a report or film

▲ to support students' presentations of what they have learned from an enquiry

▲ to evaluate students' understanding and to elicit misunderstandings: diagnostically, at the start of a unit of work; formatively, part way through a unit of work, or summatively, at the end of a unit of work

▲ by students, for revision purposes and to check their own understanding

▲ by the teacher, as a tool to help plan a unit of work, to identify the key concepts that will be introduced and the nature of links between them.

What needs to be considered when planning to use concept maps?

▲ How can the use of a concept map contribute to developing understanding of what is being investigated? Does the topic or issue being investigated lend itself to identifying links between concepts?

▲ Which aspect of enquiry could concept maps support: sparking curiosity; making sense of data; reflecting on learning?

▲ If the concept map is to be applied to source material, what concepts and links are likely to be found?

▲ Should the activity be carried out individually, in pairs or in small groups? (three or four maximum)

▲ To what extent are students to make choices or should some choices be made by the teacher (e.g. about the list of concepts, which concept to start with, which data to use)?

▲ How many concepts are to be used initially and in total (between six and 20 is usually appropriate)?

▲ How are the concepts to be presented to students (e.g. listed on a board or on a worksheet, printed on cards, printed on sticky labels, or written on sticky notes by students)?

▲ What support might students need (e.g. modelling the process, showing a finished concept map, providing skeleton concept maps and helping individuals and groups through discussion)?

▲ Do the students need to be provided with a list of possible words to write on the links: a general list for use with all concept maps, a small list appropriate to the particular list of concepts, or no list at all?

▲ How should the activity be debriefed?

What is the general procedure for using concept maps?

Ensure that students know the key question being investigated – they could write it at the top of the concept map – and that they understand the purpose of constructing the concept map (e.g. to elicit prior knowledge, to analyse sources, etc.). If students are unfamiliar with using concept maps, it is worth modelling the process by talking through a demonstration. Incomplete concept maps, with a few concepts and links already included, could be provided as an introduction or as a means of differentiation.

Present the concepts to students either in a list or on cards, sticky notes or printed on labels. Some concepts are to be used at the outset and the rest to be left in a 'parking lot'. Instructions would vary according to decisions made, but could include:

▲ Work in pairs.

▲ Choose six concepts from the 'parking lot' which you think you relate to each other.

▲ Arrange them on a sheet of paper, leaving enough space to draw links between them and to label the links.

▲ Discuss possible links between the concepts.

▲ When you have agreed, draw lines linking together concepts that you think are related to each other.

▲ On the line write down how the concepts are related to each other (or use an appropriate phrase from the list of possible relationships).

▲ Draw an arrow to indicate the direction of the relationship.

▲ When you have identified as many links as you can between the initial set of six concepts, choose another concept from the 'parking lot', place it on the concept map, identify as many links as you can and write down the nature of the relationship. Choose another concept and do the same again.

After working in pairs, students could present their work to another pair. The group of four could jot down any points to raise in a whole-class discussion. One or two pairs or groups could present their concept maps to the class. A class discussion could follow, inviting different suggestions, probing students' reasoning, inviting students to express uncertainties, correcting misunderstandings. If time and attention is given to the quality of reasoning about the links, rather than simply the number of links, this can reinforce the importance of this part of the concept map and could lead to improved concept maps in future.

Debrief the construction of the concept maps in the context of the overall enquiry question. Which concepts seemed to have clear links with others? What was the nature of the links and how strong were they? Were there networks of links? Which relationships were students unsure about? Which relationships need qualifying or further investigation?

If concept maps have been used to encourage speculation about links, this activity could lead into an investigation of links using evidence. For example, if students had speculated on links between various indices of development, the debriefing could lead to a list of hypotheses about correlation which could be checked by using a correlation technique and a database or using a website such as Gapminder.

What are the advantages and disadvantages of using concept maps?

Advantages

▲ Concept maps emphasise connections between concepts and encourage deep thinking and understanding.

▲ They encourage active participation by students.

▲ They can reveal gaps in understanding or misunderstanding of relationships.

▲ They can enhance the quality of discussion between learners or between teachers and learners.

▲ They can be used to demonstrate an increase in understanding.

▲ Many students find visual presentation of complex relationships easier to understand and to remember than textual presentation.

▲ They have been used extensively and there is evidence of their value from research into their use in higher education (Hay *et al.*, 2008; Davies, 2011) and in school geography (Leat and Chandler, 1996).

Disadvantages

▲ Concept maps are challenging to construct. Although this can be seen as an advantage in that they demand deep thinking, when they are used for the first time their construction might need a lot of teacher support.

▲ Concept maps are time consuming to construct and require thorough debriefing so that students are not left with any misconceptions they have included in their maps.

▲ Evaluation of concept maps by teachers is time consuming.

▲ Maps can become overcomplicated, with too many overlapping links, so can confuse rather than clarify. Complicated maps are not easily memorable so when a large number of concepts is used, it is the process of constructing the concept map that helps revision, not the product.

▲ Concept maps were designed as a tool to map out relationships so are not suitable for all geographical topics and issues. Where the question is concerned with arguments, counter-arguments and different points of view, Toulmin's argument pattern diagram (Chapter 8) might be more appropriate.

Example: Global patterns of health and disease

This example draws from my experience of working with teachers in Singapore in preparation for their new O-level geography syllabus, which is to adopt an enquiry-based approach to classroom practice. I emphasised the need for students to be actively involved in making sense of what they were studying and it was in this context that I introduced teachers to concept mapping, a strategy none had used before. As I presented the course ten times I had the opportunity to reflect on and experiment with different ways of using the activity.

I focused the activity on one of the key questions in the syllabus: 'What are the global patterns of health and disease?'. The syllabus required a study of social, economic and environmental factors influencing health and provided a list of terms or concepts students needed to understand (Figure 16.1). I decided to use these for the concept mapping.

I gradually refined how I presented the concepts. The first time I used the activity, I simply gave a list, which saved preparation of cards, etc. The participants wrote the concepts directly onto flip-chart paper. The second time, I gave them the list of concepts together with some small sticky notes on which they wrote the concepts they selected. The sticky notes had the advantage of flexibility; at the start of the activity they could arrange and rearrange where they placed the concepts. After that the concepts were printed on address labels. This saved time and the printed labels made the concepts stand out clearly. Until they were stuck down they could be re-arranged easily.

I found from the first few workshops that verbal and written instructions were not enough to explain exactly what to do. In subsequent workshops I chose three concepts (e.g. infant mortality rate, life expectancy and malnutrition), wrote them on flip-chart paper and circled them. I then talked through my thinking. Is there a link between infant mortality rate and life expectancy? Yes, so I'll draw a line linking them. Which way is the relationship? Infant mortality rate affects life expectancy, so I'll draw an arrow on the line. What is the relationship? High infant mortality rate lowers average life expectancy, so I wrote that on the line. Then I looked at malnutrition. Yes, it did affect infant mortality, so I drew another line. Did it always lead to infant mortality? No, so I qualified what I wrote on the line, 'malnutrition can lead to higher infant mortality rates' and drew the arrow from malnutrition towards infant mortality. Demonstrating what to do and voicing my thinking, which took only a few minutes, made a huge difference.

The teachers worked collaboratively at their tables in groups of six to produce concept maps on flip-chart paper (Figure 16.2). There might have been greater individual involvement had the groups been smaller but there was more useful discussion than if they had worked in pairs.

Concepts related to health

infant mortality rate

life expectancy

daily calorie intake

sanitation

vaccination

doctor–patient ratio

patient–bed ratio

poverty

affluence

malnutrition

obesity

lifestyle

infectious diseases

parasitic diseases

degenerative diseases

epidemics

Figure 16.1: List of concepts related to health and disease (from Singapore O-level geography syllabus).

In the first workshop the teachers attempted to use all the concepts but this made their maps very complicated. In later workshops I suggested that they chose six concepts and left the rest in a 'parking lot' to use if they had time. Because of time pressures on the course and the need for time to

Figure 16.2: Constructing a concept map. Photo: Margaret Roberts.

Figure 16.3: Two examples of concept maps.

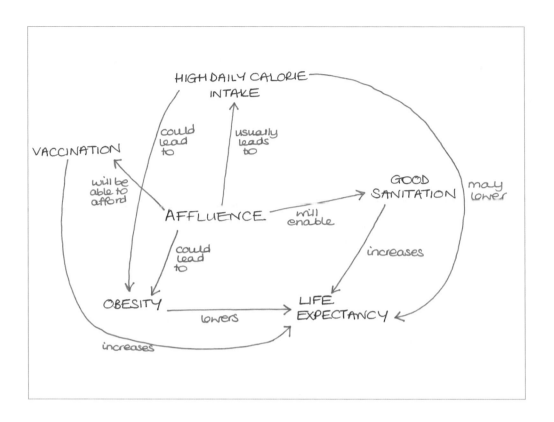

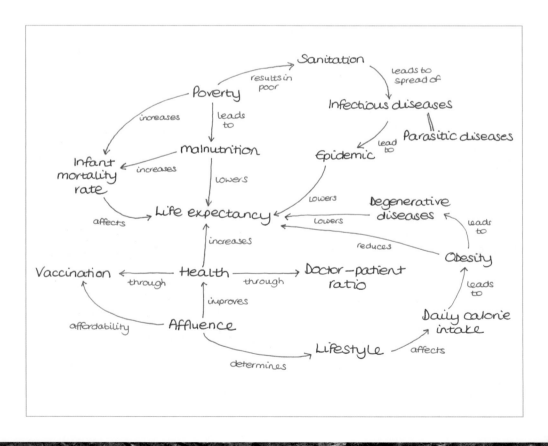

debrief the activity, the groups were allowed only 10 minutes to produce their concept maps. On one occasion one group were still debating which concepts to use when we finished the activity. On another occasion one group had chosen their six concepts but were discussing how to arrange them on the paper. In a school classroom I would have intervened, but I let this happen and used it to discuss issues related to using concept maps in schools. Although both these groups had very interesting discussions, they had not explored relationships between concepts. Some teachers decided that they would prefer to choose the six concepts for students. Some thought that if the main purpose was to discuss relationships then the concepts could be arranged and printed on a worksheet so that the first part of the activity was shortened.

Most groups worked quickly to discuss and identify relationships. Some focused on drawing lines rather than working out the nature of the relationships. Some wanted to draw as many links as possible and use a lot more concepts from the parking lot. I gradually changed the way I monitored and supported the groups, getting them to focus on the quality of their thinking about the relationship rather than the number of concepts and links they had mapped.

In the first workshops the groups put up their concept maps for others to look at. Later, before all the maps were displayed, I chose two groups to present their concept maps to the rest of the group and I probed their thinking about relationships. We then opened it up to discussion about which links they had found straightforward and what issues had arisen while they were doing it. I had learned that they did not realise the full value of using concept maps unless time was spent presenting, debriefing and discussing their maps and ideas. I also learned that it was important to challenge misconceptions and links that did not seem correct and that this was best done by listening and watching each group carefully and having dialogues with the groups rather than at the presentation stage. It was also helpful to highlight some of the misconceptions in the debriefing.

One idea that emerged during the discussion was that it could be helpful to provide students not only with the list of concepts, but with some ideas of the kinds of relationships concepts might have with each other, either as a list or as a set of cards (Figure 16.4).

Figure 16.5 provide lists of concepts related to some other geographical themes.

Link words

may indicate, can be, takes place when, influences, determines, is based on, is involved in, is increased/decreased by, requires, varies according to, will eventually lead to, may lead to, is necessary for

Figure 16.4: Possible words to be used on the links in concept maps.

Summary

Concept mapping is challenging and encourages valuable thinking and discussion about geographical concepts and relationships between concepts.

Suggestion for research

Choose a geographical theme. Use concept maps to investigate students' understanding, and misunderstandings, of concepts and relationships. If possible record some of their discussions or make observational notes. Use these together with completed concepts maps and interviews as data.

References

Ausubel, D. (1960) 'The use of advance organizers in the learning and retention of meaningful verbal material', *Journal of Educational Psychology,* 51, 5, pp. 267–72.

Ausubel, D. (1963) *The Psychology of Meaningful Verbal Learning.* New York, NY: Grune and Stratton.

Ausubel, D. (2010) *The Acquisition and Retention of Knowledge: A cognitive view.* Dordrecht: Kluwer Academic Publishers.

Davies, M. (2011) 'Concept mapping, mind mapping and argument mapping: what are the differences and do they matter?', *Higher Education,* 62, 2, pp. 279–301.

Hay, D., Kinchin, I. and Lygo-Baker, S. (2008) 'Making learning visible: the role of concept mapping in higher education', *Studies in Higher Education,* 33, 3, pp. 295–311.

Leat, D. and Chandler, S. (1996) 'Using concept mapping in geography teaching', *Teaching Geography,* 21, 3, pp. 108–12.

Novak, J.D. and Cañas, A.J. (2008) 'The theory underlying concept maps and how to construct them', *Technical Report IHMC CmapTools 2006-01 Rev 01-2008.* Pensacola, FL: Florida Institute for Human and Machine Cognition. Available online at *http://cmap.ihmc.us/Publications/ResearchPapers/TheoryUnderlyingConceptMaps.pdf* (last accessed 22 January 2013).

Novak, J. (2010) *Learning, Creating and Using Knowledge: Concept maps as facilitative tools in schools and corporations.* London: Routledge.

Globalisation

Trade
Nation states
International boundaries
Migration
Tourism
Technology
Ecology
Carbon emissions
Email
Internet
Finance
Inequality
Disease
Television programmes
Fashion
Transboundary pollution
Biodiversity
International organisations
Competition
Consumption
Food
International NGOs
Interdependence
Interconnectedness
Labour supply
Networks
Transport
Poverty
Sustainable development
Transnational corporations

Food

Staple food
Food consumption
Daily calorie intake
Disposable income
Organic food
Obesity
Malnutrition
Starvation
Scavenging
Food chain
Crop yield
Subsistence farming
Commercial farming
Intensification
Productivity
Labour
Land tenure
Land fragmentation
High-yielding varieties
Irrigation
Fertiliser
Pesticide
Green revolution
Genetically modified food
Animal breeding
Plant breeding
Organic farming
Agri-business
Extreme weather
Biofuel
Food subsidy
Food security
Stockpiling
Food distribution
Multiple cropping
Crop rotation
Soil conservation
Organic farming
Fair trade

Coasts

Waves
Tide
Currents
Geology
Ecosystem
Abrasion
Hydraulic action
Attrition
Solution
Longshore drift
Headland
Cliff
Caves
Arches
Stacks
Shore platform
Bay
Beach
Spit
Tombolo

Tourism

Honeypot tourism
Medical tourism
Health tourism
Film-induced tourism
Heritage tourism
Pilgrimage tourism
Domestic tourism
International tourism
Demand
Mass tourism
Niche tourism
Package holiday
Short-haul destination
Long-haul destinations
Eco-tourism
Budget airlines
Demand
Disposable income
Changing lifestyle
Carbon footprint

Volcanic activity

Core
Mantle
Continental crust
Oceanic crust
Tectonic plate
Convection current
Subduction zone
Divergent boundary
Convergent boundary
Transform boundary
Volcano
Pacific Ring of Fire
Shield volcano
Acid volcano
Composite volcano
Crater
Caldera
Vent
Magma
Magma chamber
Lava
Viscosity
Earthquake
Focus
Epicentre
Tsunami
Richter scale
Hazards
Aftershocks

Weather and climate

Weather
Climate
Temperature
Latitude
Altitude
Continental effect
Maritime effect
Cloud cover
Relative humidity
Evaporation
Condensation
Saturation
Clouds
Precipitation
Convectional rain
Relief rain
Air pressure
Wind
Land breeze
Sea breeze
Monsoon winds
Prevailing wind
Wind speed
Wind direction
Ocean current
Air pressure

Figure 16.5: Lists from which concepts could be selected for concept mapping.

17

The layers of inference framework

'Skills associated with answering geographic questions include the ability to make inferences, based on information organized in graphic form (maps, tables, graphs) and in oral and written narratives' (Brown and LeVasseur, 2006, p. 9).

Many history teachers, but fewer geography teachers, are familiar with the 'layers of inference' framework. This framework has its origins in the way archaeologists deal with items of evidence they collect (Collingwood, 1956). When archaeologists are investigating a find, they examine it to see what they can find out from it directly; relate what they have found out to what they already know (make informed guesses or inferences); and decide what else they would like to know to make sense of the item.

This sequence has been adapted by history teachers, originally for use in primary schools, to produce the layers of inference framework (Figure 17.1) with its sequence of four questions (Riley, 1999).

This chapter addresses the following questions:

▲ What kinds of geographical source materials are suitable for the layers of inference framework?

▲ What are the purposes of using layers of inference in geography?

▲ What needs to be considered when planning to use layers of inference?

▲ What is the general procedure for using layers of inference?

The chapter then presents two examples with comments on their use:

▲ Investigating Victorian housing in history

▲ Studying a flood hydrograph

What kinds of geographical source materials are suitable for the layers of inference framework?

The sequence of questions in Figure 17.1 can be applied to almost any type of geographical source material, e.g. pieces of text, photographs, maps, graphs, statistics or film. It is important that the source material can be examined properly, so it could be presented separately as well as within the framework. Alternatively the framework could be listed in a worksheet as in Figure 17.2, adapted from Riley (1999).

What are the purposes of using layers of inference in geography ?

The layers of inference framework encourages students to:

▲ examine geographical source material closely, identifying what it shows

▲ draw on their prior knowledge in order to make inferences or informed guesses

▲ become aware that any geographical source material presents only partial evidence

▲ be curious and to ask questions

▲ discuss their ideas with each other

▲ be critical, scrutinising what is shown and what is not shown in a piece of evidence

▲ reveal what they understand already, and possibly reveal misunderstandings.

What needs to be considered when planning to use layers of inference?

▲ Can the layers of inference framework contribute to the investigation of the key question?

▲ When would be the best time during a unit of work to use the framework: at the start, as a stimulus; later, to focus on a particular piece of evidence; or as revision?

▲ Is it reasonable to assume that students will have sufficient prior knowledge or reasoning power to make inferences or informed guesses about the source material?

Figure 17.1: Layers of inference framework.

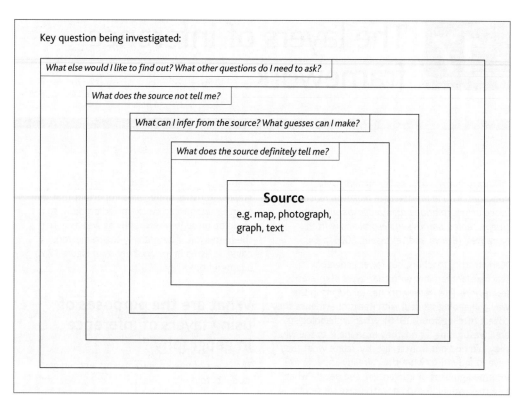

Key question being investigated:

What else would I like to find out? What other questions do I need to ask?

What does the source not tell me?

What can I infer from the source? What guesses can I make?

What does the source definitely tell me?

Source
e.g. map, photograph, graph, text

▲ What kind of source material would be most appropriate? Should different groups focus on different sources?

▲ Would it be preferable to present the questions in layers (Figure 17.1) or on a worksheet (Figure 17.2)?

Key question being investigated:
What does the source definitely tell me?
What can I infer from the source? **What guesses can I make?**
What does the source not tell me?
What else would I like to find out? **What other questions do I need to ask?**

Figure 17.2: Worksheet using layers of inference framework (based on Riley, 1999).

- Do the students need to be provided with some contextual information before they use the framework?

- If students have not carried out the activity before, should it be carried out as a whole-class activity or should it be modelled by talking through a different example?

- Would it be best for the activity to be carried out in pairs or small groups?

- How should the activity be debriefed?

- How can the activity be linked to activities that are to follow?

What is the general procedure for using layers of inference?

- Ensure that students are aware of the key question that forms the focus of the enquiry.

- Provide any necessary contextual information about the source material.

- Ask students to work collaboratively to discuss and write their ideas and questions in the framework.

- Debrief the activity going through each of the questions in turn so that students have the opportunity to share some of their suggestions. It would be helpful to correct any errors in interpretation or inference and to comment on questions.

Example 1: Investigating Victorian housing in history

The first example is taken from Riley's account (1999) of a year 9 history lesson. Although the lesson itself is not directly relevant to geography teachers, the procedure used and her comments on the lesson are useful. Riley used the layers of inference framework with students who were studying Victorian Britain. She selected a range of different sources, visual and textual. She placed them in the centre of pieces of coloured A2 card with the four boxes and their accompanying questions drawn around the source. She made students aware of the key enquiry question of the unit: 'How healthy were Victorian towns?'.

Riley started the lesson by recapping what they had already learnt about Victorian Britain to refresh students' memories and give them confidence in examining new source material. She then brainstormed the kinds of things they might look for in the sources to answer the key question. Once the students were clearly focused on the key enquiry question, she divided students into groups

of two and three and allocated the different source materials. They discussed the source and wrote their ideas and questions on the framework. Each group completed one framework and the activity was followed by discussion of what they had written down. A further lesson was spent allowing students to research some of the questions the class had suggested.

Riley was pleased with the quality of discussion, the students' reasoning and the questions it provoked. She found that students worked particularly well on the 'inference' question and used the word 'infer' in their discussions, but although most of suggestions for 'what else would I like to know?' were good, there were also questions which were irrelevant to the enquiry. She found that some students had problems distinguishing between the questions for different layers: in particular, they did not not always distinguish between facts they could identify from the source and the inferences they could make from it. She suggested that a way of helping students understand these categories would be to produce cards on which were printed definite facts and inferences and to ask students to place them in the appropriate boxes.

An example of students' work, focusing on a difficult piece of text, is shown in Figure 17.3. The links these students had made between some of their factual statements and inferences, and between what the source did not tell them and questions they wanted to ask, indicates the way they were reasoning about the source. It is worth encouraging students to make these kinds of links.

An important point about this lesson is the way the activity was sharply focused on what was being investigated. Riley achieved this partly by providing some contextual information and partly through brainstorming what kinds of things students might look for.

Example 2: Studying a flood hydrograph

This example was developed by Jane Ferretti to use with teachers on a CPD course and then with PGCE students. She used resources available on the Geographical Association website related to flooding in Uckfield (GA, 2012). The resources provided for this case study could be used for an investigation focusing on the key question, 'How should flood risk in Uckfield be managed?'. In this example, however, the activity was used to explore the potential of using the layers of inference framework rather than as an integral part of a geographical enquiry.

The PGCE group spent 35 minutes in total on the activity and could have spent longer. The first five minutes were spent showing the group a completed history example, drawing attention to the different layers, and a projected image of the hydrograph. Each group was given a large laminated copy of the hydrograph together with a layers of inference framework. They were given contextual information: the date of the hydrograph (2000); the nearest recording station (Isfield Weir, 3km downstream of Uckfield); flows in Uckfield were estimated from these recordings.

The group then worked in pairs, with one sheet between two. After a few minutes they were stopped and had opportunities to ask questions to make sure they understood the graph. Some asked questions such as 'where is the rainfall? Isn't it usually shown on these graphs?' They then continued working, some very methodically completing one layer at a time and others writing in different layers as they thought of things to write. An example from one pair of students is shown in Figure 17.4.

They then shared ideas and there was a lot of discussion about what the hydrograph definitely told them, what could be inferred and the questions they had asked. These questions included: How urbanised is the area? Was there debris in the water? Was the ground already saturated? Are there flood defences in place? What was the precipitation? What was the base flow of the river? Did the river flood?

The students found that the activity had created a 'need to know' and that it could be used to stimulate interest in the Uckfield case study. They thought that the layers of inference framework was very good for using with graphs; it really made them think about the meaning of the graph. Some suggested it would work well with photographs; statistical information about a country, e.g. indices of development; choropleth maps and eyewitness accounts, e.g. of tsunami. Some thought that it would work well as a final activity to summarise what had been learnt from the case study.

Suggestions for research

1. Carry out action research with a focus on improving your use of the layers of inference framework. Make observational notes on the lesson in which it was used, if possible supported by video or tape recordings, particularly of guidance given before the activity and of the debriefing. What issues have been raised by the findings? What is worth investigating further? Use your reflections to set up the next cycle of action research when you modify your practice and use the framework again.

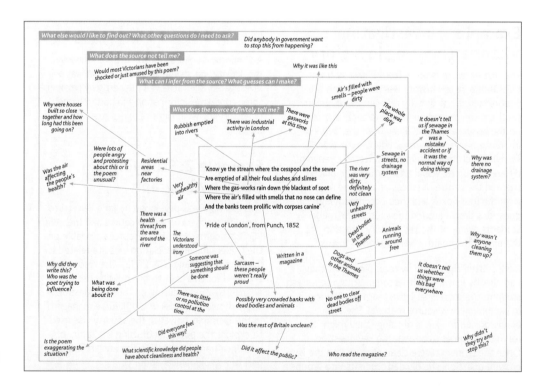

Figure 17.3: Example of students' work on Victorian Britain using layers of inference.

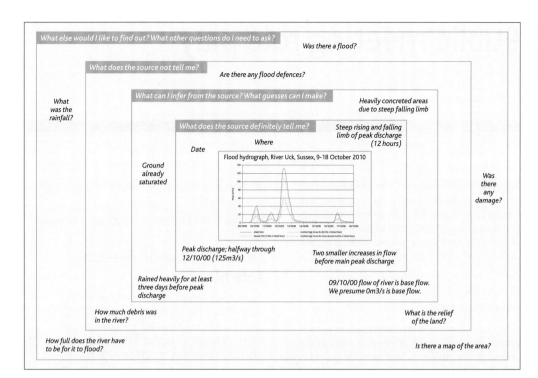

Figure 17.4: An example of PGCE work on flood hydrographs using layers of inference.

Inside the figure:

What else would I like to find out? What other questions do I need to ask?

Was there a flood?

What does the source not tell me?

Are there any flood defences?

What can I infer from the source? What guesses can I make?

Heavily concreted areas due to steep falling limb

What
was the
rainfall?

What does the source definitely tell me?

Steep rising and falling limb of peak discharge (12 hours)

Where

Date

Flood hydrograph, River Uck, Sussex, 9-18 October 2010

Ground already saturated

Was there any damage?

Peak discharge; halfway through 12/10/00 (125m3/s)

Two smaller increases in flow before main peak discharge

Rained heavily for at least three days before peak discharge

09/10/00 flow of river is base flow. We presume 0m3/s is base flow.

How much debris was in the river?

What is the relief of the land?

How full does the river have to be for it to flood?

Is there a map of the area?

---

2. Focus on the extent to which the framework helps students make sense of source material for themselves. Use different types of source material and/or with different age groups. Analyse the completed frameworks. To what extent does the framework help students to think about source material? To what extent does their work provide you with insights into what they understand and misunderstand? To what extent does it provoke curiosity? Does the framework work better with some age groups or with some types of material? How much does the debriefing contribute to the value of the framework?

References

Brown, B. and LeVasseur, M. (2006) *Geographic Perspective: Content guide for educators.* Washington, DC: National Geographic Society. Available online at *www. nationalgeographic.com/xpeditions/guides/geogpguide.pdf* (last accessed 22 January 2013).

Collingwood, R. (1956) *The Idea of History.* Oxford: Oxford University Press.

Geographical Association (2012) 'Uckfield case study: maps and data'. Available online at *www.geography.org.uk/ resources/flooding/uckfield/mapsdata* (last accessed 22 January 2013).

Riley, C. (1999) 'Evidential understanding, period knowledge and the development of literacy: a practical approach to "layers of inference" for key stage 3', *Teaching History,* 97, pp. 6–12.

Public meeting role play

'Studying a real issue rather than a topic is not only more meaningful and motivating to students, but provides a focus and direction for contextualizing and connecting information and ideas and thereby reducing the likelihood of fragmented and superficial treatment of subject matter' (Stevenson, 1997, p. 183).

Introduction

When I was working with students training to become teachers, I asked them at the end of the year what they thought their 'best' lesson had been and why. Every year, the lessons mentioned by the majority of the students were those in which they had carried out a 'public meeting role play'. It was a course requirement that they should use this strategy and reflect on it. Many were reluctant and anxious at first, but, having carried out one public meeting role play, most used the strategy several times. This chapter sets out to answer the following questions:

▲ What is a public meeting role play?

▲ What are the purposes of using public meeting role plays?

▲ How does a public meeting role play relate to geographical enquiry?

▲ What kinds of geographical issues are suitable for public meeting role play lessons?

▲ What preparations are needed for public meeting role plays?

▲ What is the teacher's role during the role play?

What is a public meeting role play?

Public meeting role play (PMRP) lessons are modelled on the procedure that takes place during public meetings and public hearings. PMRP's similarities to, and differences from, real public meetings are indicated in Figure 18.1.

What are the purposes of using public meeting role plays?

Some of the best and most memorable lessons I have observed have been PMRP lessons. What distinguished these lessons was the high degree of student engagement with geographical subject matter throughout the lesson. Students almost always left the room still debating the issue, something I did not observe often. Once when I was revisiting a school two weeks after a PMRP on the Narmada Dam a girl came up to me wanting to continue the debate.

I would justify PMRP lessons primarily in terms of their value in promoting geographical understanding of issues. In PMRP students have to make sense of

Similarities to public meetings	Differences from public meetings
There is an issue to be discussed, related to a decision that needs to be made	The issue might be the kind not actually discussed at a public meeting; it might be resolved at private meetings of government or organisations
There is a formal agenda	
There are ground rules for the conduct of the meeting	There might not, in real life, be opportunities for all groups involved to discuss the issue with each other
Evidence is presented about the issue	The time allocated to PMRP is much shorter than actual meetings so contributions are necessarily brief
There are opportunities for participants to express their views and to question the views of others	PMRP might suggest that decisions are always based on reasoned arguments when in fact there might be many vested interests that influence decisions

Figure 18.1: PMRP's similarities to, and differences from, public meetings.

the more objective evidence and the more subjective evidence related to an issue. Most decisions made about place and environment involve consideration of evidence of different kinds related to the economic, social, environmental and sometimes moral aspects of an issue. Such issues are complex and people have different opinions, underpinned by different values. PMRP lessons provide opportunities for different views to be expressed and challenged and for reasoned arguments to be developed, based on evidence. A PMRP lesson is not simply a pedagogic adventure, something carried out because it is a stimulating activity; its purpose is to deepen understanding of an issue.

There are other benefits of using PMRP. Most classrooms are dominated by teacher talk, in spite of the fact that it is through their own talk that students can make most sense of things for themselves. PMRP lessons are dominated by student talk and encourage students' reasoning skills. They can give opportunities to students who are confident orally, but not necessarily high achievers in written work, to show their ability and earn respect.

PMRP can develop skills considered valuable for the 21st century (see Chapter 2). Students develop skills of searching for information, either by doing their own research or in resources presented to them, and they develop confidence in communicating their arguments to others (information and communication). They become more aware of different viewpoints, related to local, national or global issues (civic literacy, global awareness and cross cultural skills). They develop their ability to scrutinise evidence and to challenge arguments (critical and inventive thinking).

Lastly, but not least, PMRP lessons are usually very enjoyable.

How does a public meeting role play relate to geographical enquiry?

All the key characteristics of enquiry can be developed through PMRP.

Creating a need to know/sparking curiosity

There is an explicit question to be addressed, and the activity itself creates a need to know because students have to argue their case after they have studied evidence. This is very motivating.

Using geographical sources/using evidence

In order to prepare for a PMRP, students seek relevant information to support their case using resources provided by the teacher or from their own research. Sources can include statistics, graphs, maps and photographs.

Making sense/exercising reasoning

Students draw on their existing knowledge and understanding and relate this to new information. Their geographical understanding helps them to use evidence to develop and present arguments appropriate for their role, and justify their reasoning; they evaluate and challenge opposing arguments by probing evidence and questioning assumptions.

Reflecting on learning

During debriefing the teacher asks students to consider the strengths and weaknesses of all the arguments made, reflect on what they have learnt and on the extent to which the PMRP illustrates how decisions are made in the world outside the classroom. The teacher corrects any errors in the presentation and checks that key points have been understood.

What kinds of geographical issues are suitable for public meeting role play lessons?

Clearly, where there are statutory requirements of a national curriculum and where students are working for public examinations, the issue selected for a PMRP must be one through which essential parts of the curriculum can be covered. The other prerequisite is that it must be an issue for which data is readily available. My experience suggests that decisions that have already taken place and acted upon, e.g. debating whether an out of town shopping centre that already exists should be built, are not suitable; students get confused about what the situation was before the decision was made.

Four kinds of issue are suitable for PMRP lessons.

Yes/no decisions

In this kind of PMRP the decision to be made is for or against something. For example:

▲ Should a particular site be used for new development, e.g. a supermarket, a wind-farm, new housing?

▲ Should a third runway be built at Heathrow airport?

▲ What should a country's response be to international requests to reduce carbon emissions?

In role, students argue for or against the decision. A yes/no decision is made at the end of the meeting.

Choosing one of several sites

In this kind of PMRP a decision has to be made about which of several possible locations is best for something, for example:

▲ Where should a new factory or business be located (within a country or globally)?

▲ Which venue should be chosen for an international sporting event, e.g. the Olympic Games, the World Cup?

▲ Which city should become the next European Capital of Culture?

In role, students represent the different competing places. The aim is to reach a decision on which place should be chosen.

Policy decision

In this kind of PMRP a local or national policy issue is discussed. For example:

▲ What should a country's energy policy be – which types of energy should it encourage?

▲ What policies should be adopted in relation to a coastline receding through erosion – which, if any, types of hard and soft engineering should be used?

In role, students present arguments for each of some possible options. The aim is to make a balanced judgement which might include accepting some of the options and rejecting others.

Allocating scarce resources

In this kind of role play the allocation of scarce financial resources is discussed. For example:

▲ To which of a list of proposed projects should Oxfam give money, and how should this be allocated?

▲ What should be the priorities be in allocating a limited budget for services in a town?

▲ How should a town spend limited money to prepare for the next earthquake?

In role, students argue for particular priorities or projects. The aim is to allocate the resources to one or more projects, and to decide the proportion of the total amount allocated to each.

What preparations are needed for public meeting role plays?

PMRP lessons require a lot of preparation. The work involved can be reduced if a published PMRP is used or modified, or if geography departments share what they have devised through networking with each other or through publishing their ideas in professional journals.

Stage 1: Deciding on purposes and aims

The purpose of using PMRP could be mainly to develop geographical understanding of a particular issue or it could be to develop generic and geographical skills. Where students have to meet requirements of national curricula or public examinations, then more specific aims and objectives in terms of knowledge to be remembered, concepts to be understood and skills to be developed can be incorporated into the planning.

Stage 2: Creating roles

Decide on the roles needed for the issue. I would advocate no more than six groups taking part in the debate. This could be three groups for and three groups against a decision, or groups representing six different locations or six different policies. Some students might be involved in other roles, for example, someone needs to chair the meeting. I have observed a 14 year old student being a very capable chair, but the teacher usually carries out this role. There also has to be a person or a group of people to make the decision: this could be a group of students or could be another member of staff.

Roles need to take account of the different groups of people with an interest in the issue, e.g. environmental, social and economic interests. Sometimes the roles are determined by the availability of information, e.g. on different locations for an event or factory.

Stage 3: Allocating students to roles

If the resources provided for each group are not differentiated, then it is best to have groups of mixed ability, so that those with higher reading and numeracy skills can support other students. An alternative is to differentiate the resources provided for each group, so that groups of higher achieving students have more challenging source material and groups of lower achieving students have resources which take account of their capabilities and include guidance on how to use it.

Another issue is whether to have single sex or mixed sex groups. I once observed a PMRP where the groups were mixed and the boys dominated throughout. Not a single girl spoke publicly. So, in classes in which boys tend to dominate discussion, I would recommend single sex groups as this gives both girls and boys a chance to take part in planning and speaking.

It is also worth considering which students would work well together and to ensure that every group has someone potentially strong at presenting.

Stage 4: Preparing resources

The resouces should include:

▲ General information available to everyone

▲ Role cards with information for each group (this could include a list of key arguments and some information from which they could select evidence)

▲ A list of appropriate websites, if students are to search for information

▲ Display materials: e.g. maps, posters

▲ Note-taking framework

▲ An agenda

Stage 5: Producing the agenda

Usually the preparation is best done in the previous lesson and for homework. The agenda is likely to include:

▲ Welcome by the chair: introducing the issue, the groups participating, the groups who will speak and the decision makers

▲ Chair: Information about timing and ground rules

▲ List of groups making their case

▲ List of groups asking questions

▲ Decision makers' questions

▲ Interim debrief

▲ Announcement of decision

▲ Final debrief

Stage 5: Planning the debrief

The purposes of a debrief after PMRP are to:

▲ Reflect on students' own presentation of arguments

▲ Reinforce what has been learnt (if necessary, correcting any misunderstandings)

▲ Reflect on the decision and its justification

▲ Help the students come out of role by reflecting on all the arguments presented and how well they were supported by evidence.

It is useful to use the time when a decision is being made for a short initial debrief, asking students: Which way do you think the decision will go? Why?

Debriefing a PMRP is very worthwhile. It has the greatest impact if it can start immediately after the decision is made, but to get the most out of the experience it is worth continuing debriefing in the following lesson.

Some debriefing questions might arise from notes made by the teacher during the role play but it is worth preparing a few questions in advance. The actual questions will depend on what is being discussed but might include:

▲ Which were the strongest arguments for, and why? Which were the strongest arguments against, and why?

▲ What were the strongest arguments for each site/policy/funding proposal and why? (Probe the extent to which they were supported by evidence.)

▲ Which underpinning values seemed to be most important to the decision makers and why (economic, social, environmental)?

▲ What would be the implications of this decision for the future? Who would be affected by it? Who would gain? Who would lose?

▲ Why do you think the decision went the way it did?

Stage 6: Planning follow up activities

Students could complete a note-taking framework during or after debriefing. The debriefing discussion could be used to prepare students to write a report about the issue, presenting the arguments and the evidence. If the main purpose of written work is to help them get out of role, they could write something more creative, e.g. a letter to a newspaper arguing the case made by one of their opponents.

Stage 7: Getting the classroom ready

The best layout for a PMRP is conference-style horseshoe arrangement of tables so that students can all see each other. However, consideration has to be given to how easy it is to rearrange a room and then restore it; it might be easier to have tables for each of the groups and tables at the front for the chairperson and decision maker(s). Name cards for the groups could be prepared in advance or students could make their own. Maps, posters and the agenda need to be displayed. There should be a clock or watch with a second hand to keep track of timing and possibly a bell to ring to indicate when time is up.

What is the teacher's role during the role play?

An important role for the teacher is to listen carefully to the arguments being made, how students use the information provided, and to jot down things to be taken up in the debriefing: good points, inaccuracies, misunderstandings.

It is also important to manage the role play so that all the presentations, questions and answers can be heard. The ground rules need to be explicit, e.g. only one person talking at a time in the meeting, and enforced. If the teacher is acting as chair, then this is best acted in role, using the authority of the chair to draw attention to the rules of the meeting.

It is also crucially important to manage the time, to have strict time limits on presentations and on responses to questions and to allow for the inevitable short gaps between presentations.

Although I have used PMRP many times with PGCE students and they used the strategy many times with secondary school students, the example I have chosen is based on my recent experience of working with teachers in Singapore.

Example: Should Mauritius aim to double the number of tourists by the year 2020?

Context

I devised this example of a PMRP to use with teachers in Singapore who were on a course preparing them to teach the new enquiry-based geography O-level syllabus. I wanted to explore with them the potential of PMRP for investigating geographical issues and for developing an understanding of key concepts and the skills required by the syllabus.

I chose to focus on global tourism which is framed by the key question: 'Is tourism the way to go?' There are three subsidiary questions:

▲ How does the nature of tourism vary from place to place?

▲ Why has tourism become a global phenomenon?

▲ Developing tourism: at what cost?

The syllabus requires an investigation of the economic, socio-cultural and environmental impacts of tourism and of the role of different groups involved in tourism, e.g. government, travel writers, media, etc. Concepts that need to be understood include: international tourism, long haul and short haul destinations, infrastructure, conservation, fragile environment, sustainable tourism, foreign exchange and regional fluctuations in tourism.

The first reason I chose Mauritius for the role play was because there was a genuine controversial issue to be investigated: the Mauritian government was planning to double the number of tourists by 2020. Second, it was possible to get up-to-date information. Third, it related to another issue in the syllabus: the future of coral reefs. I was also fortunate that, because my daughter's mother-in-law is Mauritian and lives there, I had the opportunity to visit Mauritius and talk to a number of local people about the issue.

Before the group started preparing for the role play, I explained the purpose of using it, outlined the issue, explained the procedure and provided some basic information about Mauritius, including its location, size and population. Because of time constraints on the course, teachers had only 20 minutes to prepare their presentations. The PMRP was timed to last no more than 40 minutes to demonstrate that it was feasible within the length of a single period of geography.

Roles

There were six groups, representing:

▲ the Mauritian government (focusing on economic arguments for the proposal)

▲ the Mauritius Tourism Authority (focusing on environmental arguments for the proposal)

▲ hoteliers (focusing on social arguments for the proposal)

▲ 'We Love Mauritius', a non-govermental organisation (focusing on economic arguments against the proposal)

▲ a group of local residents (focusing on social arguments against the proposal)

▲ 'Reef Conservation Mauritius', an environmental organisation (focusing on environmental arguments against the proposal)

Additional roles included:

▲ a chair, who prepared an introduction to the issue

▲ the decision makers: a group of six, who had to weigh up the evidence, ask questions of each group and decide what to recommend to the government as a result of the meeting.

Although each group could have spoken about economic, social and environmental factors influencing their viewpoint, I decided that each group should focus mainly on one aspect, partly because of time constraints, partly to ensure that all these aspects were discussed and partly for clarity in distinguishing between these factors.

Resources

▲ Map to show location of Mauritius in Indian Ocean – projected on screen

▲ Map of Mauritius

▲ Photographs of Mauritius – projected on screen

▲ Background information for all participants

▲ Role cards

▲ Note-taking frame

▲ An agenda for the meeting.

Each participant had the same background information (Figure 18.2). Each group had role cards that outlined the main arguments that people in their role would make and provided information from which they could select evidence to support their arguments (see Appendix 1).

Agenda

1. Chair: welcome and introduction to the issue and to the groups

2. Presentation of cases (two minutes for each group, stopped by bell if necessary) in the following order:

▲ Government representatives

▲ We Love Mauritius

▲ Hoteliers

▲ Local residents

▲ Tourism Authority

▲ Reef Conservation Mauritius

Five-minute interlude during which each group devises questions for one of the opposing groups

3. Question time (one minute per question and response)

▲ Each group asks a question and the appropriate group responds

▲ The decision makers ask each group a question and the appropriate group responds

4. The decision makers leave the room to consider their decision

5. Interim debrief while decision is being made:

▲ What do you think the decision will be? Why?

▲ Which of the arguments for seemed the strongest?

▲ Which of the arguments against seemed the strongest?

6. The decision makers present and explain their decision to the group.

Debriefing after the public meeting

To the decision makers:

▲ What were the most important issues that influenced your decision?

To all groups:

▲ Do you think the decision was fair?

▲ What were your weakest arguments?

▲ What was the strongest argument against you?

▲ Who stands to gain most if tourist numbers are doubled?

▲ Who loses most?

▲ Which group is likely to have most influence on the decision and why?

▲ Which groups are least likely to have an influence on the decision and why?

Some reflections on how the role play worked in practice

Timing was a big issue and the main debriefing took place after the 40-minute period. The good thing about having a short preparation time meant that each group really focused on the issue, the arguments and the evidence. Most groups split the work between them, some concentrating on their two-minute presentation and others studying the case to be made by the group they were going to question. However, almost all presentations were stopped by the bell and some groups managed to say only half of what they wanted to. Depending on what questions they were asked, most groups had the opportunity to add more to their argument during questioning.

Mauritius background information

The Mauritian government aims to increase tourist arrivals from 980,000 in 2011 to 2 million by 2020. It is promoting investment in new hotels. It plans to diversify and attract more visitors from countries such as India, Russia, China and South Africa. Vision 2020, the National Long-Term Perspective Study, estimated that the total capacity could be increased from the present 5300 hotel rooms to a maximum of 9000. Beyond this 'green ceiling' increased earnings would have to come, not from higher numbers, but from higher spending per visitor.

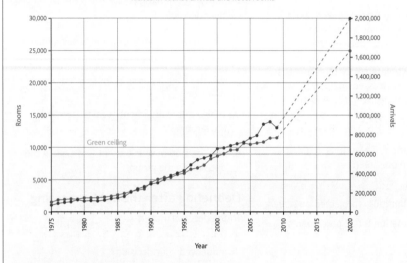

Trends in tourist arrivals and hotel rooms

The island of Mauritius

▲ Mauritius, a popular tourist destination, is famous for its white sandy beaches and coral reefs. It lies in the Indian Ocean, within the tropics, east of Madagascar at 20° N, 57° E. The island is 45km across east to west, 65km north to south and has 330km of coastline. The island's capital and largest city is Port Louis.

▲ The climate in Mauritius is typically tropical with forests in the mountainous areas. Mauritius is of volcanic origin and is generally sheltered by barriers of coral reefs forming natural, safe, crystal clear lagoons.

▲ The temperature in the coastal areas varies between 22°C in winter and 34°C in summer. The sea temperature varies between 22°C and 27°C. In the central part of the island, the maximum daytime temperature varies from about 19°C in August to about 26°C in February.

▲ Mauritius has a population of roughly 1,250,000, mainly descendants of people from India, continental Africa, France and China. 52% are Hindu, 36% Christian and 17% Muslim.

▲ The Mauritian economy is based on four sectors: textiles, tourism, sugar and services.

▲ All tourist development is on or near the coast.

The five-minute interlude for groups to decide on questions was introduced after running the role play several times and enabled everyone to discuss the arguments of their opponents. It was during the question and answer session that the meeting came alive and people got really involved in the arguments and evidence. Timing had to be strict at this point. Long questions were discouraged and in later versions of running this role play, we used a bell to limit replies to questions. If there is more time available for a PMRP, then I would suggest keeping the initial presentations very brief and allowing a longer period for question and answers.

While the groups were preparing their cases, I eavesdropped on their discussions and made notes of things I would follow up in the debriefing session. I also asked each group what were the main points they intended to make in their presentations. This was to ensure that some key economic, socio-cultural and environmental arguments were made publicly and to give each group confidence. I also answered questions, provided additional information and corrected some misunderstandings.

Sometimes participants filled in a note-taking frame during the PMRP. Sometimes I asked them to make notes before the debriefing, remembering as much as they could. What was impressive was that few knew much about Mauritius before the activity but through discussion and debate they all felt they had acquired knowledge and understood the key issues.

The decision-making group had copies of all the resources. In the first use of the role play they did not have individual roles, but later each person focused their attention on the arguments of one of the groups, studied their resources, listened carefully to their presentation and devised a question to ask that group. This made this group feel more involved.

During the interim and final debriefing, in an attempt to get people out of role, I tried to get each group focusing on the strengths of their opponents' arguments and the weaknesses of their own.

I would not want participants in PMRP to conclude that those who make the best arguments supported by the strongest evidence necessarily have the most influence on decisions. In the majority of decisions about geographical issues, some groups have more power to influence decisions than others. In this particular example, the groups for expansion – the

government, the hoteliers and the tourist agency – are powerful and well funded. The groups against – We Love Mauritius, the local residents and Reef Conservation – are smaller, less powerful and less well-financed and were in reality not likely to have so much influence. It seemed important to me that the issue of power to influence and power to decide should be discussed in the debriefing session. I ran this PMRP ten times and usually the decision went in favour of expansion. Arguments about the economic needs of Mauritius usually outweighed arguments about employment and about conservation, however well these arguments had been presented. Sometimes the decision makers qualified their decision in favour of expansion by saying they would establish procedures to consult with the Reef Conservation group and with local people. These were all useful points to probe and discuss.

Summary

PMRP lessons can enable students to investigate and discuss geographical issues and examine different viewpoints, the evidence supporting them and their underpinning values. Students increase their knowledge and understanding through discussion and also develop a wide range of enquiry and generic skills.

Suggestion for research

Investigate the use of a public meeting role play lesson. Examine the extent to which it enables students to understand complex issues and to gain a critical understanding of the kinds of evidence used by interested parties and power relationships in decision making. Collect data in the form of: observational notes of the preparation for PMRP, the role play itself and the debriefing; film or audio recordings; students' written work; questionnaire surveys or interviews.

Reference

Stevenson, R. (1997) 'Developing habits of environmental thoughtfulness through the in-depth study of select environmental issues', *Canadian Journal of Environmental Education*, 2, pp. 183–281. Available online at *http://jee. lakeheadu.ca/index.php/cjee/article/viewFile/361/340* (last accessed 22 January 2013).

19 Directed activities related to text

'We know that the ability to take on complex ideas, to handle the notion of a multiplicity of viewpoints, to deal in abstract thought, relies on a person's experience of reading widely and often – in combination with open-ended but challenging discussion' (Rosen, 2008).

Directed activities related to text, usually abbreviated to DARTs, were originally devised by the Schools Council Effective Use of Reading project in the 1970s (Lunzer and Gardner, 1979). From its research across the curriculum, the project found that little time was spent in classrooms helping students to read text. Most reading was done in short bursts which were unlikely to lead to understanding. More sustained reading was often set as a homework activity. Typical classroom activities required students to find bits of information in the text rather than to discuss the meaning of the text as a whole. The project devised a range of activities that focused on the structure and meaning of texts.

This chapter addresses the following questions:

▲ What are DARTs?

▲ What are the purposes of using DARTs?

▲ What needs to be considered when planning to use a DART?

▲ What is the procedure for using DARTs?

▲ What issues are related to using DARTs?

The chapter then provides some examples of how DARTs have been used:

▲ Where does my iPod come from?

▲ Tackling eutrophication on the Norfolk Broads.

▲ Drumlins.

What are DARTs?

DARTs are structured activities, planned by the teacher, designed to help students understand the meaning of a piece of text. There are two types of DARTs.

Reconstruction DARTS

Reconstruction DARTS require students to put together text which has been broken up in some way. There are two main types of reconstruction DARTs:

▲ Diagram completion: Students are presented with a piece of unaltered text, e.g. about the structure of a volcano, together with a diagram that has had all the labelling removed. The task for students is label the diagram correctly, from their careful reading of the text. This type of DART focuses on structure.

▲ Sequencing text (which can be supplemented with diagrams): Students are presented with text describing a sequence, e.g. of an industrial process, of growth of towns, of coastal erosion, which has been broken up into separate stages. The task for students is to put the pieces of text into the correct sequence. If there are also diagrams, then the task includes matching the text to the diagrams. This type of DART focuses on change and process.

Analysis and reconstruction DARTs

In analysis and reconstruction DARTs the text is presented to students as a whole. However, the text might have been modified to make it more accessible to students or to make it more relevant to what is being investigated. In this type of DART activity, students need to mark the text, so if textbook passages of text are to be used they need to be copied beforehand. There are two stages:

▲ analysis of the text using underlining or by writing headings for paragraphs

▲ reconstructing the text in a different form, usually in some sort of table.

What are the purposes of using DARTs?

The main purpose of using DARTs is to develop students' understanding of what they are reading. In contrast to activities that require students to find bits of information in a text to answer comprehension questions, DARTs help students understand texts as a whole. DARTs can help students develop their understanding of geographical ways of thinking as they use various geographical categories (Figure 19.1) to analyse their text. A completed reconstruction DART can provide a useful focus for discussion.

DARTs can help students develop analytical skills which they can apply to other texts they study independently. DARTs can introduce students to different ways of making notes from text, e.g. in tables, diagrams, flow charts.

What needs to be considered when planning to use a DART?

▲ How should the activity be introduced so that students are aware of how it contributes to understanding the issue they are investigating?

▲ Is there a piece of text which provides useful geographical source material for an investigation of the topic or issue?

▲ Does the text need to be modified in any way, to make it appropriate for the age and literacy capabilities of the students?

▲ If the text is accompanied by diagrams, would it be suitable for breaking up, separating the diagram(s) from the text, to use as a reconstruction DART (sequencing or diagram completion)?

▲ Does the text have a clear structure so that it would be easy to analyse? What categories could be used to analyse it (Figure 19.1)?

▲ How could the text be reconstructed to bring out the meaning of the text as a whole (Figure 19.1)?

▲ Will the activity be done individually, in pairs or in small groups (three or four students)?

▲ How long should students have to complete the activity?

▲ What support might students need, e.g. modelling the process, showing a finished reconstruction of a similar type for a different text or helping individuals and groups through discussion?

▲ How should the activity be debriefed?

What is the procedure for using DARTs?

Students need to be aware of the key question that is being investigated and the purpose of using the DART, and the teacher needs to create some sort of stimulus so that students have a 'need to know'.

Usually, students work in pairs or small groups. This encourages discussion between students about the meaning of the text. They are presented with the text as evidence to be scrutinised. Reconstruction DARTs are presented in an envelope with one envelope per pair. Analysis and reconstruction DARTs are presented on a resource sheet with one copy per student.

Analysing geographical texts	Different ways of reconstructing text
Geographical texts can be analysed in many different ways, using different categories, e.g.:	After a text has been analysed it could be reconstructed in different ways, e.g.:
▲ Economic, social, environmental, cultural, political, technological (factors or effects)	▲ A table
▲ Local, national, international, global (factors, effects or implications)	▲ A spider diagram
▲ Causes, effects, implications	▲ A mind map
▲ Physical causes	▲ A concept map
▲ Human causes	▲ A flow diagram
▲ Physical impacts, human impacts	▲ A picture
▲ Short term effects, long term effects	▲ An annotated diagram
▲ Who gains, who loses?	▲ A storyboard
▲ Advantages, disadvantages	▲ A physical construction, e.g. model
▲ Arguments for, arguments against	
▲ Facts, opinions	
▲ Big points, little points	

Figure 19.1: Analysis and reconstruction DARTs

The teacher reads the text out loud as recommended by the original DART project. This has the advantage of students hearing the language of geography and could give them the opportunity to clarify the meaning of vocabulary before they analyse the text. It is particularly useful to do this in classes with a wide range of reading abilities.

Students are given instructions (Figure 19.2), preferably both read out loud and in written form, and a time limit to carry out the DART.

For analysis and reconstruction DARTs students should be encouraged to analyse the whole text before starting to reconstruct it. While they are working the teacher eavesdrops on the discussions, making a mental note of things that could be raised in the debriefing, and provides support if necessary.

The activity is debriefed by asking questions that probe the meaning of the text. If the DART is closed, i.e. with correct answers, the debriefing focuses on the answers and possibly on different versions of the reconstruction. If the DART is more open, some students could present their reconstruction to the rest of the class and explain it. Debriefing could focus on how they have represented everything in the text and the extent to which they have grasped the full meaning of the text. The activity could also be debriefed in the context of the investigation of the topic, asking questions such as: how reliable is this text as evidence? What other information do we need about this topic? Where might we find this?

When students are familiar with using DARTs and with categories for analysing geographical information, the strategy could be used for a homework exercise.

What issues are related to using DARTs?

If DARTs include reconstruction in tables with 'right answers', students could think of the task simply as an exercise. In order for the text to be used as evidence, the DART needs to be debriefed

---

Using a DART

These instructions should be adapted so that they are appropriate for particular texts.

Instructions for diagram completion

▲ Your task is to replace the missing labels from your diagram of ...

▲ Read the text about ...

▲ Underline all the words related to the structure of ...

▲ Make a list of all the words related to the structure of ... (if using a textbook)

▲ Look at the list of words provided and try to label the diagram correctly.

Instructions for sequencing text and diagrams

▲ In your envelope you will find some pieces of text and some illustrations.

▲ Match the text to the correct illustration.

▲ Now put them into the correct sequence.

Instructions for analysis and reconstruction DART: paragraph labelling

▲ Read the text about ...

▲ Discuss what each paragraph is about.

▲ Write a suitable heading for each paragraph.

▲ Now write a suitable heading for the whole text (either on the text or on paper).

▲ For each heading give an example of information in that paragraph. Either circle the information on the text or write it under the title you have given the paragraph.

Instructions for analysis and reconstruction DART: underlining and reconstruction

▲ Read the text about ...

▲ Underline all the parts of the text related to ...

▲ Underline in a different way parts of the text related to ...

▲ Underline in a third way parts of the text related to ...

▲ Now use the information you have underlined in one of the following ways:

1. (For reconstruction using a table.) Produce a table, using the categories as headings at the top. List important information about each category under each heading in note form (you could subdivide the table by using side headings).

2. (For reconstruction using a mind map.) Use your underlining to make a mind map of the article, where the main branches are the main categories underlined and where the sub-branches are related to information about that category.

3. (For reconstruction using a pictorial representation). Draw a pictorial or diagrammatic representation of the text, making use of the categories of information. Try to ensure that all the information in the text is included in the picture or diagram. NB the picture can use stick people or simple drawings; you do not need to be a great artist.

Figure 19.2: Instructions to students for using a DART.

to discuss how it contributes to answering the key question being investigated. When students first use a DART they are dependent on the way the teacher has structured the activity. However, DARTs give students a strategy for analysing text through underlining and reconstructing it independently, for their own note-taking, for revision purposes or to make sense of text found on a website.

The piece of text needs to be relatively well structured for students to be able to analyse it. From their analysis, students can learn how texts convey meaning clearly, through their paragraphs and through the way they structure arguments. This could help them think about structure and argument for their own written work.

Examples

Reconstruction DART: Sequencing: Where does my iPod come from?

Lesson 2 in *Going Global?* (Owen, 2010), a Geographical Association publication for GCSE level, includes a DART activity aimed at helping students understand the different stages and locations in the production of iPods. Students are provided with a set of cards. The DART task is to arrange the cards to show the sequence of production and then to categorise the primary, secondary, tertiary and quaternary stages of production. Additional questions on who receives what proportion of the selling price and about the location of the different stages of production are useful to discuss in a debriefing.

Analysis and reconstruction DART: Tackling eutrophication on the Norfolk Broads

This DART, on the concept of eutrophication, is a variation on the original suggestions for DARTs in that, following analysis of a piece of text, the reconstruction is in pictorial or diagrammatic form. This has the advantage that students have to think harder about how to represent the text than if they had to use only words in the reconstruction, because they are translating text from words to images. The activity gives more scope for creativity and has proved to be motivating and enjoyable.

The instructions (Figure 19.3) ask students to analyse a piece of text by underlining

---

Eutrophication

Definition: Eutrophication is the nutrient enrichment of bodies of water, resulting in excessive plant growth and loss of oxygen to wildlife.

Task

1. Read the text carefully.
2. Underline things that cause eutrophication.
3. Underline, in a different way, the effects of eutrophication.
4. Underline, in a third way, solutions to the problems of eutrophication.
5. Reconstruct the text diagrammatically or pictorially to represent everything you have underlined.

The Norfolk Broads – a series of rivers and lakes – provides valuable habitats for wildlife and is one of Britain's most popular boating areas. Eutrophication has been an issue in the Broads for many years.

Most of the land next to the Broads and its waterways is used for farming. The use of chemical fertilisers such as nitrates to increase yields has increased substantially in the last 60 years. Rain washes out the nitrates from farmland into the Broads. In addition, an increase in the local population and in the number of tourists have led to an increase in the quantity of phosphates which are released into the waterways from sewage treatment plants. The lack of tertiary sewage treatment in this area means that phosphates are not removed from the effluent before it is released.

The nitrates and phosphates are a rich source of nutrients for plant life, including algae, which can multiply very quickly. Many of the Broads have become covered in 'algal blooms' making the water look green. The rapid growth of algae means that the oxygen levels in the water decrease and the 'algal blooms' block out the sunlight. Many water plants and animals cannot survive the lack of oxygen and sunlight. Life other than algae soon dies. The algae also die quickly and this leads to an accumulation of rotting algae on the bed of the Broad. The material formed is called necron mud which consumes oxygen slowly as it decomposes. This reduces the oxygen level even further and also fills up the Broad with mud making it shallower. Animals that require deep water begin to disappear. If this process is allowed to continue, the Broad will eventually fill up with necron mud and disappear. In addition, tourist boats in the area can stir up the necron mud, which is rich in nutrients, encouraging the process of eutrophication.

This problem can be solved. Since 1990, investment in sewage treatment works has reduced the quantity of phosphate being discharged leading to a reduction in nutrient concentrations in the Norfolk Broads. This has reduced the amount of algae and allowed other plants and animals to re-establish themselves. It has also improved the clarity of the water.

The Norfolk Wildlife Trust has also undertaken restoration programmes. For example, Cockshoot Broad was sealed off from the river and the necron mud pumped out from the bottom of the broad. After a year or so, native plants and animals began to reintroduce themselves. This solution isn't always practical, however, as it makes the Broads inaccessible to tourist boats.

Figure 19.3: A DART focused on the process of eutrophication on the Norfolk Broads. Source: adapted from Naish and Warn, 1994.

different categories of information: causes, effects and solutions.

When I have used the activity I have asked small groups to work together to represent their analysis in pictorial form on flip-chart paper. Some groups have interpreted this as drawing a pictorial representation (Figure 19.4) or an instruction to draw a mind map (Figure 19.5). Others have reconstructed the text as a diagram.

My role when the groups were working on their reconstruction was to get them to explain to me what their picture was showing, to probe their understanding and to encourage them to check whether they had included everything in the text.

What is interesting about using a DART is that students have to read the text several times, going back to check details. Often when their representations were 'complete' groups would re-read the whole text to see if there were any extra details they could add or label. This kind of reading and making sense is more intensive than the usual classroom reading of a text as a comprehension exercise.

I usually asked two groups who had produced very different pictures to use them to explain the process of eutrophication. They could always do this without reference to the text and had a good overall grasp of the process from carrying out the activity. Debriefing could probe what had been emphasised in some representations and not others, which ideas were difficult to represent and what they had learned from the process of doing the DART.

It is worth keeping some good examples of flip-chart mind maps, pictorial or diagrammatic reconstructions to show to other groups who are doing a similar DART on a different topic.

Drumlins (provided by Rachel Atherton)

A-level students analysed the text on drumlins (Figure 19.7) by underlining anything that they could represent in a model. They then reconstructed the text by building one drumlin out of builder's sand and labelling it (Figure 19.8).

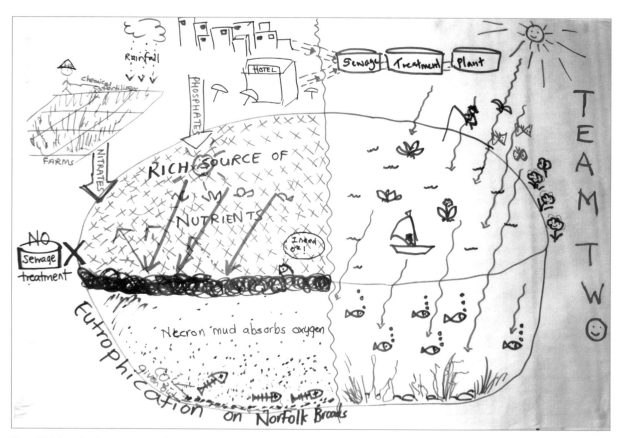

Figure 19.4: Example of a reconstruction of eutrophication text as a picture. Photo: Margaret Roberts.

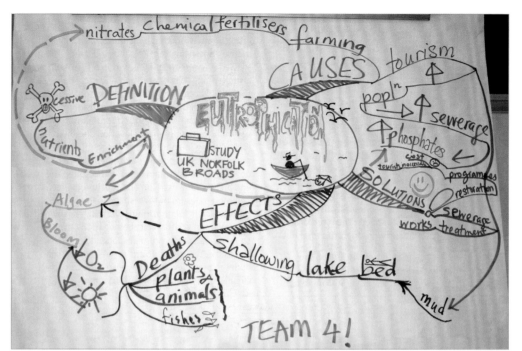

Figure 19.5: Example of a reconstruction of eutrophication text as a mind map. Photo: Margaret Roberts.

Figure 19.6: Using the eutrophication text to create a diagram. Photo: Margaret Roberts.

Figure 19.7: Text on drumlins for analysis and reconstruction DART. Source: *www.sheffield.ac.uk/drumlins/drumlins.*

Drumlins

An oval-shaped hill, largely composed of glacial drift, formed beneath a glacier or ice sheet and aligned in the direction of ice flow. There are no strict definitions relating to their size but they tend to be up to a few kilometres long and up to 50m in relief. They are widespread in formerly glaciated areas and are especially numerous in Canada, Ireland, Sweden and Finland. Drumlins are considered to be part of a family of related landforms including flutes, mega-scale glacial lineations, and rogen moraine which are collectively referred to as subglacial bedforms. Their formation remains controversial (see below) but in spite of this they are extremely useful for reconstructing former ice sheets. The word drumlin is a derivation of a Gaelic word for a rounded hill.

While there are many variations in shape, the 'classic' drumlin is a smooth, streamlined hill that resembles an egg half buried along its long-axis.

They tend to exist as fields or swarms of landforms rather than as isolated individuals, with a typical swarm comprising tens to thousands of drumlins. Viewed en masse, drumlins within a swarm display a similar long-axis orientation and morphology to their neighbours, and are closely packed, usually within two to three times the dimensions of their drumlin length. The majority of drumlins in a swarm have their highest elevation and blunter end pointing in an upstream direction, with the more gently sloping and pointed end, or tail, facing down-ice. The upstream blunt end is called the stoss end and the downstream end is called the lee. A common measure of their shape is the elongation ratio, which is the maximum drumlin length divided by maximum width. Typical elongation ratios are 2:1 to 7:1. Variations in drumlin shape include spindle-like forms, two-tailed forms resembling barchan dunes in plan view, and they also exist as perfect circular hills with an elongation ratio of 1:1.

Figure 19.8: Example of reconstruction of drumlin text in builder's sand. Photo: Margaret Roberts.

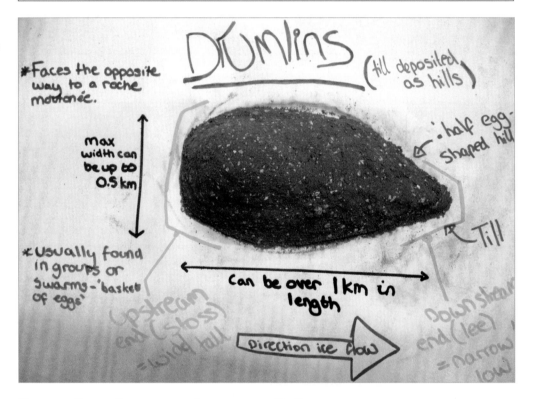

Suggestions for research

1. Devise some DARTs and collect data on their use, from work completed by students and from interviews.

2. Encourage students to use a DART strategy for homework or for text found on the internet. Evaluate the extent to which DARTs support learning.

References

Lunzer, E. and Gardner, K. (1979) *The Effective Use of Reading.* Oxford: Heinemann.

Naish, M. and Warn, S. (eds) (1994) *16–19 Core Geography.* Harlow: Longman.

Owen, C. (2010) *Going Global? A study of our interconnected world.* Sheffield: Geographical Association.

Rosen, M. (2008) '*Death of the bookworm*', the *Guardian*, 16 September.

20 Using questionnaires

'... a carefully structured and ordered set of questions designed to obtain the needed information without either ambiguity or bias. Every respondent answers the same questions, asked in the same way and in the same sequence, which contrasts with more open-ended formats used in interviews' (Johnston et al., 2000).

Although questionnaire surveys are usually associated with fieldwork, they can be used for enquiry work taking place mostly in the classroom.

This chapter addresses the following questions:

▲ What are the purposes of using questionnaire surveys in geography?

▲ What kinds of geographical issues and topics are suitable for questionnaire surveys?

▲ What is involved in devising and using a questionnaire survey?

▲ How can students be helped to produce good questionnaires?

▲ What are the limitations of questionnaire surveys?

What are the purposes of using questionnaire surveys in geography?

There are several justifications for using questionnaire surveys. If students collect their own first-hand data, they are aware of what the data relate to in the 'real world'. They can be involved in the whole enquiry process: identifying questions; collecting evidence; interpreting evidence; reaching conclusions and evaluating their investigation. They are also better able to critique data and conclusions as they are aware of how they have been collected and presented.

Students can develop geographical and generic skills in a purposeful context, skills such as: devising clear geographical questions; choosing category boundaries; aggregating numerical data by addition or averaging; communicating with those answering

the questionnaire; representing data graphically and writing reports. They can also develop an understanding of the concepts of sampling, reliability and validity (Figure 20.1).

Some of the secondary data encountered by students in textbooks or in the media originates in questionnaire surveys. If students are to become aware of how this kind of knowledge is constructed, it is advantageous for them to have used questionnaire surveys themselves. They can become aware that 'factual' information collected through surveys is selective of reality, highly dependent on the questions asked, the category boundaries chosen, the sample used and when and where the data were collected. This can enable them to deal with information generated by questionnaire surveys more critically. Questionnaire surveys can be used as a diagnostic assessment of students' prior knowledge and understanding (Figure 20.2).

What kinds of geographical issues and topics are suitable for questionnaire surveys?

Questionnaires can provide information about:

▲ the person answering the questionnaire, e.g. their age group

▲ their behaviour, e.g. shopping habits

▲ their opinions, e.g. attitudes towards an issue

▲ their existing knowledge, e.g. naming the countries in the EU.

Questionnaire surveys can be used to investigate a wide range of geographical questions related both to facts and to people's values, attitudes and opinions, for example:

▲ What? Where? When? How often? Why?

▲ What do you think? Do you agree/disagree?

▲ What is most important to you?

Many of the themes and issues investigated in geography could be studied partly through the use

Sampling

It is not possible to collect data from everyone who could be researched for a particular question. Researchers therefore collect data from a sample of the possible total population using various ways of sampling:

▲ Probability sampling is based on the idea that the sample selected will be representative of the whole and includes random, systematic and stratified sampling.

▲ Random sampling is used for a very large sample, often using a set of random digits, e.g. to choose pages and lines to select people from telephone directories.

▲ Systematic sampling is similar, but would choose, for example, every 'nth' person from the directory.

▲ Stratified sampling is used to ensure that the relevant categories of people are included in the survey, e.g. an appropriate proportion of age-groups, genders etc.

▲ Non-probability sampling is used when the number of people being surveyed is smaller or where people are hand-picked for a specific purpose, e.g. to provide additional information about existing knowledge or to modify thinking.

▲ Convenience sampling is based on selections to suit the researcher because they are easiest to obtain but cannot be used for reliable, valid research.

Reliability

Data from questionnaire surveys are reliable if the same results would be obtained on another occasion or if the questionnaire was administered by another person. Reliability is about whether the questionnaire itself is reliable, and whether the evidence it produces is consistent and credible. Questions to consider:

▲ Would the findings be the same if I used the questionnaire on a similar occasion?

▲ Are the findings consistent with information from other sources?

If the questionnaire is not reliable, then the data produced from it are unreliable too and it is not possible to generalise from the data.

Validity

Data from questionnaire surveys are valid if the survey finds out what it intends to find out and the data collected are accurate. Questions to consider:

▲ Has the questionnaire found out what it was intended to find out?

▲ Are the findings accurately and honestly presented?

Figure 20.1: Sampling, reliability and validity.

of questionnaire surveys. The examples given after each of the themes listed below indicate a range of questions that could be asked. Each question would need to be developed and refined to make it suitable for use in a questionnaire.

▲ Perceptions of place (What do you associate with the following countries/continents? Which country would you most like to visit? Why? Which countries would you least like to visit? Why?)

▲ Day trips and holidays (Where? Why? For how long? Mode of transport? What type of accommodation? What kinds of activities?)

▲ Visiting relations (Which relations? Where do they live? How long are the visits? What occasions? What do you like/dislike about the visits?)

▲ Journey to school (Distance to be travelled? Mode of transport? Time taken? Likes and dislikes about the journey?)

▲ Shopping (Where do you shop? Which shops? How often? What for? What features of shops/shopping centres do you like or dislike? Do you shop online? What for? Do different age groups/genders shop differently?)

▲ Moving home: migration as common experience (Have you moved house? In which places have you lived? Why have you moved house? What do you think of the area you last lived in? What do you like/dislike about your new area?)

What is involved in devising and using a questionnaire survey?

The process of devising and using a questionnaire survey can be broken down into eight stages.

Stage 1: Establishing the scope of the survey

There needs to be a clear purpose to the survey, framed by a key question or series of questions. This could be negotiated with students. Once the overall purpose has been established, decisions need to be made about how many questionnaires are to be completed and by whom, e.g. members of the public; another class in school; people living in the same household as the students; relations; particular age groups, etc., and to what extent these need to provide any kind of representative sample.

Stage 2: Devising questions

Eight common question types, including closed and open questions, are shown in Figure 20.3, based on Denscombe (2010).

Closed questions invite respondents to tick, cross or circle something already on the questionnaire (question types 1–5) and are much easier to analyse than open questions. 'Fill in the blank' questions (type 6), asking for a single word or a numerical response, are also easy to analyse. Closed and 'fill in the blank' questions produce data that can be quantified.

Open questions invite respondents to answer a question in a word or phrase, a list, or comments (types 7 and 8). Open questions allow for a range of responses that the person devising the question has not anticipated. They enable respondents to express their views in the way they want to, rather than being limited to predetermined categories decided by others. It is, however, time consuming to analyse open responses. They are usually coded in some way and care has to be taken in reporting them fairly.

Students could work initially in pairs to generate a standard set of questions to be used by the whole class, and then discuss their questions in fours. These could be shared with the class and suitable questions selected. Attention should be given to the order in which questions are listed on a questionnaire. It is best to start with short 'simple' factual questions and to leave more personal and open questions to the end. Ideally the questionnaire should be trialled, possibly with students in the class, to find out whether there are problems with any of the questions.

A common questionnaire to be used by all students is printed.

Stage 3: Preparing to use the questionnaires

It is worth rehearsing the use of questionnaire surveys so that students can consider how to introduce and explain them, how to relate to members of the public and how to use them in public places.

Stage 4: Collecting responses

Students find appropriate people to complete their questionnaires.

Stage 5: Collating the data

When a class is using a common questionnaire survey, the responses need to be combined.

Diagnostic assessment

Although taking account of prior knowledge is thought to be a good thing, it can be difficult to find out about the prior knowledge of all the students in a class. Short questionnaires can be used for this purpose before the start of a new investigation. Students should be aware that the purpose of such a questionnaire is to identify what they already understand and to reveal any misunderstandings so that these can be taken into account in developing the investigation.

Borowski (2011) used a questionnaire as one way of finding out about primary school pupils' perceptions of Africa before they were involved in a project about Africa. The pupils were asked to:

▲ Choose, from a list of adjectives, the words they thought described what Africa was like.

▲ Choose, from a selection of images, pictures that they thought showed what Africa was like.

▲ Rate various characteristics of African people.

As well as using questionnaires, Borowski asked students to draw or write on a blank map of Africa what they knew and followed up the questionnaires with focus group discussions.

Walshe (2007) researched year 8 students' understanding of sustainability partly through asking students to draw spider diagrams and partly through interviews. She found from a pilot study that she got more detailed responses about their understanding of sustainability when she asked them about it within a specific context, such as sustainable tourism. Diagnostic questions could include:

▲ What do you understand by sustainable tourism?

▲ What kind of tourism do you think would not be sustainable?

▲ What would a sustainable school/town be like?

▲ What would an unsustainable school/town be like?

Figure 20.2: Using questionnaires for diagnostic assessment.

Data needs to be entered on a spreadsheet by students and/or the teacher, or added via an online system such as Google Forms or Survey Monkey. If qualitative data are collected through open questions, responses need to be studied to see what common themes emerge and examples found to illustrate these themes.

Stage 6: Presenting the data

Students consider how the data could be presented graphically, in tables or in a report. They choose appropriate methods of representation.

Types of questions

1. Choosing one answer from a list of options provided in the questionnaire

Yes/No	e.g. Have you been to a country outside the UK in the last 12 months?
Categories	e.g. Do you live in: a terraced house; a detached house; a semi-detached house; a flat; a caravan; other
Grouped data	e.g. How old are you: under 16; 16-40; 41-65; over 65 (make sure that the categories do not overlap)

2. Choosing one or more answers (or none) from a list of options

For example: Which of the following EU countries have you ever visited? Austria; Belgium; Bulgaria; Cyprus; Czech Republic; Denmark; Estonia; Finland; France; Germany; Greece; Hungary; Ireland; Italy; Latvia; Lithuania; Luxembourg; Malta; Netherlands; Poland; Portugal; Romania; Slovakia; Slovenia; Spain; Sweden. NB If using this question outside UK include the UK in list.

3. Ranking

For example: Which of the following are most important to you when choosing a holiday? Indicate your order of preference with 1, 2, 3 etc.

Holiday feature	Order of preference
Weather	
Attractive scenery	
Interesting towns to visit	
Opportunities for sporting activities	
Night life	
Opportunities to see wildlife	
Cultural events: art; museums; music	

4. Expressing agreement/disagreement using the Likert scale

The Likert scale, developed by Rensis Likert in 1932, invites respondents to express the extent of their agreement or disagreement with given statements, e.g.

Statement	Strongly disagree	Disagree	Neither agree nor disagree	Agree	Strongly agree
Geography should be compulsory until the end of year 11					

5. Semantic differential

In these questions, respondents are given pairs of contrasting words and asked to indicate their viewpoint on a scale which can vary between 1 and 10. For example, Smith Street is:

Dirty	1	2	3	4	5	Clean
Boring	1	2	3	4	5	Interesting
Noisy	1	2	3	4	5	Quiet
Unsafe	1	2	3	4	5	Safe

6. Fill in the blank

e.g. Which country would you most like to visit?

e.g. How many times have you visited a cinema in the last month?

7. Open list

This type of question is used when there are too many possible responses to list them all.

e.g. Which countries have you visited in the last 12 months?

8. Open response

This type of question leaves a space for the response. The size of the space can indicate what length of response is wanted.

e.g. What changes would you like to see in this town/place in the next five years?

Figure 20.3: Eight common types of questions used in questionnaires. Source: based on Denscombe, 2010.

Stage 7: Interpreting the data, reaching conclusions

Students describe what they have found out, identifying significant features and drawing conclusions. The findings could be presented to a wider audience in a display, or in a report for those who contributed to the survey.

Stage 8: Evaluating the survey

The findings are discussed critically. To what extent do the data answer the questions? Could the data be misleading in any way? In what ways might the data be unreliable or invalid? In what ways could the questionnaire have been better?

How can students be helped to produce good questionnaires?

Students could be introduced to the use of questionnaires by omitting stages 1–5 and by presenting them with data already collected as shown in the example in Figure 20.4. The statistics presented on this worksheet were modified from the data collected and are not presented as reliable data on the use of the Peak District National Park. Indeed, it would be useful to go beyond what is suggested in question 4 and discuss why the data are unlikely to be reliable or valid. This example could be adapted and applied to many different contexts.

If students have no experience in devising questions, then it is useful for them to be introduced to only two or three of the question types in Figure 20.3 and use these well. If the teacher has devised the questions, then again it is useful to select a limited range of question types and to make explicit what types of questions have been used, so that students can become familiar with them.

Students could be alerted to some of the common pitfalls which can occur in questionnaires by providing examples of good and bad questions for them to discuss. Figure 20.5 lists categories of bad questions with some examples. Alternatively, rather than providing examples of all the types of bad questions initially, it might be preferable to discuss any problems with questions as and when they are suggested by students.

What are the limitations of questionnaire surveys?

General limitations

▲ Questionnaires are not good at eliciting complex reasoning about issues. They do not usually allow

Instructions (for a year 7 class)

An A-level geography student has carried out a study at Padley Woods in the Derbyshire Peak District. She wanted to know how the area was used by visitors. Using a questionnaire, she asked 100 people visiting the area a series of questions. This is a copy of some of the data that she collected.

1. Represent the data collected using a different type of graph for each question. Each must have a title and, if needed, a key.

2. Write a sentence describing what each graph shows.

3. The questionnaire survey was carried out during two sunny weekends in summer. Suggest how the answers might have differed if it had been carried out in winter.

4. Suggest one other question which could have been included in the questionnaire and explain why you think it would be a useful question.

How did you get to Padley Woods today?	CAR	BUS	TRAIN	OTHER
	ЦНТ ЦНТ ЦНТ ЦНТ ЦНТ ЦНТ ЦНТ ЦНТ ЦНТ ЦНТ ЦНТ ЦНТ ЦНТ ЦНТ	ЦНТ ЦНТ II	ЦНТ III	ЦНТ
How will you spend your time here?	WALKING	PICNICKING	CYCLING	OTHER
	ЦНТ ЦНТ ЦНТ ЦНТ ЦНТ ЦНТ ЦНТ ЦНТ IIII	ЦНТ ЦНТ ЦНТ ЦНТ ЦНТ ЦНТ III	ЦНТ I	ЦНТ ЦНТ ЦНТ II
Do you think the area has been damaged by visitors in any of these ways?	LITTER	FOOTPATH EROSION	DAMAGED VERGES FROM PARKED CARS	NONE OF THESE WAYS
	ЦНТ ЦНТ ЦНТ ЦНТ ЦНТ ЦНТ ЦНТ I	ЦНТ ЦНТ ЦНТ ЦНТ ЦНТ ЦНТ ЦНТ ЦНТ III	ЦНТ ЦНТ ЦНТ ЦНТ ЦНТ ЦНТ II	ЦНТ ЦНТ II

Figure 20.4: Using data collected from a questionnaire survey.

space for respondents to qualify responses, explain what they mean or justify their viewpoints.

▲ Pre-structured questionnaires reflect the thinking of those who wrote them and might have inbuilt bias.

▲ The extent to which human behaviour can be studied through the collection of quantitative data and generalisations based on them is debatable.

▲ Great care must be taken to avoid ambiguity. It is important that all respondents understand the same question in the same way. Piloting the use of the questionnaire can reveal problems. If people interpret questions differently the findings would be invalid.

▲ There is no guarantee that respondents have answered the questionnaire honestly.

Limitations of the use of questionnaire surveys by school students

▲ The data are unlikely to be reliable because of the limited sample size and because data have to be collected at a time convenient for school students. It is unlikely, therefore, that the findings would be replicated.

▲ The sample is likely to be too small to generate valid generalisations; students should not accept the findings as reliable knowledge.

▲ There will be a limit to how frequently friends, neighbours, relations, teachers or other possible respondents are willing to take part in surveys.

▲ Some commercial premises, e.g. department stores and supermarkets, might not give permission for school students to stand outside and ask questions of their customers. It is advisable to seek permission before students are expected to use questionnaires outside particular shops.

Summary

Through using questionnaire surveys students can increase their geographical understanding and develop a range of skills. They can become aware of how some of the geographical information they encounter in textbooks and the media has been constructed and become aware of subjectivities involved in producing this information. They can learn to be more critical. Questionnaires are not straightforward to produce and students could be given guidance on types of questions to ask. They should be aware that findings from their own questionnaires are unlikely to be reliable or valid and to know why.

References

Borowski, R. (2011) 'The hidden cost of a Red Nose', *Primary Geography,* 75, pp. 18–20.

Denscombe, M. (2010) *The Good Research Guide: For small scale research projects* (4th edition). Maidenhead: Open University Press.

Johnston, R., Gregory, D., Pratt, G. and Watts, M. (2000) *The Dictionary of Human Geography* (4th edition). Oxford: Blackwell Publishers.

Walshe, N. (2007) 'Year 8 students' conceptions of sustainability', *Teaching Geography,* 32, 3, pp. 139–43.

Types of questions	Examples
Questions with overlapping categories where some possible answers could be in two categories	In which age group are you? 0–10; 10–30; 30–50; 50 and over.
Questions in which not all possible categories are included and no 'other' category is provided	How did you travel to school today? Bus; train; tram.
Questions which invite one response from a list when several might be appropriate	How did you travel to school today (tick one box): bus; train; car; tram; bicycle; walk; other.
Double-barrelled questions which cover more than one topic	Do you think the town centre is modern and attractive?
Leading questions which suggest that the researcher wants/expects a certain response	Which items do you recycle?
Loaded questions suggesting particular responses	Do you think there are too many foreigners coming to Britain taking British jobs?
Questions using a negative	Do you agree that people should not be allowed to throw litter in towns? Yes/No.
Questions with words that might be interpreted differently by different respondents	Have you been to the cinema recently? (Words to avoid: recently, often, sometimes, regularly, local.)
Questions to which some respondents might not know the answer	Have you visited an EU country in the last 12 months? (Respondents might not know which countries are in the EU.)
Questions which rely too heavily on detailed memory	How many times did you go to town last year?
Intrusive, personal questions	How much do you earn a year?

Figure 20.5: Types of bad questionnaire questions, with examples.

CHAPTER 21

Using the World Wide Web: web enquiries

'Young people are growing up in a world so dense with information and sources of knowledge that the education system has a duty to help them deal with it effectively' (Payton and Williamson, 2008, p. 9).

Introduction

The World Wide Web (WWW) was created in 1989 by Tim Berners Lee, making use of the underlying structure of the internet, through which computers are linked worldwide. The WWW is a vast collection of interlinked web pages which hold information or links to other pages and its growth has been phenomenal. It is possible to find information about any geographical theme on the WWW as well as ideas for teaching them and articles related to geographical education. This chapter addresses the following questions:

▲ What kinds of geographical information can be found on the WWW?

▲ What are some of the issues related to using the WWW in school geography?

▲ How can students be supported in their use of the WWW in an enquiry-based approach?

What kinds of geographical information can be found on the WWW?

Geographical information in every possible format can be found on the WWW:

▲ Maps of all kinds: topographical, thematic, street maps, weather charts, route-maps, Worldmapper, Gapminder, etc.

▲ Photographs and diagrams: through searching on Google Images or through particular websites

▲ Film: e.g. from YouTube; live webcams; recent TV programmes

▲ Statistics: e.g. access to large national and international databases which are updated regularly; data about weather and climate; census data.

▲ Facts and figures of all kinds, simple answers to simple questions

▲ Graphs and diagrams: e.g. climate; population pyramids; scatter-graphs (Gapminder)

▲ Reports: e.g. official reports; reports from various organisations; recent radio and TV news reports; newspaper articles

▲ Music and voice: e.g. listening to experts

▲ Animation: e.g. animated maps, graphs and diagrams.

Many websites designed for specific purposes, e.g. charities, NGOs, Gapminder, are multimedia and include a combination of content forms including text, audio, still images, animation, video and/or interactivity.

In addition to using general search engines such as Google, Google Images and Google Maps, the Geographical Association and the Royal Geographical Society's websites both have a large number of pages specifically designed for geography teachers, together with links to other useful resources. The subscription site *www. geographyalltheway.com* provides curriculum ideas and resources prepared by geography teachers specifically related to the requirements of geography public examinations.

What are some of the issues related to using the WWW in school geography?

There is too much information

Looking through web pages to find information relevant to the geographical themes and issues being studied can be very time consuming as there is so much information. Figure 21.1 shows the results of a few quick searches, each producing astounding results in less than half a minute. I feel sure that not many people search beyond the websites listed on the first few pages on the screen but there is no guarantee that these are the most appropriate for a particular enquiry.

Word or words typed in	Searched on:	Number of results
Volcanoes	Google: search	423,000,000
Volcanoes	Google: images	5,150,000
Volcano maps	Google: images	2,280,000
Vesuvius	Google: search	6,670,000
Vesuvius	Google: images	2,590,000
Vesuvius maps	Google: images	414,000
Antarctica	Google: search	178,000,000
Antarctica	Google: images	153,000,000
Antarctica maps	Google: images	3,690,000
Antarctica maps for kids	Google images	1,390,000

Information from varied interests and viewpoints

Whereas geography textbooks aim to present authoritative information about the subject, the sources of information on the WWW vary in reliability. For example, if students searched for 'nuclear power' using the Google search engine, on the first page of results they could come across the information shown in Figure 21.2. Of the websites listed, only Wikipedia and Andy Darville's sites present themselves as neutral, and students might accept them as authoritative although there are problems with both sites. Information on

Wikipedia might be correct but has not undergone the kind of scrutiny that academic material is subject to before being published so is not always reliable. Darville's site, immediately after criticising viewpoints opposing nuclear power, suggests that students should make up their own mind about the issue. Also the hyperlinks from the Wikipedia website to Greenpeace, for example, do not take the reader to the Greenpeace site but to a Wikipedia representation of Greenpeace.

In contrast, the websites produced by Greenpeace, the US Department of Energy and Horizon Nuclear Power present information influenced by the

WWW information

A search on Google of 'nuclear power' produces 227,000,000 results. The information provided in the websites listed on the first page of results includes the extracts below. The numbers refer to the order in which these websites appeared in the list in September 2012.

1. Wikipedia: *http://en.wikipedia.org/wiki/ Nuclear_power*

'There is an ongoing debate about the use of nuclear energy. Proponents, such as the World Nuclear Association, the IAEA and Environmentalists for Nuclear Energy, contend that nuclear power is a sustainable energy source that reduces carbon emissions. Opponents, such as Greenpeace International and NIRS, believe that nuclear power poses many threats to people and the environment.'

4. Website created by Andy Darville, an ex-science teacher: *www.darvill.clara.net/altenerg/nuclear.htm*

'There are many different opinions about nuclear power, and it strikes me that most of the people who protest about it don't have any idea what they're talking about. But please make up your own mind.'

5. Greenpeace: *www.greenpeace.org.uk/global*

'Greenpeace has always fought – and will continue to fight – vigorously against nuclear power because it is an unacceptable risk to the environment and to humanity.'

6. The US Department of Energy: *www.ne.doe.gov*

'The Office of Nuclear Energy (NE) promotes nuclear power as a resource capable of meeting the Nation's energy, environmental and national security needs by resolving technical and regulatory barriers through research, development and demonstration.'

9. Horizon Nuclear Power: *www.horizonnuclearpower.com*

'Horizon Nuclear Power was formed in January 2009 with the aim of developing up to 6,600MW of new nuclear power station capacity to help meet the UK's need for stable and sustainable low carbon energy.'

Figure 21.2: Examples of varied information found on WWW.

purposes of their organisation. They declare their interests clearly and give students an opportunity to read different viewpoints.

Some information is difficult to use

Much of the text found on the WWW was written for adults and demands a high reading age. For example, useful articles that can be found on the websites of UK newspapers such as the *Guardian*, the *Independent* or the *Telegraph* often require reading ages of over 20. Also, although there is a lot of valuable statistical information on the WWW, the information in large data sets can be difficult to search and to interpret.

Accessibility of computers at home and school

There are sometimes issues related to access to the WWW both at home and in school. In spite of the increase in the number of computers in UK schools in recent years, not all geography classes have access to them when they need them.

The WWW is potentially very useful for geography homework. Valentine *et al.* (2005) found that, for geography, students used ICT at home to find information, to create presentations and for revision. Using ICT increased their motivation. They found that the majority (89%) of students had access to home-based ICT. This percentage will have increased but there could still be some students who have no access at home or cannot easily use home-based ICT. It is important, therefore, before requiring students to use the WWW for homework,

to check that they are able to access it easily out of school and that they have sufficient guidance on its use, as suggested by Valentine *et al.*:

'*The clear relationship identified in this study between subject specific use of ICT in the classroom and subject specific use of ICT for school work outside of lessons highlights the need for good scaffolding in terms of introducing children in the classroom to how technology can be used in specific subjects across the curriculum and showing them how this ICT use can be developed at home for school work in specific subjects*' (2005, p. 10)

What students do with the information they find

I remember once asking a student who had just found some information on the WWW 'what are you going to do with this information?' He replied, 'I am going to print it out.' 'Then what?' 'I am going to stick it in my book.' This student is probably not representative but there is a danger that students, having found information, do nothing with it; they do not make sense of it by working on it, discussing it, interpreting it and critiquing it. Valentine *et al.* (2005) commented:

'*It is clear from the interviews that children and young people felt that they could acquire this information quickly and thoroughly through the use of the Internet. However, how effective their strategies for information retrieval were was not clear from the interviews. At times, the searching techniques children and parents described appeared to be*

WebQuests

The WebQuest model was devised in 1995 by Bernie Dodge at San Diego State University. Dodge described a WebQuest as:

'an inquiry-oriented activity in which most or all of the information used by learners is drawn from the Web. WebQuests are designed to use learners' time well, to focus on using information rather than looking for it, and to support learners' thinking at the levels of analysis, synthesis and evaluation' (Dodge, 1995).

Since 1995, the model has been developed and applied to different subjects in many countries and is supported by a dedicated website: *http://webquest.org*

WebQuests are underpinned by a social-constructivist view of learning in which discussion is valued. They are therefore planned as group investigations. They have a clear structure designed by the teacher and detailed guidance designed to prevent students from surfing the web in a purposeless way. They are structured in the following way:

The task

The task is what the students have to achieve through the WebQuest. The task requires students to transform the information they collect rather than simply reproduce it. The task could be:

▲ solving a problem or a mystery

▲ designing a product, e.g. a brochure or PowerPoint presentation

▲ producing a report or journalistic account.

The process

This comprises instructions for the students, broken down into stages, to enable them to accomplish the task. It might include advice on how to organise the information collected.

Resources

These are the online resources the students should use, given as links to specific websites in the instructions. Sometimes off-line resources can be included in the enquiry.

Evaluation

Students need to be aware of the criteria by which their work will be evaluated.

Conclusion

This is time for reflecting on the task and considering how the enquiry might be extended.

In addition to describing the structure and characteristic attributes of the WebQuest, Dodge identified 'Five rules for writing a great WebQuest', summarised by the mnemonic FOCUS (Dodge, 2001):

Find great sites

Orchestrate your learners and resources

Challenge your learners to think

Use the medium

Scaffold high expectations

---

rather vague and random. There was little evidence of the pupils being reflective about the process of information retrieval from the web' (p. 34).

How can students be supported in their use of the WWW in an enquiry-based approach?

The potential of the WWW for enquiry-based education was soon recognised. Bernie Dodge, based at San Diego State University, USA, developed the WebQuest model to support 'inquiry based learning' (Figure 21.3). Ways of using the WWW in school geography have been developed by the Staffordshire Learning Network (SLN), which has many examples of 'Web Enquiries' on its website. Fisher (2002) showed how the WebQuest model could be applied

to a decision-making exercise in geography (Figure 21.4).

Both WebQuests and SLN Web Enquiries address many of the issues raised above. Instead of using the WWW as a resource for students to use completely independently, they both provide the scaffolding that Valentine *et al.* (2005) identified as being necessary. They have the advantages of:

▲ preventing students wasting time searching the WWW for relevant information

▲ providing students with links to suitable websites, within which they can search and select

▲ possibly providing students with choice

▲ presenting a web-based enquiry in a purposeful context

WebQuest component	Detail of component	Outline example
Introduction to the task	This is usually a short statement giving some background. It sets the context for the WebQuest task.	A paragraph explaining the National Forest and a proposal for extending it.
Process	The process should be broken down into clear, appropriate steps or stages. This might also involve guidance on parallel activities undertaken by different group members. Clear guidance about timescale is important; time allocation should provide challenge and require interdependence. Guidance may also be given on how to organise material in order to complete the task.	Research current location and uses of the National Forest. Identify contiguous areas and make a reasoned choice of area for extension by identifying characteristics of area (land use, topography and soils, settlement, economic activity, tourism and infrastructure). Develop presentation. Make presentation to class.
Resources	Resources will include at least some web-based sources. These will have been identified by the teacher and will ideally be hyperlinked from within a computer-based document, e.g. a web page or a word-processed task sheet. Other sources might include books, documents, video, etc., as resources permit or the task requires.	Full WebQuest guidance. National Forest website. Other related websites. Ordnance Survey, land use and atlas maps. Remote sensing images. Documentary information about National Forest and surrounding areas.
Evaluation	The task should include criteria which can be used by learners to evaluate their level of success in the task. Learners should be encouraged to identify and make explicit their approach(es) in undertaking the task and the effectiveness of the strategies employed.	What did the group learn about the National Forest and issues of resource use and environmental management? How effective was the group's presentation? How did the group organise the task?
Conclusion	A point of closure for the activity, possibly including a recap of what has been learned.	Which group presented the most convincing case? Would it be a good idea to extend the National Forest? What would be the probable costs and benefits?

Figure 21.4: Example of a WebQuest framework applied to geography. Source: Fisher, 2002, p. 27.

▲ suggesting challenging and interesting ways of increasing students' knowledge and understanding of geography through using the WWW

▲ providing structures and frameworks within which students can work, e.g. subsidiary questions, newspaper templates.

Drawing on the WebQuest and SLN Web Enquiries models, together with ideas presented in this book, I have provided a list of what is involved in planning a web enquiry in Figure 21.5.

There are some possible disadvantages to using these teacher-structured frameworks for web-based enquiry work.

▲ If the web enquiry is very tightly structured, leaving students with few choices, they might feel that they are carrying out the teacher's enquiry, rather than getting fully involved in carrying out their own. This could mean that they learn to follow instructions accurately rather than get involved in the subject matter they are investigating.

Figure 21.5: Framework for planning a web enquiry.	**What is involved in planning a web enquiry?**	**Comments**
	The key question and creating a need to know Identifying a challenging, motivating key enquiry question Deciding how to 'create a need to know' for the web enquiry	The key question provides the title for the web enquiry. Subsidiary questions could be built into the enquiry, or negotiated with students before they embark on it. Subsidiary questions could be guided by the route for enquiry (Figures 5.4 and 12.4).
	Devising an appropriate context for the enquiry Devising a realistic, purposeful task for the enquiry, one which requires an end product	The task should involve students in making sense of information by transforming it in some way rather than simply reproducing it, e.g. as TV or newspaper journalists, in the preparation of a report for a particular group or in a decision-making exercise.
	Finding suitable evidence Searching for and selecting websites which are: ▲ relevant to the enquiry ▲ sources of good evidence ▲ accessible and easy to use ▲ varied, e.g. photographs, maps, animations, text, graphs ▲ interesting Deciding whether to recommend any off-line resources for some evidence or contextual information	Providing links to a limited number of websites saves students' time searching and can ensure their suitability. Providing links to several websites gives students choice and also the experience of selecting relevant information.
	Making sense Deciding on activities to be incorporated into the web enquiry that would require students to examine information and make sense of it for themselves, e.g. using analytical frameworks, translating information from one form into another, e.g. text to map	If students work in pairs or small groups, their discussions will help them work on their understanding. The teacher has an important role during the web enquiry: interacting with students; probing their understanding of information and key concepts; listening to their ideas for the finished product and providing help if necessary. Students might need guidance on selecting, analysing or interpreting information.
	Reflecting on learning Considering whether the finished products will be shared within the class or with a wider audience, e.g. parents. Deciding how work (process and final product) is to be evaluated. Considering whether peer evaluation would be appropriate Planning the debrief of the web enquiry	The teacher should ensure that students are aware of the criteria by which their work will be evaluated or negotiate the criteria with them. After the web enquiry students need to consider: ▲ To what extent has the WWW provided evidence for their investigation? ▲ To what extent is the information they found reliable? ▲ What other information might be needed to answer the key question?

▲ Students need to learn how to search for appropriate websites themselves if they are going to be able to use the WWW independently. At some stage during a geography course it would be useful for them to select sites and justify their selection.

▲ Part of the excitement of using the WWW is the search for information and finding good websites. Could it be with web enquiries that the teacher has all the fun and students miss out? Are there enquiries on some themes that students could carry out successfully with minimal guidance, or where for parts of the web-based enquiry they could search for websites themselves?

Suggestions for research

1. Follow up the research carried out by Valentine *et al.* (2005) on students' use of computers at home. Compare their use of computers for geography, for other subjects and for recreation.

2. Develop and evaluate a web enquiry using observational notes, reflection, students' work and possibly questionnaires and/or focus groups. To what extent did the web enquiry:

   ▲ remain the teacher's enquiry, or become the students' enquiry (see Figure 3.6)?

   ▲ give access to different information than off-line enquiry work (more, more varied, as reliable, more interesting)?

   ▲ encourage reasoning about the information?

   ▲ encourage conceptual development and understanding?

   ▲ encourage students to be critical? (see Figure 10.5)

   ▲ encourage rigorous assessment?

References

Dodge (1995) 'Some thoughts about WebQuests'. Available online at *http://webquest.sdsu.edu/about_webquests.html* (last accessed 29 April 2013).

Dodge, B. (2001) 'Five rules for writing a great WebQuest', *Learning and Leading with Technology*, 28, 8, pp. 6–58. Available online at *http://webquest.sdsu.edu/focus/focus.pdf* (last accessed 30 January 2013).

Fisher, T. (2002) *Theory into Practice: WebQuests in Geography.* Sheffield: The Geographical Association.

Payton, S. and Williamson, B. (2008) *Enquiring Minds: Innovative approaches to school reform.* Bristol: Futurelab. Available online at *www.enquiringminds.org.uk/pdfs/Enquiring_Minds_year4_report.pdf* (last accessed 22 January 2013).

Staffordshire Learning Network: *www.sln.org.uk/geography/enquiry/listing.htm* (last accessed 18 March 2013).

Valentine, G., Marsh, J. and Pattie, C. (2005) *Children's and Young People's Home Use of ICT for Educational Purposes: The impact on attainment at key stages 1–4.* London: DfES. Available online at *www.education.gov.uk/publications/eOrderingDownload/RR672.pdf* (last accessed 22 January 2013).

Mauritius public meeting role play cards

Government of Mauritius

Your role is to argue the case for the expansion of the tourist industry, focusing especially on economic reasons. After all the presentations, you will ask the non-governmental organisation 'We Love Mauritius' a question, and they will ask you a question.

The key arguments

The tourism industry is growing in importance. The target is 2 million tourists, and an increase in the number of hotel rooms from 9000 to 20,000, by 2020.

There has been a decline in the relative importance of agriculture and textiles:

▲ Mauritius's economy suffered at the turn of the millennium as longstanding trade preferences in textiles and sugar were phased out.

▲ Sugar cane occupies 40% of the total land area of Mauritius and accounts for 15% of exports, but is vulnerable to bad weather (droughts and cyclones).

▲ The textile industry has been hit by strong competition from production in emerging countries.

The tourism industry has the potential to contribute to GDP and to earn foreign exchange.

Information you can use as evidence for your case

Government action to support the tourist industry

▲ Investment in a new airport so that super-jumbos can land.

▲ Construction of dams to deal with the increase in demand for water.

▲ Encouragement of upmarket tourism, attracting wealthy tourists and promoting the use of the island for conferences.

Background information

'*Since independence in 1968, Mauritius has developed from a low-income, agriculturally based economy to a middle-income diversified economy with growing industrial, financial, and tourist sectors. For most of the period, annual growth has been in the order of 5% to 6%. This remarkable achievement has been reflected in more equitable income distribution, increased life expectancy, lowered infant mortality, and a much-improved infrastructure. The economy rests on sugar, tourism, textiles and apparel, and financial services, and is expanding into fish processing, information and communications technology, and hospitality and property development. Sugarcane is grown on about 90% of the cultivated land area and accounts for 15% of export earnings. The government's development strategy centers on creating vertical and horizontal clusters of development in these sectors.*' (Source: www.africa.com/mauritius)

Selected economic facts and figures

Natural resources: none

Contributions to GDP (2011):

▲ Agriculture: 3.6% (includes sugar cane production)

▲ Manufacturing: 17.7% (includes food processing, textiles, clothing)

▲ Hotels and restaurants: 7.1%

Main countries of origin of tourists (2011): France 31%; Reunion 12%; UK 9%; South Africa 9%; Germany 6%

Number of hotels: 116

Total employment: 559,700. Employment in hotels and restaurants: 38,000. Numbers employed in agriculture and manufacturing have declined since 2010, but the numbers employed in hotels and restaurants has seen an increase.

Source: *www.mcci.org/economy_figures.aspx*

Hoteliers in Mauritius

Your role is to argue the case for the expansion of the tourist industry, focusing mainly on socio-cultural reasons, but you could also include economic and environmental arguments. After all the presentations, you will ask the local residents a question, and they will ask you a question.

The key arguments

Hotels and restaurants provide employment for local people. In 2011 there were 116 hotels. The National Tourism Development Plan provided guidelines on land management, architectural design and eco-friendly practices – geared towards attracting foreign investment.

Hotels provide opportunities for small enterprises in the area and for employment related to developing the infrastructure.

The majority of tourists are from outside Mauritius, so they contribute to foreign exchange.

Under the Environmental Protection Act 2002 hotel developers are required to submit Environmental Impact Assessment reports.

Information you can use as evidence for your case

Hotels

At the end of December 2011, there were 116 registered hotels of which 109 were in operation, with a total room capacity of 11,925. The average room occupancy rate for all hotels in 2011 was 65% (same as in 2010).

Employment

The total number of Mauritians in employment in 2011 was estimated to be 559,700 (358,200 males and 201,500 females). Of these 38,000 (25,200 males and 12,800 females) were employed by hotels and restaurants, i.e. 6.8% of the workforce.

Some examples of average monthly earnings in 2011 (in Mauritian Rupees):

▲ Agriculture: 14,818

▲ Manufacturing: 11,930

▲ Hotels and restaurants: 15,875

▲ Finance: 36,353

▲ Health and social work: 24,000

▲ Average all sectors: 19,967

Compared with manufacturing and construction, which employ large numbers of people from outside Mauritius, the tourism industry employs mainly local people. It employs only 335 foreign workers, compared with 19,000 in manufacturing.

Contribution to infrastructure

Under the Tourism Fund Act, hotels contribute to a tourism fund for infrastructure development.

Source: Mauritian Government statistics

Tourism Authority

Your role, as representatives of the Tourism Authority, is to argue the case for the government's aim to double the number of tourists. In your presentation you should emphasise what you are doing to safeguard the environment. After all the presentations, you will ask the environmental group 'Reef Conservation' a question, and they will ask you a question.

The key arguments

The Tourism Authority promotes the sustainable development of tourism by:

▲ inspecting hotels, restaurants, and agencies for car and windsurf rental before issuing them with a licence

▲ monitoring tourist enterprises to ensure that standards are maintained

▲ registering, licensing and regulating the use of pleasure boats

▲ conducting training sessions for skippers of boats

▲ cleaning tourist areas.

Information you can use as evidence for your case

The Tourism Authority Act

The Tourism Authority Act of 2006 and its amendments in 2008 provided a framework which set out regulations for tourist services so that they could meet international standards and Mauritius could develop as a high-quality, safe tourist destination. The Tourism Authority is responsible for issuing licences and for supervising the activities of tourist enterprises.

Tourist enterprise licenses

These are required for establishments and activities providing services for tourists, including: hotels, restaurants, golf courses, ferry boats, pleasure craft, rental agencies for jet skis, kite surfing, paragliding, windsurfing, scuba diving, canoes, and people working as tourist guides.

Pleasure craft licences

These must be issued to vessels used for fishing as a sport, for water sports, or pleasure purposes and includes a recreational platform. Pedal boats, canoes, kayaks, surfboats or non-motorised rubber inflatable boats are not regarded as pleasure crafts.

Skippers' licences

These are required by skippers of boats, and they must pass both theoretical and practical tests to obtain them.

Cleaning project

The Tourism Authority has set up a project to clean tourist areas such as beaches and bare lands.

Source: *www.tourismauthority.mu*

Local non-governmental organisation 'We Love Mauritius'

Your role, as representatives of a local non-governmental organisation, is to argue the case against the government's aim to double the number of tourists. In your presentation you will focus on the economic arguments against. After all the presentations, your group will ask the representative of the government a question, and they will ask you a question.

The key arguments

▲ The Mauritian tourist industry is dependent on long-haul flights. As the cost of flying increases there could be a decline in the number of tourists.

▲ The number of tourists varies from year to year and can be affected by terrorist attacks, financial recession or the weather (Mauritius is in the cyclone belt).

▲ The government's airport expansion, to take super-jumbo jets, is misguided. These planes need to be full to be economic. Because of variations from year to year it is not possible to guarantee filling the planes to capacity.

Extract from Geographical

'As the cost of flying increases (whether it's due to increases in the cost of aviation fuel, tax rises or the imposition of emissions trading) and "carbon guilt" sets in – meaning we no longer feel entirely comfortable boasting about our overseas holidays – the "why" and "how" of travel will surely become more important … Smart destinations will no longer just pursue more tourists per se. Instead, they will focus more on the types of tourists they need and matching these to the most suitable areas and communities within their country. As a result, economic benefits will be maximised, while social and environmental costs are kept to a minimum.'

(Source: *www.responsibletravel.com/resources/ future-of-tourism/pdfs/FutureOfTravel.pdf*)

Hotels

At the end of December 2011, there were 116 registered hotels of which 109 were in operation, with a total room capacity of 11,925. The average room occupancy rate for all hotels in 2011 was 65% (as in 2010).

Source: Questions to Minister of Tourism and Leisure: *http://welovemauritius.org/node/18*

Information you can use as evidence for your case

Tourist arrivals in Mauritius by country of residence

Country of residence	2002	2004	2006	2008	2010
France	202,869	210,411	182,295	260,054	302 185
Germany	53,762	52,277	57,251	61,484	52 886
India	20,898	24,716	37,498	43,911	49 779
Italy	38,263	41,277	69,407	66,432	56 540
Reunion	96,375	96,510	89,127	96,174	114 914
South Africa	42,685	52,609	70,796	84,448	81 458
UK	80,667	92,652	102,333	107,919	97 548
Other countries	146,129	148,409	179,569	210,034	179 517
Total	681,648	718,861	788,276	930,456	934 827

(Source: Statistics selected from Table 28, *Digest of International Travel and Tourism Statistics 2010*, published in 2011 by the Ministry of Finance and Economic Development Data: *www.gov.mu/portal/ goc/cso/report/natacc/tourism10/digest.pdf*)

Local residents

Your role, as a group of local residents, is to argue the case against the government's aim to double the number of tourists. In your presentation you should emphasise the social case against. After all the presentations, you will ask the hoteliers a question, and they will ask you a question.

The key arguments

▲ Although the hotels provide employment, wages are low.

▲ The hotels are mostly under foreign ownership so local people do not benefit enough.

▲ Land is scarce and an increasing amount of land is being taken for tourism.

▲ Local people have less access to beaches because hotels are built along the coast.

▲ Local roads are already too congested because of tourism.

▲ Only wealthy Mauritians can afford to fly so most local people would not benefit from the money spent on the airport.

▲ An increase in tourists with different cultural practices could have a negative influence on local cultures.

Information you can use as evidence for your case

English is the official language of Mauritius but it is spoken by less than 1% of the people. About 80% of the population speak Creole. The other languages are Bhojpuri (12.1%) and French (3.4%). The population of Mauritius is multi-ethnic:

▲ 68% are Indo-Mauritian (descendants of people from India)

▲ 27% are Creole (descendants of slaves from Africa and Asia)

▲ 3% are Sino-Mauritian (descendants of people from China).

Comments from 'We Love Mauritius' website

'Mauritius's appeal is as a quality destination, exotic, safe, beautiful and peaceful. An equally appealing feature is the harmonious coexistence of diverse cultures which make up the Mauritian nation. Over-development would destroy this appeal, threaten the ecology of the lagoons, and deprive Mauritians of a proper share of their own beaches. Accordingly it has been estimated that total capacity can be increased from the present 5,300 hotel rooms only to a maximum of 9,000 rooms. Beyond this "green ceiling", increased earnings will have to come, not from higher numbers, but from higher spending per visitor, with still higher standards of provision and a wider range of activities, including, perhaps, inland and eco-tourism.'

'Most jobs in hotels and servants in villas earn a pathetic salary in Mauritius. How does this sector help them to improve their standard of living?'

'How can our island support more resource-hungry tourists and foreign élites when, for example, there is insufficient water to properly supply the local population?'

'In 1968, when we gained independence, all the coastal land was transferred from the British Crown to the Mauritian people. Today, while wealthy foreigners enjoy the best of it, we are treated like trespassers in our own country.'

Employment

The total number of Mauritians in employment in 2011 was estimated to be 559,700 (358,200 males and 201,500 females). Of these 38,000 (25,200 males and 12,800 females), i.e. 6.8% of the workforce, were employed by hotels and restaurants.

Some examples of average monthly earnings in 2011 (in Mauritian Rupees):

▲ Agriculture: 14,818

▲ Manufacturing: 11,930

▲ Hotels and restaurants: 15,875

▲ Finance: 36,353

▲ Health and social work: 24,000

▲ Average all sectors: 19,967

Local non-governmental organisation 'Reef Conservation Mauritius'

Your role, as representatives of local environmental group 'Reef Conservation Mauritius', is to argue the case against the government's aim to double the number of tourists. In your presentation you will emphasise the environmental arguments against. After all the presentations, you will ask the Tourism Authority a question and they will ask you a question.

The key arguments

The expansion of the tourist industry would have several negative effects:

▲ It would lead to further damage to the coral reefs.

▲ It would threaten the ecology of the lagoons behind the coral reefs and lower the quality of water in them.

▲ If coral reefs are lowered, beaches would be threatened by wave action.

▲ Laws related to protecting the environment are often ignored.

Information you can use as evidence for your case

Information and quotations from the 'Reef Conservation Mauritius' website www.reefconservation.mu/index.php

'Reef Conservation Mauritius is a non-profit organization dedicated to the conservation and the restoration of the marine environment of Mauritius. It promotes sustainable use of the biodiversity of our marine ecosystems through local and regional efforts in a partnership approach with all concerned stakeholders. Reef Conservation Mauritius employs professional, qualified biologists and support staff to manage and implement its projects.'

Reef Conservation Mauritius's objectives are to promote marine conservation and management through research, education and training to encourage people to respect laws on marine environment and to protect underwater and coastal ecosystems through awareness-raising activities and campaigns.

Reef Conservation Mauritius provides:

▲ Educational resources, training on their use and field trips for schools

▲ Fixed Mooring Buoys and Reef Monitoring Project: buoys are used at popular dive and snorkel sites to protect the coral from anchor damage. Corals and fish populations are monitored to assess regeneration at these sites.

'Tourism also has its direct and associated impacts, with snorkel and dive boats dropping anchors and breaking the coral. Collection of shells and corals for sale to visitors has depleted the number of shells and people holding, walking and sitting on coral all contribute to the demise of the lagoon habitats the visitors have come to see.'

Damage to coral reefs

Extract about coral reefs from:
http://welovemauritius.org/node/5

'Although sea levels are rising, the slow growing massive and encrusting corals that break most of the energy of waves and storms grow sufficiently fast to keep up. Branching corals grow much faster and probably provide the bulk of coral debris that replenishes the sand reservoir within the lagoon. However, physical impact caused by contact with boats, anchors, fishermen, snorkellers and divers damage even the massive and encrusting corals. Man-made environmental stressors such as pollution from boat engines and industry; siltation resulting from deforestation; and increases in competing algae due to sewage, agricultural run-off and over fishing of herbivores are reducing growth rates.'

Websites which provide information on Mauritius

Statistics Mauritius: *www.gov.mu/portal/site/cso*

Ministry of Tourism, Leisure & External Communications: *www.gov.mu/portal/site/tourist*

Mauritius Tourism Promotion Authority: *www. tourism-mauritius.mu*

Association of hoteliers and restaurants in Mauritius: *www.mauritiustourism.org*

Reef Conservation: *www.reefconservation.mu*

Map of Mauritius (showing extent of coral reefs) and map showing location in relation to Africa:

www.worldatlas.com/webimage/countrys/africa/ mu.htm

Map of Mauritius showing coral reefs: *www. travelnotes.org/Africa/mauritius.htm*

Go Africa map of Mauritius: *http://goafrica.about. com/library/bl.mapfacts.mauritius.htm*

www.africa.com/mauritius

Google Earth (Coral reefs and lagoons can be seen when zooming in)

Planning an enquiry-based unit of work

Things to consider in planning an enquiry-based unit of work

The creative process of curriculum making does not necessarily follow the logical steps often set out in curriculum planning advice. The inspiration for a unit of work might come from specific geographical source material, a television programme, from discussion with colleagues in other subjects, from conferences or from one's own particular interests and wider reading. The list below is not presented as a sequence for planning but simply as things that need to be considered when planning an enquiry-based unit of work.

Things to consider	Questions to consider in relation to the theme/place/issue being investigated
Geographical content of unit of work	What aspects of geography might be included? Are there specific requirements, e.g. from national curriculum or examinations, which have to be included? What key concepts and ideas might be introduced? What case studies might be used?
Students	What relevant knowledge will students bring to this unit of work (from everyday experience or from prior learning in school)? What skills (e.g. literacy, numeracy, graphical, ICT) will they already have? What are their likely needs e.g. do they need to learn new skills/techniques or will they need support when using challenging source materials? In what ways will their geographical thinking be extended beyond their prior knowledge and understanding?
Focus of enquiry	What key question might frame this unit of work? Is the key question intriguing and challenging? How will the key question and subsidiary questions be established (by teacher or through discussion)?
Role of teacher	Is the unit of work to be tightly or loosely structured? To what extent will students have opportunities to choose content, questions to investigate, activities, choice of techniques to use? If controversial issues are being investigated, what will the teacher's stance be? How will support be provided to students throughout the unit of work?
Sources of information	Will students be presented with specific sources of information? Will students have opportunities to search for information themselves? Will students be provided with guidance on sources of information, e.g. websites, references? How will students be encouraged to examine information critically?
How will students work?	Will students work individually, in pairs or in groups for all or part of the unit of work? What guidance will they be given on working collaboratively? Will there be presentation of information/ideas/explanations to the whole class? What opportunities will students have to discuss their work with each other (in whole-class, paired and group discussion)?

Things to consider	Questions to consider in relation to the theme/place/issue being investigated
Classroom processes and activities	What initial stimulus will be provided to engage students? What activities might be incorporated into the unit of work to encourage students to makes sense of it for themselves and to think geographically? Will there be a final outcome activity to provide a focus for the investigation?
Learning	What part will students play in negotiating learning outcomes? Which of the following will be important: acquiring specific knowledge of places; developing conceptual understanding; applying ideas to new case studies; investigating different viewpoints; learning new skills/techniques? How will the unit of work be debriefed, so that students reflect on what and how they have learnt?
Assessment	What will be assessed e.g. students' work during the unit of work, written work, oral work, final product? What will the assessment criteria be? Will students play a part in determining criteria? How will students' progress be assessed formatively? Will they become aware of what they need to do to improve? Will there be self or peer group assessment?
Dissemination	Will students' work be shared with others in the class through discussion or presentations? Will there be wider dissemination of students' work, e.g. through displays or through information presented on computers, to other classes or to parents?

03 Activities and strategies referred to in *Geography Through Enquiry*

Someone commented to me, after the publication of *Learning Through Enquiry*, that it would have been useful to have had an appendix listing all the activities and strategies mentioned in the book. This is why I have included this list for reference purposes. I am not suggesting, however, that using one or two of these strategies in a unit of work or lesson means that an enquiry approach is being adopted and that students are necessarily actively engaged in investigating questions, problems and issues. If students are to learn geography through enquiry then it is important to establish a culture of enquiry within the classroom, one in which students are encouraged to question, to examine geographical sources critically and to learn to think geographically for themselves. These activities might contribute to that process.

Activity/strategy	Chapter/Figure	Page number
5Ws	Figure 5.1	44
7Ws and an H: an octagon planning framework	Figure 5.2	45
Amazon or not?	Figure 7.2	64
Argumentation	Chapter 8, Figures 8.4 and 8.6	66–7
Big questions/little questions	Figure 5.5	48
Brainstorming	Chapter 5	47
Compass Rose	Figure 5.3	46
Concept maps	Chapter 16	148–54
Critical enquiry	Figure 10.5	103
DARTs (directed activities related to text)	Chapter 19	168–74
Deconstruction	Figure 8.3	74
Definitions: e.g. globalisation	Figures 9.6, 9.9	89, 92–3
Dialogic teaching: strategies to encourage whole-class discussion	Chapter 11	105–13
Diamond ranking	Figure 12.9	126
Five Key Points	Chapter 14	135–40
Identifying tensions in meanings of words/terms	Figure 8.3	74
Intelligent guesswork	Chapter 13	128–34
Jigsaw pictures of contrasting images	Figure 4.2	40
KWL framework and variations	Chapter 5	43–4
Layers of Inference	Chapter 17	155–59
Mind maps	Chapter 15	141–47
Photo editor	Figure 7.2	64
Pictionary	Figure 9.6	89

Bibliography

The following books have been important in helping me developing my thinking. They include some that have not been referenced directly in the chapters.

Alexander, R. (2011) *Towards Dialogic Teaching: Rethinking classroom talk* (fourth edition). York: Dialogos.

Butt, G. (ed) (2011) *Geography, Education and the Future.* London: Continuum.

Leat, D. (1998) *Thinking Through Geography.* Cambridge: Chris Kington Publishing.

Lambert, D. and Morgan, J. (2010) *Teaching Geography 11–18: A conceptual approach.* Maidenhead: Open University Press.

Marsden, B. (1995) *Geography 11–18: Rekindling good practice.* London: David Fulton.

Mercer, N. and Hodgkinson, S. (eds) (2008) *Exploring Talk in Schools.* London: Sage.

Morgan, J. (2012) *Teaching Secondary Geography as if the Planet Matters.* London: Routledge.

Nichols, A. and Kinninment, D. (2000) *More Thinking Through Geography.* Cambridge: Chris Kington Publishing.

Rawling, E. (2007) *Planning your Key Stage 3 Geography Curriculum.* Sheffield: The Geographical Association.

Roberts, M. (2003) *Learning Through Enquiry: Making sense of geography in the key stage 3 classroom.* Sheffield: The Geographical Association.

Taylor, L. (2004) *Re-presenting Geography.* Cambridge: Chris Kington Publishing.

Index